EXPOSING MEN

CYNTHIA R. DANIELS

E X P O S I N G   M E N

THE SCIENCE AND POLITICS OF MALE REPRODUCTION

UNIVERSITY PRESS

2006

OXFORD
UNIVERSITY PRESS

Oxford University Press, Inc., publishes works that further
Oxford University's objective of excellence
in research, scholarship, and education.

Oxford   New York
Auckland   Cape Town   Dar es Salaam   Hong Kong   Karachi
Kuala Lumpur   Madrid   Melbourne   Mexico City   Nairobi
New Delhi   Shanghai   Taipei   Toronto

With offices in
Argentina   Austria   Brazil   Chile   Czech Republic   France   Greece
Guatemala   Hungary   Italy   Japan   Poland   Portugal   Singapore
South Korea   Switzerland   Thailand   Turkey   Ukraine   Vietnam

Copyright © 2006 by Oxford University Press, Inc.

Published by Oxford University Press, Inc.
198 Madison Avenue, New York, New York 10016

www.oup.com

Oxford is a registered trademark of Oxford University Press

Library of Congress Cataloging-in-Publication Data
Daniels, Cynthia R.
Exposing men : the science and politics of male reproduction / Cynthia R. Daniels.
    p. cm.
Includes bibliographical references and index.
ISBN-13 978-0-19-514841-1
ISBN 0-19-514841-X
1. Men.   2. Sex role.   3. Masculinity.   I. Title.
HQ1090.D36   2006
305.31—dc22   2005027745

9 8 7 6 5 4 3 2 1

Printed in the United States of America
on acid-free paper

To the memory of my father,

Raymond J. Daniels

...taken from the dance floor far too soon

ACKNOWLEDGMENTS

Like human reproduction, the production of a book is always dependent on the labor of many people. I owe intellectual debt to the many people who have read and often challenged my work, including Janet Golden, Eileen McDonagh, and Nancy Hirschmann. The gender scholars in the women and politics program at Rutgers—Sue Carroll, Drucilla Cornell, Jane Junn, Leela Fernandes, and Mary Hawkesworth— have built an intellectual environment that encourages the questioning of "gender knowledge" and helps to imagine gender equality beyond equality just for women. Without that institutional support, this work would not have been possible.

My undergraduate students at Rutgers—a lively group of critical thinkers—read drafts of chapters and provided me with the questioning that only students brave enough to challenge the accepted knowledge of their professors can provide. I recognize their contribution to the clarity of these arguments. I would like to especially thank Anna Goldfild, one of my undergraduate assistants, for her support of this project. She is a model of organization and often provided support out of enthusiasm for the project, if not always for wages. My graduate students also provided insightful criticisms and challenging exchanges which helped to deepen this work. I would specifically like to thank my research assistants and

the students too numerous to name in my gender seminars who took the time to read and comment on chapters in their development.

A number of research centers at Rutgers, including the Institute for Research on Women and the Center for the Critical Analysis of Contemporary Culture, provided material and intellectual support for a project that often crossed the boundaries of disciplinary scholarship. The vitality of these centers provided me with the ability to transgress boundaries between theory and practice, masculine and feminine, politics and culture.

My editor at Oxford, Dedi Felman, provided the kind of enthusiasm for this project that every author wishes for in an editor. As the manuscript went through various transformations, her insightful comments provided me with critical direction and encouragement and forced me to sharpen the central arguments of this work.

Throughout this book's production, my primary research assistant, Judith de Vries, organized research materials, carefully edited my work, and succeeded at keeping track of multiple versions of each chapter. Imagine a research assistant who combines the precision of a mathematician with the intellectual care and curiosity of a historian and you will have Judith. She has been an ideal "partner" in work, in midnight hours, and in intellectual exchange at some of the best diners in New Jersey.

Outside of academia, I am most indebted to those scientists and advocates who have had the courage and imagination to question "accepted knowledge" about male reproduction despite the personal and professional costs of doing so. They work in labor unions, in state bureaucracies, and in science labs. This book is built upon the foundation of their brave work.

I wrote most of this book while living on a family farm. The daily labor of mucking, hauling, and caring for animals provided a different kind of perspective on the reproduction of all life, both eternal and deeply social, even for the smallest of living beings. I would like to thank Monte, Louie, Ollie, Bonnie, Pete, the hens, and the "Hags" for comic relief.

A book project engenders costs to one's family that cannot be measured in simple time. I hope that my daughters, Katherine and Julia, will benefit from this work in living lives less constrained by what we

think men and women have to be. I thank them for their love and inspiration throughout the writing of this book. My mother, Margaret Daniels, who had to take on the task of both mothering and fathering four children too early in life, provided inspiration in real life. I thank her for that . . . and also for the meatballs. Finally, I thank my life partner, Bob Higgins, who represents what I hope to be the future of manhood—a future where fathers are recognized as true partners in the production and sustenance of human life and where manhood is measured not by an abstract and often damaging notion of masculinity, but by each person's true humanity.

CONTENTS

EXPOSING MEN

INTRODUCTION

I

At the turn of the twenty-first century, news stories reported a dramatic drop in sperm counts worldwide. Other stories warned of increasing rates of reproductive cancers in men, a sharp rise in the number of baby boys born with genital deformities, and a decline in the male-to-female birth ratio. Stories of Gulf War veterans, like Vietnam veterans before them, reported soldiers with high rates of infertility and soldiers fathering babies born with bizarre, often fatal, childhood disorders. News accounts noted the striking growth of the multimillion-dollar sperm bank industry in the United States, where male seed was stocked, packaged, and sold on the open market as if it were just another market product. Like few times before in history, stories of men's reproductive disorders publicly exposed the private reproductive troubles of men.

Such stories of men suffering reproductive disease and disability were disturbing not only because they suggested possible men's health problems but also because they flew in the face of traditional ideals of male reproduction. Ideally, men are virile, capable of impregnating women and producing their own biological children. Ideally, men are relatively invulnerable to harm, able to withstand the hazards and risks of the public world, and capable of denying the pains of the human body and the suffering of others. Ideally, men are the protectors of women, children,

and the nation, capable of fighting wars, accepting threats of bodily harm, and shielding others from external risk. Ideally, men are the providers for children, distant from the daily work of child care so that they may earn the resources needed for children's economic well-being. The man who fulfills these functions is a worker, a soldier, a father, a self-sustaining man, dependent on no one and needing neither the protection nor the assistance of others.

Images of men suffering reproductive ailments confounded these ideals by revealing the needs and vulnerabilities of the male reproductive body. If men were as vulnerable as women to the harms of the outside world, if the male reproductive system was equally damaged by the toxins of war and work, and if men, through sperm, could pass on harm to the children they father, then how were we to justify the ideal of men as superior in strength and as the protectors and providers of women and children? Public exposure of men's private reproductive troubles threatened to throw into question not just the health of the male body but these deeper ideals of masculinity as well.

Exposing Men examines how such ideals of masculinity have skewed the science of male reproductive health and our understanding of men's relationship to human reproduction. It argues that such ideals are double-edged, for while they perpetuate assumptions about the superior strength of the male body, they lead to a profound neglect of male reproductive health and a distorted view of men's relationship to human reproduction. It looks at the conditions under which male reproductive health needs have emerged on the public scene at the turn of the century, the charged public responses to such exposure, and the implications of these for how we think about not only men's relationship to human reproduction but also broader social relations between men and women.

Assumptions of reproductive difference have historically presumed a differential division of reproductive labor between men and women. This division of labor presumes not just biological difference but differences in the social functions that men and women play in both human reproduction and society at large. Men impregnate; women gestate. Women's investment in reproduction is long-term; men's is fleeting.

Women produce eggs and milk; men produce "throwaway sperm." This reproductive division of labor, presumed to be imprinted in biology, is often used to justify different capacities and temperaments for men and women. Women breed, nurture, and conserve human life; men rule the world, often at the expense of human life. If women are more caring and men more tactical in human relations, it is because men and women perform different functions in the reproduction of the species.

Such assumptions may seem antiquated in a time when social movements and feminist scholarship have challenged gender inequalities in nearly every realm of human life. Men have been increasingly drawn into the work of family and child care as women have moved into the masculine worlds of work and politics. Feminist scholars argue that even the grouping of bodies into just two sexes—male and female—distorts a more complex biology of sexual differentiation. Yet while such critiques seem ubiquitous, deeply embedded in the collective consciousness remains the assumption that, in the end (or beginning), the biological functions that men and women perform in reproduction are beyond social contestation.

Exposing Men is a book not just about men's reproductive health but about, in addition, reproductive difference. I am not arguing for a denial of all biological differences between men and women in reproduction— in gestation, lactation, or even the hormonal differences between the sexes—but that these have taken on social meanings far beyond biology. I do not argue that men and women play equivalent roles in the reproduction of the species but that these differential roles have been highly exaggerated. Indeed, denying all biological differences between men and women would get us no closer to a system of gender equity than their exaggeration. But I do argue that men and women are more similar than different in their contributions to reproduction and that assumptions of reproductive difference have been used to justify social, political, and economic inequalities between men and women. I argue that until assumptions of reproductive difference are challenged, gender inequities for both men and women will continue.

Exposing Men is also a book about the paradoxes of masculine privilege. It argues that such assumptions of reproductive difference do not

just privilege but burden men. The scholarly literature on the politics of reproduction has focused almost exclusively on the costs to women of assumptions of reproductive difference—of the disproportionate burdens women bear in human procreation and caregiving. Yet men pay a price as well. Is it privilege that we neglect ailments like male infertility in the interest of maintaining illusions of male virility? Is it privilege to spend the bulk of a lifetime in dreary or dangerous work, separated from their children, in order to perpetuate ideals of men as providers? Is it privilege to man the front lines of war while women provide primary care for children? Is it privilege to ignore the hazards of both work and war to the male reproductive system to maintain the illusion of men as invulnerable? Although men may enjoy the economic and social advantages of assumptions of reproductive difference, they pay a high price for such advantage as well.

In this age of war and political retrenchment, of rollbacks in affirmative action and challenges to women's reproductive rights, it is not only difficult but also, some might say, politically problematic to write a book about the suffering of men. But only through recognition of the vulnerabilities of men can gender injustices be transformed. We must see, and believe, evidence of male weaknesses and vulnerability. We must see, and recognize, men's intimate connection to human reproduction. Only then can we achieve a more equitable system of gender relations for both men and women.

Reproductive Masculinity

The chapters to follow examine these questions through the lens of male reproduction. Central to this study is the concept of reproductive masculinity—a set of beliefs and assumptions about men's relationship to human reproduction. Reproductive masculinity can be defined in terms of four interrelated elements: First, men are assumed to be secondary in biological reproduction. Although both men and women contribute essential genetic material to conception, women's role in gestation, birth, and lactation presumably renders men secondary in human reproduc-

tion. Second, men are assumed to be less vulnerable to reproductive harm than women. The male reproductive body is seen as less susceptible to the hazards of the world than the female reproductive system. The science of andrology—the study of male reproductive health—has historically been and remains marginalized. Third, men are assumed to be virile, ideally capable of fathering their own biological children. Although reproductive technologies and medical interventions make it possible for infertile men to become fathers, the infertility of men is still understudied, a source of personal shame, and shrouded in comparative secrecy. Fourth, men are assumed to be relatively distant from the health problems of children they father. Birth defects in children, miscarriage, and reproductive disorders are most often still traced to women's and not men's exposures to drugs, alcohol, and environmental and workplace toxins. Despite a growing body of scientific evidence that suggests otherwise, men remain uninformed about how their toxic exposures can affect both pregnancy and the children they father.

Each of these elements of reproductive masculinity has a social history and has increasingly come under social contestation. The following chapters examine the history of each of these assumptions, the conditions under which each has come to be challenged, the social and political resistance to such challenges, and the implications of these assumptions for how we understand men's and women's relationship to human reproduction.

Chapter 2, "Powers of Conception," examines the first element of reproductive masculinity—the assumption that men are secondary in biological reproduction. It visits the history of assumptions about the male role in reproduction, from the ancients through the twentieth century. The male role in biological reproduction has been highly contested. This chapter charts these contestations through the scientific discovery of sperm in seminal fluid (in the seventeenth century) and the debates that discovery produced in the scientific and philosophical communities. Some argued that sperm contained the entire preformed being, ready to be implanted into the uterus. Others argued that "seminal worms" played no substantive role in procreation and simply "excited" the egg into development. Such debates were the result not just of the limits of

science but of competing cultural assumptions of masculinity and femininity that cast men as either primary or peripheral to biological reproduction. In the twenty-first century, the recognition of men's and women's equal genetic contributions to biological reproduction has clarified but not resolved questions about reproductive difference between the sexes. Instead, such debates have shifted onto new grounds of hormonal gender difference.

Chapter 3, "Dropping Sperm Counts," examines the second element of reproductive masculinity—the assumption that the male reproductive system is less vulnerable to the harms of the outside world than the female reproductive system. It explores the historical neglect of andrology, produced by the need to disguise the weaknesses of the male body, which continues today. It looks into these questions by examining the evidence of a dramatic drop in sperm counts, as well as reports of the increase in male reproductive diseases and disorders at the turn of the twenty-first century.

Chapter 4, "Commodifying Men," examines the third element of reproductive masculinity—the assumption of male virility—by studying the historical neglect of male infertility and the rise of the sperm banking industry in the United States. It traces the transformation of the secretive practice of artificial insemination in the nineteenth and early twentieth centuries into the public, multimillion-dollar sperm banking industry. It explores how racial politics (which sought to use artificial insemination for eugenic purposes), market forces (which sought to profit from these efforts), technological innovations (which made it possible to increase rates of success), and social movements (for reproductive rights) have pushed male infertility into public light. Such forces seem to at once reaffirm the ideal of men as fathers even as they expose the reproductive "failings" of those men seeking infertility services.

Chapter 5, "The Children Men Father," examines the fourth element of reproductive masculinity—the presumption that men are more distant from the children they father. Historically, research into the field of paternal fetal harm has faced formidable barriers, with most finding the scientific evidence of male-mediated fetal harm simply unbeliev-

able. The politics of fetal hazards continues to focus almost exclusively on damages to fetal health through the female body. This chapter suggests that ideals of reproductive masculinity have skewed the science of male-mediated fetal harm at a price not just to men but to the children men father.

Chapter 6, "Reproducing Men," examines the implication of these public exposures for broader ideals of masculinity. It argues that challenges to reproductive masculinity hold implications for the broader ideals of men as fathers, workers, soldiers, and citizens. It analyzes the processes of social change that have led to both challenges to ideals of masculinity as well as resistance to these challenges. It argues that a transformation of gender relations and of the historical inequities that have defined not just reproductive relations but the economic, social, and political roles of men and women requires both a recognition of reproductive difference and an acknowledgment of the commonalities of men and women.

POWERS OF CONCEPTION 2

W hat is the male role in human reproduction? The first presumption of reproductive masculinity is that men play a secondary role in biological reproduction. This presumption may seem self-evident. Although men, through sperm, contribute genetic material to conception, women provide ova, gestate, and give birth to children. Despite the advent of reproductive technologies such as in vitro fertilization, artificial insemination, and surrogate mothering that complicate this process, biology still presumably renders men both essential and secondary in biological reproduction. Yet the history of the reproductive sciences, explored in this chapter, suggests that the discovery of the male role in reproduction and the secondary social value given to that role are relatively recent developments.

Since antiquity, scientists and philosophers have debated the significance of men to human procreation. Some gave all procreative power to men, casting them as the creators of life, with superior "fluids" capable of ensouling the fetus or with sperm containing the entire miniaturized human being ready to be "planted" into the womb. Others gave men only a minimal role in conception, with human beings encapsulated in ova and stimulated to growth by "parasitic worms" in sperm. It was not until the end of the nineteenth century that investigators in the biological sciences reached a consensus on the role of sperm in human conception.

Some might argue that advances in the reproductive sciences have now ended such debate over the biological role of men in human reproduction. Microscopic technologies make it possible to see processes of fertilization and implantation and to observe the development of the conceptus into the embryo and fetus. The genetic sciences now provide the framework for understanding how paternal and maternal traits are passed to children through sperm and ova. Yet the biology of male reproduction, studied far less than women's reproductive biology, is still not fully understood. Assumptions that reproduction is the primary domain of women have led to a historical (and continuing) neglect of male reproduction. The production of sperm in the male body and the causes of male infertility are not completely understood. The role of sperm in causing miscarriages or transmitting birth defects to the fetus remains understudied. This chapter analyzes the history of debates over the male contribution to biological reproduction as prelude to analysis of the particular reproductive problems of men, addressed in later chapters.

Perceptions of men's role in human reproduction have been more than just a matter of scientific debate and progressive discovery. Historically, biological arguments were often used to justify a *social* division of reproductive labor between men and women, sometimes to assert men's power over reproductive decision making (like the power of infanticide in ancient societies or the authority of men over households), or to justify women's primary "natural" responsibility for the work of bearing and raising children. This chapter suggests that biological knowledge of reproduction has been, and remains, inseparable from the social relations of reproduction and the social constructions of masculinity.

I am not arguing that the biological differences between men and women in reproduction can be dismissed as a product of the social imagination, for clearly they cannot. Reproductive differences cannot be collapsed into some simplistic notion of reproductive equality or "sameness" between men and women. But the minimal role now given to men in reproductive processes is a relatively recent social construction that should be subject to a critical rethinking.

This chapter is not intended as a comprehensive history of the reproductive sciences but as an illustration of how cultural influences inform even the most fundamental understandings of men's role in reproductive biology. Early theories of reproductive difference were framed by the dominant "one-sex" paradigm, the belief that the male and female bodies were mirror images of each other, with the female "internal" organs simply a reverse construction of the male "external" reproductive organs. As this one-sex theory was historically contested, three dominant paradigms competed for legitimacy in understandings of the specific processes of procreation: (1) preformation theory, which presumed either that the sperm or the egg contained an entire preformed being in a miniaturized form; (2) epigenesis theory, which posited a developmental model of human creation but still attributed differential reproductive importance to men and women; and the paradigm now dominant, (3) the genetic/hormonal difference model, which recognizes the equivalent genetic contributions of men and women to human procreation but shifts assumptions of reproductive difference onto gestational and hormonal grounds.

The History of Male Reproduction

Although the scientific imagination has speculated about the male role in conception since antiquity, certain knowledge of the role of sperm in the reproductive process was not established in the medical sciences until the end of the nineteenth century. Sperm itself was discovered much later than human ova, and historical investigation of semen was met with deep suspicion until well into the nineteenth century. Despite the fact that the Dutch scientist Antoni van Leeuwenhoek observed the male "animalcula" in 1677, scientific paradigms did not recognize the equal contributions of sperm and egg in conception for more than another 200 years.[1]

The late discovery of sperm and its role in human procreation can be explained only partly by the limitations of early scientific methods. After all, the mechanics of the human body made sperm more readily accessible than eggs to human investigation. Yet cultural beliefs cast

semen, as well as the male reproductive system, as "inappropriate" for scientific investigation and, as a result, the male reproductive body remained relatively understudied.

For much of ancient and modern history, Western science and medicine believed that the male and female bodies were mirrored versions of the same one-sex body. This paradigm set the larger framework for understanding men's and women's contributions to human reproduction. One-sex theory posited that the male and female genitals were essentially equivalent in structure, with the male body the more perfect construction. Ovaries were likened to the testicles (and, in fact, were called the female "testes" until the early nineteenth century), and the cervix or vagina was likened to the penis, turned inward.[2] As Galen put it in the second century A.D.: "Think first, please, of the man's [external genitalis] turned in and extending inward between the rectum and the bladder. If this should happen, the scrotum would necessarily take the place of the uterus with the testes lying outside, next to it on either side."[3]

This one-sex model, although contested throughout medical history, consistently privileged the masculine sex and dominated medical and philosophical thought from antiquity through the early seventeenth century.[4] Aristotle, for instance, believed that both males and females produced "sperma" from their blood—seed from the male and menstrual fluid from the female. Yet women's fluid was inferior. They could not turn sperma into seed because of their "cold" nature and hence could not produce the essence of human life. As evidence, Aristotle suggested: "A sign that the female does not emit the kind of seed that the male emits, and that generation is not due to the mixing of both as some hold, is that often the female conceives without experiencing the pleasure of intercourse."[5] It was the active male seed that produced life from the passive menstrual fluid. Aristotle portrayed women as being little more than incubators. Semen tried to produce the highest form of life, the male, and in its failing produced the less perfect product, the female.[6] "A woman," Aristotle argued, "is as it were an infertile male; the female, in fact, is a female on account of an inability of a sort, viz. It lacks the power to concoct semen out of the final state of nourishment (that is either blood, or

its counterpart in bloodless animals) because of the coldness of its nature."[7] Aristotle also believed, like a number of Greek physiologists before him, that the sex of the offspring was determined by which testicle had produced the conceiving sperm, with males coming from the father's right testis and female from the left. Early accounts of reproductive physiology also mistakenly believed that male offspring developed only on the right side of the womb, and females on the left. Presumably, natural divisions between men and women were so deeply rooted that segregation began before birth.

Greek mythology had also often characterized the male as the creator of life, with Zeus giving birth from his head to Athena and from his thigh to Dionysus. And as Greek philosopher Aeschylus cast it, "She who is called the mother is not her offspring's parent, but nurse to the newly sown embryo. The male, who mounts, begets. The female, a stranger, guards a stranger's child."[8] Plato argued that "the woman in her conception and generation is but the imitation of the earth and not the earth of the woman."[9] Despite women's passive role in procreation, women were held responsible for the quality of the "environment" in which the fetus grew and also for the care of children after birth.[10] One might think that procreative theories that placed so much importance on the male contribution would also place the burden of reproductive responsibility on the man.[11] But not so, as men retained power over children but not responsibility for their daily care. Plato called for state-based (masculine) supervision of reproduction, with prohibitions on pregnancy (through forced abortions) for women deemed inappropriate for reproduction, such as women over the age of forty.[12] The father's formative role in procreation also endowed him with the power of life over infants. The Greek father retained the right to infanticide or "exposure" of the newborn infant (leaving the infant outside to die of exposure to the elements) in the early weeks of life.[13]

The Aristotelian one-seed model was dominant but not uncontested. Others argued for a more egalitarian model of procreation. Hippocrates, for instance, suggested that "seminal fluids" were produced by both male and female bodies and were similar in nature. Such fluids were generated

by all parts of the human body, which explained the likeness of offspring to their parents. A child, as such, might look more like one parent than another if the fluids of one parent predominated in that particular conception.[14] The Roman anatomist Galen argued for a two-seed model of reproduction, with women, like men, possessing "seed" and with women's pleasure equally necessary to procreation.[15] Despite this presumption of procreative equality, Roman families were ruled by the tyrannical authority of fathers, including the power to put to death both their wives and children.[16]

These assumptions of men's primary importance to human conception and reproduction were evident throughout the centuries. During the sixteenth and seventeenth centuries, some even speculated that human generation was possible without women at all, if male seed could be deposited in the stomach of a horse and nurtured by human blood.[17] Reproductive texts often cast women as the passive "landscape," "orchard," or "vessel" within which the seed was stored and grown, with the reproductive contributions of the female seen as farming, orchard keeping, or craft work. In this way, procreation was considered to be men's work.[18]

Such assumptions of male predominance in biological reproduction were not uncontested. "Learned women" of the early 1700s offered more generous interpretations of women's role in biological reproduction, with the female contributing both substance and character to their offspring. Yet this alternative account appears to have received little hearing in the dominant medical texts of the day.[19] More typical were those who attributed to women a more active role in both sexuality and reproduction, even as they saw only males producing "human seed" and more biologically important to the production of offspring. Medical texts in the late seventeenth century, for instance, sometimes characterized women as the sexual aggressors, with the womb pursuing the seed of man: "in some Women the wombe is so greedy and lickerish that it doth even come down to meet nature, sucking, and (as it were) snatching the same."[20] In another account, the womb "delightfully opens, ravenously attracts the mans Seed."[21] The womb "skipping as it were for joy, may

meet her Husband's Sperm, graciously and freely receive the same, and draw it into its innermost Cavity . . . sprinkle it with her own Sperm . . . that so by the commixture of both, Conception may arise."[22] But despite the active role of the "wombe," men remained the progenitors of life.

Preformation Theory

Social and technological developments in the seventeenth century, particularly the development of the microscope, triggered new controversies over human conception. Earlier models of reproduction gave way to theories of human preformation. Preformationism was first articulated in 1674 by the French priest Nicolas Malebranche:

> We may say that all plants are in smaller form in their germs.
> By examining the germ of a tulip bulb with a simple magnify-
> ing glass or seen with the naked eye, we discover very easily
> the different parts of the tulip. It does not seem unreasonable
> to say that there are infinite trees inside one single germ, since
> the germ contains not only the tree but also its seed. . . .
> Perhaps all the bodies of men and animals born until the end
> of times were created at the creation of the world.[23]

Preformation theory is the idea that the complete human being exists preformed inside the male or female body before conception. As science historian Angus McLaren notes, "They presented an image of a mono-parental embryo in which conception implied simply an enlargement of what was already there. Human beings didn't themselves 'create,' but simply brought to fruition that which God had already created at Genesis, that all human being had been 'concealed in the loins of Adam and Eve.'"[24] Such theories were driven by religious conviction, presupposing the existence of a higher being who had produced all life in complete miniature form at the moment of genesis. As one late-seventeenth-century theologian put it, "It seems most probable that the fibers of all the Plants and all the Animals that have ever been, or ever shall be in the World,

have been formed at the origin of the world by the Almighty Creator within the first of each respective kind."[25]

Preformation theories reached their height of popularity in the 1670s and continued through the middle of the eighteenth century. Preformation theorists were divided into two camps: the "ovists," who believed the embryo was housed inside the female egg, and the "spermists" or "animalculists," who believed the preformed being existed inside the sperm. Both theories managed to allocate primary generative power to the male. Ovists argued that the preformed being rested in the egg, activated into development by sexual excitement or the jostling of seminal fluid. As one embryologist of the seventeenth century suggested: "the egg is weak and powerless and so requires the energy of the semen of the male to initiate growth."[26] During the seventeenth and early eighteenth century, this characterization was quite common: the human egg was "shaken" into development by the active sperm; the fetus was "excited" into life by the "seminal worms."[27] In 1768, the Italian naturalist Lazzaro Spallanzani claimed to have discovered a "preformed tadpole folded up and concentrated" inside the egg of a frog before fertilization.[28] As Spallanzani put it, "the spermatic fluid is the stimulating fluid, which, by penetrating the heart of the tadpole, excites more frequent and stronger pulsations and gives rise to a very tangible augmentation of parts and to that life which follows fecundation."[29]

By contrast, animalculists argued that the being rested within the male seminal fluids, like a tiny homunculus, coming to fruition only once planted in the "soil" of the woman's womb, where it was nourished by the female fluids.[30] Animalculists presented women as little more than passive recipients of the male gift of the child.[31] Human ova were sometimes cast as the product, not the source, of reproduction or as a product of semen itself, "globules" formed by animalcules that were unused after intercourse.[32]

If women were not the true progenitors of human life, they often still retained the power to ruin human development. While denying women the power of procreation, animalculists, like many ancients before them, attributed to women the power to "alter the figure of the fetus,"

the theory of maternal impressions.[33] This was the power not only to impart maternal traits but also to disrupt human development: "Her nourishment, her work, her sleep, all must contribute to the formation of a new creature . . . the very air she breathes may become the food or the poison of the fetus, and she must put a stop to her passions and stay away from the enticements of her unleashed imagination."[34]

The power of the female imagination could render the child deformed at birth. Maternal imprint could thus be perceived as the source of all mystery and evil in birth, including physical deformities, diseases, and disabilities. Women could in this way produce children born with the attributes of animals if they stared too long at an image of a beast, or they could produce children of a different skin color if they gazed too long at a portrait of a dark-skinned man.[35] Others disclaiming such power on the part of the mother asserted the dominance of the father in the production of fetal traits, as one early-eighteenth-century critic noted:

> By what Right has the Mother's Fancy any Influence upon the
> Body of the *Foetus*, which comes from the *Semen virile* and
> which is, in respect to her, but a *Passenger*, who has taken
> there his Lodging for a short time? If the Father could not
> cause, by the Strength of Imagination, any change in the
> Animalcule which was originally in his Body: I desire to know
> why the Mother should plead that Priviledge in Exclusion to
> the Father?[36]

Preformation theory was bolstered by the development of the microscope and with it the "discovery" of human sperm in semen. The Dutch investigator Antoni van Leeuwenhoek was reportedly obsessed with what the microscope could reveal. He cut fine slices of animal tissue, nerves, and his own skin for observation under the small glass beads that powered his early microscope. He observed fleas and mites, blood and saliva, and "little animals" in fluids of all sorts.[37] He collected anatomical parts from local butchers and fishermen and infested grains from local merchants, and recruited a seaman to bring back a whale penis to him.[38] But while human blood, saliva, and skin were thoroughly examined, Leeuwenhoek

expressed frustration that cultural beliefs seemed to make human semen inappropriate for scientific observation.

It wasn't until 1677 that Leeuwenhoek turned his instrument to human semen and discovered in it a "vast number of living animalcules." As Leeuwenhoek wondrously observed:

> They all have the same size and the same shape, they move
> their tails in a way that is clearly meant to make them swim,
> and in consequence they are true animals. Whereas one is
> going to the right, another is going to the left; one comes up
> and another goes down. Some start moving in a certain
> direction and then turn themselves around by a swing of the
> tail to go back the way they came.[39]

Leeuwenhoek's discovery of such microscopic organisms generated from the scientific, philosophical, and religious communities both intense interest and skepticism about the significance of sperm and men to processes of human reproduction. What was the function of sperm in human generation? Perhaps sperm existed only to "excite the male to perform the sexual act" or to prompt the preformed embryo in the ovum to grow. Or perhaps, as the ancients had suggested, buried in the sperm lay the entire generative principle—a ready-made animal that the fluids of the uterus would stimulate to full development.

Leeuwenhoek himself attributed will to these little creatures. He used what he perceived as their volition as evidence that sperm contained the whole of the developing human being. Such "evidence" lent credence to the established spermist paradigm, this time suggesting that these male "animals" were the source of human generation. Leeuwenhoek spent much of the rest of his career dissecting spermatozoa in search of vascular systems and internal organs that could grow into a complete fetus.[40]

But there were also many critics: those who believed that what Leeuwenhoek had observed were simply the bacterial products of decay, those who believed that the egg contained within it the preformed being, and those who contested the preformation theorists altogether, a

stance that would later lead to theories of epigenesis. To such interlocutors, Leeuwenhoek responded:

> Those who have always tried to maintain that the animalcules were the product of putrefaction and did not serve for procreation, will be defeated. Some also imagine that these animalcules do not live, but that it is only the fire that is present in the sperm. But I take it that these animalcules are composed of such a multitude of parts as, such people believe, compose our bodies.[41]

Theories of preformation, whether *ex animalculo* or *ex ovo*, held important implications for assumptions about which sex held the ultimate power of human creation.

The discovery of the human ovum in 1827 combined with the development of human autopsy, which enabled extraction of the conceptus from the female corpse, to reveal a quite different story of procreation. In 1828, the German biologist C. E. von Baer was the first to actually see the human egg. This observation threw into question assumptions that the male animalcule contained the human being preformed. As a result of observations of the human egg and the presence of the embryo within the female body, many in the scientific community largely dismissed animalculists. The work of Italian physiologist Spallanzani, who had pioneered work in artificial insemination in spaniels, gave much credence to naturalists in the ovist tradition. By the early nineteenth century, many naturalists had accepted his position that "the parts were preformed in the egg; the male semen . . . stimulated the egg to develop; and the spermatic animalcules, accidentally parasites of the testes, had no role in generation."[42]

One might guess that, as the ovist tradition took hold in the early nineteenth century, the reproductive power balance might shift from men to women. Instead, arguments that the embryo existed preformed in the egg were used to justify the social division of labor between men and women, not just in reproduction but in society at large: As the science historian John Farley has argued:

Sex was simply the means of procreation used by organisms that had, by the division of labor, placed the task of procreation into the hands (or, more appositely, ovaries) of a special individual, the female. Socially and biologically, the female existed solely to bear and raise offspring. The nineteenth-century biological attitude toward sex mirrored that century's social attitude toward women. The status of women was therefore a law of nature; to argue otherwise was to threaten the social and biological fabric of the race.[43]

Farley argued that the biological sciences were used to dictate the division of society into a private female sphere and a public male sphere, justifying, throughout the nineteenth century, the subordination of women in both work and politics and men's primary responsibility and power in both.

From the perspective of the division of labor, sexual reproduction was very simply the means of reproduction employed by those species in which a distinctive reproductive individual, the female, had been formed. In social terms, this division of labor into males and females allowed the male to expend his energies in more noble and civilized pursuits while placing the entire burden of procreation and childbearing on the female.[44]

Reproduction thus became a uniquely female occupation, with the male freed to pursue higher social functions. Such theories reflected the nineteenth-century move to specialized divisions of labor in work, with the male and female segregated into distinct reproductive functions.

Despite women's central role in life creation, throughout the nineteenth century men continued to be cast as critical to human reproduction. It was men who were responsible, through sexual stimulation, for the release of the egg and for providing the semen that remained critical for stimulating the egg into growth. Until the mid-nineteenth century, it was widely believed that human ova were released only if the woman experienced sexual pleasure. Endowing men with another kind of pro-

creative power, it was the responsibility of the male—and the sperm—to excite the woman into production of her seed.[45] Indeed, because the pleasures of sexual stimulation were seen as necessary to conception, until the beginning of the nineteenth century, pregnancy could be used as evidence of the victim's complicity in cases of sexual assault.[46] One-sex theories had also presupposed that because men needed to be aroused to ejaculate, as mimics of the male, women's internal organs required the same.[47] Shifts in the mid to late nineteenth century to an ideology of middle-class, domestic, "passionless" womanhood, as well as the discovery of evidence of ovulation in women who had never had heterosexual intercourse, would later undermine theories that women's sexual pleasure was necessary to ovulation.[48] Patterns of ovulation—that women released eggs in cycles and not at sexual stimulation—were not well understood until the end of the nineteenth century.

Overall, from the ancients through the early nineteenth century, there was no consensus on the nature of the biological processes by which human beings were conceived and developed. The physical limits of scientific observation into the biological processes left much room for the cultural imagination, which often, but not always, constructed these processes in favor of men.[49]

Epigenesis

By the mid-nineteenth century, some scientists had documented the penetration of the egg by the sperm.[50] This observation supported a developmental, or epigenetic, model of conception and creation. Refined methods of dissection allowed scientists to see that fertilized eggs changed in both substance and form as they developed. Cell theory, the idea that the human body was a composite of particles that transformed and developed as humans grew to maturity, provided the foundation for understanding these transformations. Darwin's work also contributed to the view that human beings did not exist preformed but instead adapted, through the gradual transformation of shared traits, from one generation to the next.[51]

Beginning in the mid-nineteenth century, German scientists bolstered the idea of epigenesis by leaving behind the dominant "mechanical" model of reproduction (the preformed whole simply grew into larger form) in favor of a "chemical" model of human reproduction in which a combination of distinct elements came together and reacted to produce and develop an entirely new being.[52] Postmortem autopsy, which did not fully develop until the early to mid-nineteenth century, lent support to epigenetic theories.[53] Autopsies could now be performed on women who had died during pregnancy or childbirth, and technologies of preservation made it possible to more carefully examine the fetuses of miscarriages at different stages of pregnancy and development. Embryos at ten weeks of gestation had relatively no internal organ development, whereas fetuses at twenty or thirty weeks had complex and sophisticated internal biological structures.

With the advance of embryology in the mid-nineteenth century, researchers could see (and finally believe, because embryology had been practiced in crude form since the time of Aristotle) that not all human organs existed preformed in the egg, sperm, or conceptus.[54] Yet this observation did not settle the question of men's role in biological reproduction. As early as 1820, French scientists (Prevost and Dumas) had found that sperm could penetrate the mucous membrane surrounding the egg, but they interpreted this as evidence that the sperm provided only the rudimentary cerebral spinal system of the developing embryo.[55] Even with recognition that the sperm penetrated the egg, many continued to argue that the sperm were merely parasites that lived within the testicles, like intestinal worms often found in the digestive system, and that spermatic parasites gave energy but no material structure to the developing fetus.

This belief in sperm as a form of parasite persisted throughout the nineteenth century. Scientists claimed to have dissected and found internal animal structures inside sperm, this time not to prove that the sperm carried within it a preformed human being but to prove that sperm were parasitic creatures with their own structures of anatomy. Indeed, scientists in the nineteenth century tended to discount the idea that sperm

contributed materially to the embryo because it "seemed too near the discredited theory of animalculism."[56] But a sperm stimulating an egg hardly seemed sufficient to transmit paternal traits to offspring. By the mid-nineteenth century, there seemed no resolution to the question of the material role of sperm in human reproduction. Even those who argued for theories of epigenesis did not always recognize the equal importance of sperm and egg to human generation.

Science historians have argued that the ability of science to observe processes of fertilization was limited not so much by the technologies of science as by the cultural lens through which this work was viewed. As Farley has observed, reproductive scientists cannot be divorced from their social contexts: "The biological theories to which the nineteenth-century scientists subscribed, an almost sexless egg-laying female and a reproductively insignificant energizing male, were as much a reflection of . . . middle-class values as they were the result of the biologists' scientific discoveries."[57] A host of social institutions flowed from the assumptions underneath this biological reality: Men's limitless sexual desire must be constrained by marriage and family structure. Women's primary role lay in conceiving, bearing, and rearing children. Males contributed "force and vitality" (even brain and spine) to the next generation, and women "housed and fed" the developing fetus.[58]

Such assumptions of gender difference led medical scientists to focus almost exclusively on the female reproductive system as an object of study. The turn of the twentieth century brought gynecology as a new medical specialty. Women became identified as a "distinct type within the human species."[59] Reproductive sciences in the nineteenth and early twentieth centuries focused primarily on the "diseases and disorders" of female reproduction through the development of gynecological and obstetrical investigations. As such, the science of reproduction was "management" of female reproductive health. Philosophers and anatomical scientists renewed their attempts to document the natural differences between men and women not only in reproductive organs but also in brain size, bone structure, muscle form, cells, hair, and even blood vessels.[60] Not only were men and women not of "one sex" but also they

hardly seemed of the same species. Sex difference was not just skin deep or confined to the sexual organs, as earlier anatomists had argued, but permeated the whole of the human body.[61] By the late nineteenth century, this dichotomization of the sexes dominated not just the reproductive medical field but all of medical study. Cellular physiology sought even to justify sex difference by documenting the inherent passivity of "female" cells and the active nature of "male" cells.

By the middle of the nineteenth century, physicians searching for the "heart" of sexual differences between men and women focused on the ovaries. As Virchow, a founding father of the field of physiology, noted in 1848:

> It has been completely wrong to regard the uterus as the characteristic organ. . . . The womb . . . is merely an organ of secondary importance. Remove the ovary, and we shall have before us a masculine woman, an ugly half-form with the coarse and harsh form, the heavy bone formation, the moustache, the rough voice, the flat chest, the sour and egoistic mentality and the distorted outlook. . . . in short, all that we admire and respect in woman as womanly, is merely dependent on her ovaries.[62]

This focus on the ovaries as the "place in the body where the 'essence' of femininity was located" led to an upsurge in medical interventions in ovarian surgeries and treatments. Central to this femininity was that idea that women alone had the primary nature to reproduce the species.

Genetic Equality/Hormonal Difference

By the early twentieth century, scientific investigation had come to relative consensus over the role of sperm in human reproduction: that sperm contributed not just "force" and "energy" but substantive structure to the egg.[63] This recognition shifted larger debates over reproductive difference from reproductive physiology to reproductive hormones. The concept of hormones was coined in 1905, and endocrinology was well

established by the 1920s and 1930s. The field of sex endocrinology introduced the concept of female and male sex hormones as chemical determinants of femininity and masculinity.[64] Endocrinologists argued that hormones not only drove reproductive cycles but also influenced women's moods, behaviors, and overall temperament. As Oudshoorn has observed of the endrocrinological sciences in the 1930s and 1940s:

> based on the female sex hormone blood test, gynecologists
> now suggested that men and women could be characterized
> by the specific nature of their hormone regulation, emphasiz
> ing the cyclic nature of female sex hormone production in
> women and the continuous, stable nature of male sex hor
> mone production in men. Sex endocrinology thus attached
> the quality of cyclicity to femininity, and stability to mascu
> linity.[65]

The development of hormonal theory further justified beliefs that men and women had different reproductive functions rooted in their biologies. The biological (hormonal) imperative for women was to procreate. Male hormones, on the other hand, fostered aggression and sexual drive, with fatherhood a secondary consequence of these nonreproductive desires.

Women were presumed to be "ruled" by their hormones, an expression of the centrality of the female to reproduction and the centrality of reproduction to women, as it influenced the whole of the female life. Women's biology produced a temperament that suited her for caregiving, and male biology produced in men a lesser emotional investment in reproduction. Despite scientific recognition of the equivalence of male and female genetic contributions to conception, the larger accepted paradigm presumed fundamental biological differences on both hormonal and emotional levels.

From the 1950s through the mid-1970s, sociobiology constructed a new story of reproductive difference. Some argued that the very size of the reproductive cells offered evidence for differing reproductive strategies by men and women. Such assumptions remained common within biological textbooks, with sperm cast as the aggressor and eggs

the passive recipient in processes of fertilization.[66] Sociobiologists argued that, whereas women produce a single large egg, men produce millions of sperm and that this biological structure reflected men's natural tendencies toward infidelity and women's toward monogamy. As the British sociobiologist Jeremy Cherfas argued, "Males, with their cheap throwaway sperm" are naturally more promiscuous. "Mating costs them so little [that men] seek sexual opportunities wherever they can."[67] In addition, evolutionary biologists argued that the differing strategies of men and women lead to differing psychological structures, with men more distant from human procreative processes and women more deeply entwined in them. As Donald Symons, one sociobiologist, has put it:

> Since human females, like those of most animal species, make a relatively large investment in the production and survival of each offspring, and males can get away with a relatively small one, they'll approach sex and reproduction, as animals do, in rather different ways from males. . . . Women should be more choosy and more hesitant, because they're more at risk from the consequences of a bad choice. And men should be less discriminating, more aggressive and have a greater taste for variety of partners because they're less at risk.[68]

Although many presumptions of essential biological differences between the sexes were challenged throughout the 1980s and 1990s, assumptions about essential reproductive differences persisted. Like their historical predecessors, biological scientists studying human reproduction often imparted great social significance to men's and women's distinct physiological structures. Studies focused on the hormonal differences between the sexes, with aggression attributed to male testosterone levels and estrogen controlling women's monthly mood swings.[69] Even more progressive sociological accounts of reproduction often carried within them presumptions of essential reproductive difference going well beyond simple biology. As the sociologist William Marsiglio has argued:

Men are anatomically and hormonally different from women. ... The biological realities of sexually induced reproduction have limited men's experiential opportunities during pregnancy and childbirth. The biological processes associated with sex and reproduction therefore represent the foundation for men's emotional and psychological alienation from the reproductive process.[70]

The story of reproductive difference was thus constructed in this way: Men and women are anatomically different in their reproductive functions. Men may conceive, but only women gestate. Hormonal differences between men and women are a product of (and in turn reproduce) these anatomical distinctions. These innate functional differences then produce the different interests and social roles of men and women in reproduction. These different social roles in reproduction then produce differences in men's and women's roles in familial, political, and economic structures. Although we might modify social reproductive roles by drawing men more deeply into caregiving functions, we cannot alter the basic biological building blocks of human reproduction. Reproductive biology is the bottom line of sexual difference and is beyond social critique. Anatomical difference presumably places women at the heart and men at the periphery of biological reproduction.

But even at the level of simple biology, culture continues to construct—and, more important, distort—understandings of the male role in human reproduction. In times when the science of reproduction was in its infancy, when there was so much unknown about biological reproductive processes, the cultural imagination that constructed stories of men's and women's relative functions in human reproduction is easier to see. But even the scientific certainty that we now presume to have reached in our knowledge of human reproduction does not lay to rest questions of the cultural construction of biological reproduction.

At the most basic level of reproductive biology, we can question the differential importance given to men and women in reproduction. Even before conception, it is often considered less important to study the

production of sperm, to understand the infertility of men, or to treat male reproductive disorders than it is to study and treat women. At conception, it is often assumed that the genetic contribution of men is less important in causing miscarriage or in transmitting genetic disorders to the fetus. As pregnancy progresses, it is assumed that the behaviors of women and the exposures of the female body are more important in determining birth defects and disorders than the behaviors and exposures of men who produce the sperm necessary to conceiving children. The disproportionate attention to women, while sometimes justified, often unjustly minimizes the role of men. This minimizing is a product not only of the "realities" of biology but also of the social value we impart to male reproduction.

The secondary biological role of men in reproduction—the first assumption of reproductive masculinity—has both privileged and burdened men. It has privileged men by casting them as less responsible for concerns of reproduction, less vulnerable to the harms of the outside world, and more distant from the children they produce. But at the same time it has led to a distorted view of men in human reproduction, a neglect of the male reproductive system, and a devaluation of the male role in producing healthy children.

DROPPING SPERM COUNTS 3

The Science and Politics of Male Reproductive Health

In 1992, a team of Danish researchers reported a drop of more than 40% in sperm count rates worldwide over the previous fifty years. They noted as well an almost fourfold increase in rates of testicular cancer in men and a doubling of genital birth defects in baby boys. Others noted a decrease in the male-to-female birth rate; it seemed that fewer baby boys were being born. In the ten years to follow, these claims would be among the most highly disputed in both science and politics. It would seem that these measures would be simple to assess: Had testicular cancers increased or declined? Had sperm counts risen or fallen? Had the proportion of baby boys gone up or down? How was it possible that we didn't know or hadn't noticed? But no one seemed certain about the state of men's reproductive health. The lack of historical attention to male reproductive health meant that there were few baseline measurements to recall, little information about the extent to which such reproductive ailments had afflicted men in the past. Neglect throughout the twentieth century meant that there were few tracking systems to assess the simplest measures of male reproductive health.

When such issues spilled over into public consciousness, as they did in the ten years following the Danish team's initial report, the response displayed many of the elements of public panic, with deeply conflicted

responses in the scientific community, the media, government agencies worldwide, and the general public. Some declared a crisis of epic proportions—the "feminization" or "chemical castration" of men and the potential end of the human race. Others denied such claims as social and scientific hysteria. At one extreme, claims of a monumental health crisis appeared to eclipse scientific reason. At the other, the doubts with which these measures were met appeared to exceed reasonable scientific skepticism.

What was at stake, it seemed, was more than just male reproductive health but masculinity itself. This failure to agree on even the simplest measures of male reproductive health is evidence not only of the difficulty of tracking rates of disease or disability but also of cultural barriers to the recognition of the potential reproductive vulnerabilities of men and the volatile nature of any suggestion of male reproductive failure.

Social, scientific, and political controversies surrounded male reproductive health disorders at the end of the twentieth century. These controversies, as well as the public response, were informed by the second element of reproductive masculinity—the presumption of the invulnerability of the male reproductive body. This presumption has led, first, to a historical lack of attention to male reproductive problems and now to conflict-ridden responses to such issues. Ultimately, appropriate attention to these problems, including simple assessments of the level of risks men truly face, hardly seems possible until this second presumption of reproductive masculinity is challenged as well.

The "Diseases of Men"

There is no question but that those afflictions peculiar to the male have been more neglected, less fully understood, and more frequently treated "for what there is in it," rather than a desire to benefit the patient, than was ever true of the diseases of women. We believe that to-day fully as barbarous, slipshod, and dishonest work is being done in this class of affections as was ever to be observed in gynic disease.

Diseases of men have ever been the fruitful field of the quack and the charlatan." (1891 editorial in the *Journal of the American Medical Association*)[1]

Historically, the singular focus of reproductive medicine on the female reproductive system was paralleled by a concurrent neglect of the male system. Men, it seemed, with their peripheral role in human creation, had elementary reproductive systems that needed no special study or medical attention. Like a simple mechanical instrument, the male system either worked or it didn't. Because women were seen as primary in reproduction, problems of fertility were typically assumed to be female in origin. The vulnerable female system stood in contrast to the virile male system, despite nineteenth-century appeals by some physicians that "there is no part of the body that so quickly and painfully resents incompetency and tinkering as does the genito-urinary apparatus of the male."[2]

While the field of gynecology grew throughout the nineteenth century, there was little similar development in andrology—the study of the nature and diseases of male reproduction. As a result, reproductive sciences in the nineteenth and early twentieth century focused primarily on the diseases and disorders of female reproduction through the development of gynecology and obstetrics. The science of reproduction focused primarily on the "management" of women. Although the term *andrology* made a brief appearance in the professional medical lexicon in the late nineteenth century, it was then absorbed (and virtually disappeared) into the field of urology for more than fifty years. The term *andrology* was not reintroduced into medical terminology until 1951, when it was coined by a professor of gynecology in Germany. The first medical journal to address the field (*Andrologie*) was not established until 1969. Although an informal medical association of physicians and researchers focusing on male reproductive health was active in the United States from 1969 onward, not until 1975 was the American Society of Andrology founded.[3] As medical historian Nelly Oudshoorn has rightly observed, "It was only in the late 1970's that scientists and clinicians established andrology as a medical specialty devoted to the study and medical treatment of male

reproductive bodies . . . today, andrology is still a small and marginal profession compared to gynecology."[4]

By the year 2001, the International Society of Andrology (founded in 1981) had thirty-six national societies and more than eight thousand members worldwide.[5] Still, this was a far cry from the size and scope of medical associations, schools, and centers dedicated to the study and treatment of female reproduction. As earlier chapters have suggested, the initial assessments of male reproductive health focused either on male "underproduction" or on "overproduction"—either treatment of male infertility or, even more marginally, control of male fertility through male birth control methods.

As the one of the earliest analysts of male infertility observed:

> Now, when a man is unable to beget children by his wife, although his virility is unimpaired, he is said in common parlance to have a cold nature. To my mind, however, it would be more apt to say that no living animalcules will be found in the seed of such a man, or that, should any living animalcules be found in it, they are too weakly to survive long enough in the womb. (Leeuwenhoek, Letter to the Royal Society, London, March 30, 1685)[6]

Despite Leeuwenhoek's early investigations and concerns, male fertility has been a subject historically understudied. As previous chapters have suggested, ancient physiologists and philosophers proposed different theories of sperm production. One medical historian recounts: "Aristotle thought semen arises from the brain, Hippocrates wrote that semen was transported to the testicles via the arteries behind the ears, and Plato considered that semen originates from the spinal cord." Reproductive disorders of the male system received only limited attention, and not all of this positive. In 1585, Pope Sixtus V apparently decreed that "all marriages in which men do not have two testicles in the scrotum should be dissolved."[7] One of the first clinical practices to treat male reproductive ailments was not established until 1905.[8]

Although the field of andrology has expanded considerably, basic functioning of the male reproductive system remains somewhat of a mystery. As researcher Richard Sharpe put it in 1992:

> We can't monitor sperm production. All we can do is look at the end product. It's like investigating the production of a motor car by looking at whether it's come out of the factory or not, and whether it's got doors on back to front, but not being able to go inside the factory to see where in the production cycle something has gone wrong.[9]

Very few studies have been conducted on the general population of men to determine average sperm counts over extended time periods or even correlations between sperm counts and actual male infertility. Sperm shape and movement appear to be as important as count or, as one news headline personified the findings, "Shapely Swimmers Win Fertility Race!"[10] Sperm count may vary from day to day or week to week, but we're not certain by how much or for what reasons. Sperm count may decrease with age, but it's unclear at what rate. Counts appear to vary by season and by geography, but not enough data exist to determine predictable patterns. Although we know, for instance, that heat slows sperm production, sperm counts are not necessarily lower in tropical climates. We have, therefore, few baseline estimates for establishing what is normal for men, despite the fact that, technically speaking, collecting semen from the male body is relatively easy.

Historically, semen analysis has relied on subjective measures taken by lab technicians who were trained to count sperm under a microscope and observe abnormalities, like dual heads or missing tails. Technicians simply placed sperm samples under a microscope equipped with a grid screen, counted the number of sperm in each grid, and extrapolated total sperm count from this sample. They also assessed normal versus abnormal structure and noted levels of sperm movement. At the end of the twentieth century, sperm was microanalyzed through more objective computer-aided assessment measures.[11] Sperm samples are now

videotaped under a microscope, and sperm shape, size, and speed are assessed with standardized computer assistance.[12]

In contrast to earlier assumptions of the male body as machinelike and sperm as relatively invulnerable to harm, researchers have noted that sperm are apparently fairly fragile—sensitive to both temperature and movement. Evaluation must take place within two hours of being "produced." Samples are prewarmed in an incubator or on a warming plate before being placed under a microscope. Technicians are warned to avoid "vigorous shaking" of the sample to avoid damage to the sperm. If sperm were "produced" by the female body, researchers might have said they were "delivered," but mechanical and production metaphors seem to dominate in studies of men's sperm count.

As the media response to reported drops in sperm count will illustrate, male sperm count, despite its questionable relationship to male fertility, is still considered a primary sign of one's manhood; consequently, low sperm counts typically carry with them stigmas of "unmanliness." As a result, it is not always easy to find willing donors to study. Male participants are subject to a level of sexual surveillance not typically experienced by men: They are asked to refrain from ejaculation at least two days before producing a specimen and may be asked for an "ejaculation calendar" (because sexual frequency may have an effect on sperm levels). They may be asked about alcohol, cigarette, and drug use or be monitored for such use during the study period. As a result, sperm count studies are typically not drawn from the general population but from men who have some other motivation for participating (sperm donors, couples at fertility clinics, or men working in toxic environments) or from men already under state surveillance (in prison or in the military).

Sperm Count Crisis: Scientific Evidence (or Not?)

In the 1980s, Danish pediatrician Niels Skakkebaek noticed an alarming trend in the school-aged boys he saw in his pediatric practice. A surprisingly high number of them were appearing with malformations of the genitals or with one or both testicles undescended—conditions that could

lead to sterility or higher rates of testicular cancer as they grew older. Skakkebaek had already noted a dramatic rise in testicular cancer rates for men. Denmark had the highest rates in the world—nearly one in a hundred men in Denmark would be diagnosed with the disease in their lifetimes. By the mid-1980s, Skakkebaek had documented in his practice a relationship between abnormal cells in the testes, low sperm count, and adult testicular cancer, and he and his colleagues began to investigate this relationship.[13]

Along with other Danish scientists, Skakkebaek had also noticed the difficulties sperm banks were having in recruiting adequate sperm donors, some centers reporting that they had to test ten men to find one good donor.[14] He suspected a relationship between rising rates of cancer and falling sperm count rates. With a group of other researchers, Skakkebaek decided to initiate a preliminary study of sperm quality as the simplest measure of the health (or failure) of the male reproductive system. Their first preliminary study of male airport workers in Denmark found that 50% had abnormal forms of sperm, much higher rates than expected.[15]

To see how widespread this trend might be, the Danish team then collected evidence from all of the sperm count studies they could find that had been conducted worldwide between 1938 and 1990 and combined data from almost 15,000 men to examine long-term sperm count trends. Although varying in their methodology, most of these studies had been conducted to assess sperm quality because of the rise of artificial insemination and sperm banking. Skakkebaek and his associates found a greater than 40% drop in sperm count over the fifty-year period.[16] They noted as well that data from the United States and Europe indicated that testicular cancer had increased "twofold to fourfold over the past 50 years."[17] Because the rates of testicular cancer had risen fairly dramatically over a short time period and sperm counts had dropped in a similar time frame, Skakkebaek and his associates suggested that the cause was "probably due to environmental rather than genetic factors." In conclusion, they suggested that "some common prenatal influences could be responsible both for the decline in sperm density and for the increase in cancer of the testis.

... Whether oestrogens or compounds with oestrogen-like activity ... or other environmental or endogenous factors damage testicular function remains to be determined."[18]

Despite the cautious conclusions of Skakkebaek and other major researchers, critics immediately attacked research findings suggesting any decrease in sperm counts by questioning both the validity of sperm count drops and any association with environmental estrogens. The aggregated studies upon which the Danish team based their findings were questioned on a number of levels: Geographical variation might account for the apparent decline; methodological differences might have skewed the research; subject selection might have produced the appearance of a decline, when in fact there was none. Follow-up analyses sought to take these critics' questions into account.

Some researchers suggested that changes in research methods over the same time period might have skewed the sperm count numbers. Because the sixty-one original studies were conducted before the advent of standardized techniques for semen analysis, critics argued that sperm evaluations could have varied as much as 40% upward or downward, depending on the quality of equipment and the subjectivity of technical readers.[19] The *New England Journal of Medicine* ran a 1995 editorial questioning the validity of the studies' methods and evidence: "The men in these studies ranged in age from 17 to 64 years, the duration of abstinence was for the most part neither controlled nor recorded, and the mean sperm concentration varied threefold." In addition, most studies relied on a single sperm sample, when sperm count levels can vary "two to fourfold" in a single week for an individual man, even under "disciplined conditions of abstinence."[20] Any of these elements could have skewed sperm count assessments up or down, although it was not clear that any one of these complicating factors would have systematically created the appearance of a sperm count decline.

Researchers also looked more carefully at the original sixty-one studies examined by the Danish team. Studies controlled for abstinence time, age, percent of men with proven fertility, and specimen evaluation methods confirmed the decline in sperm density for the United States and

northern Europe but noted that not enough data were available to assess sperm count rates for non-Western countries.[21] In 1996, a prominent group of nineteen scientists issued a statement that "several aspects of male reproductive health have changed dramatically for the worse over 30 to 50 years . . . [including a] striking decline in sperm counts in the ejaculate of normal men."[22]

Yet critics contested these conclusions and argued that sperm count rates vary by geographical location and that comparisons between East Coast and West Coast or First World and Third World countries could create the appearance of a decline that didn't exist. Researchers Harry Fisch and E. T. Goluboff of Columbia Presbyterian Hospital in New York disaggregated the original sixty-one studies, first eliminating all those containing fewer than a hundred subjects. Of the remaining twenty studies, they found that all of the studies before 1970 were from the United States, and 80% of these were from New York City, which, they argued, has typically higher sperm counts than other locations. In contrast, 80% of the studies conducted after 1970 were from locations with typically lower counts—Europe and five Third World countries.[23] Others argued that these geographical variations might be due to ethnic differences between cities, with some evidence that Chinese men have naturally lower sperm counts than white, African-American, or Hispanic men.[24] These conclusions were limited by the fact that they were drawn on only twenty of the original sixty-one studies. Nevertheless, many welcomed this study. As one commentator reported, "There is no longer a need to feel impotent in the face of mass extinction."[25]

Sperm count studies multiplied across the globe. Declines were found in the United States, Pakistan, Germany, Hong Kong, Sweden, and Belgium.[26] One study of four European cities cited significant geographical variations in sperm count, with the lowest sperm counts for Danish men, followed by French, Scottish, and Finnish men.[27] French researchers found that the sperm count of men in Paris had declined 2–3% every year from 1973 to 1992, along with increases in the percentage of abnormal sperm and decreases in sperm concentration and motility.[28] A study of more than 48,000 Canadian men showed similar declines.[29] Danish

scientists found that 43% of army recruits tested in one study had sperm count levels low enough to lead to decreased fertility.[30] Studies that held geography constant seemed to confirm the decline.

Others suggested the data on sperm count drop could be skewed by subject selection. Over the forty-year period, most studies of sperm quality have been conducted at fertility clinics or on sperm donors—men with either especially low or especially high counts.[31] If the early studies came from fertility clinics and the later ones from sperm donors, that difference might also create the false appearance of a decline. Follow-up studies tried to hold subject selection constant. One study collected semen from men who were seeking fertility treatment with their partners at the University of Southern California Medical Center in Los Angeles. Sperm counts of these men, compared with semen collected in a 1951 study, showed only a 1% decline.[32] Researchers in Australia said that sperm donors in Sydney remained "as fertile as ever," with no decline between 1983 and 2001, and no decline in sperm counts was found in one study of donors in Seattle.[33] It would be reasonable to assume, researchers suggested, that if there had been a drop in sperm count worldwide, this would be reflected in a decrease in the counts of sperm donors.[34]

Other critics looked at male infertility rates, under the assumption that if sperm counts had been dropping, then male infertility should be rising, but there was no apparent drop in male fertility during the past fifty years. On the contrary, studies suggested that "time to pregnancy"—the number of months it takes a couple to achieve conception—had improved.[35] As a *Lancet* commentary accompanying the report of study suggested: "At present, the near-panic sometimes expressed in the lay press about the effects of environmental pollution on sperm quality and male fertility is not justified."[36] Such studies of time to pregnancy provided ammunition for those who questioned the validity of sperm count studies more broadly, even though researchers also noted that any decline in male fertility might have been compensated for by improvements in techniques for predicting ovulation and achieving conception over the same time period.[37] Nevertheless, stories such as "Potent News" in the

Milwaukee Journal Sentinel reported that "the virility of American men hasn't changed much in the past four decades."[38]

Countering such hopeful sentiments, others warned that the natural overabundance of sperm in a man's semen is no reason to be complacent about male fertility. Even if they were in decline, sperm counts still remained, on average, well above the level needed for male fertility. But as researcher Richard Sharpe of Scotland noted, "If we are being exposed to something that is having this effect and we don't know what it is, then we don't know whether we've reached the bottom of that decline. . . . If we were to come along in another 50 years' time and find our sperm counts had fallen by another 50 per cent then we would be extremely concerned."[39]

Data from the sixty-one studies on the nearly 15,000 men examined over five decades, burdened as they were by methodological difficulties, didn't seem to be able to resolve the question of dropping sperm counts. Studies conducted on thousands of men in the 1990s didn't seem to hold definitive answers either, although much of the research confirmed Skakkebaek's original conclusions. The evidence, while still contested, seemed to suggest that sperm counts had decreased, at least in some parts of the globe, over the preceding fifty years.

Male Reproductive Deformations

While debate continued on the question of sperm count drops, others explored the evidence presented by Skakkebaek and his colleagues of a substantial increase in malformations and diseases of the male reproductive system. Hypospadias is a developmental malformation in which the urethra opens on the underside of the penis or on the perineum. This malformation can lead to male infertility or a range of health problems. Reports had suggested increased rates of this malformation from the 1960s to the 1980s. Researchers also reported increases in cryptorchidism—a condition in which one or both of the testicles fail to descend. Undescended testes had been suspected as a cause of increases in testicular cancer in men, as well as a cause of male infertility. Two U.S. studies

showed increases in this condition. As researchers framed the discussion, both hypospadias and cryptorchidism represented forms of "feminization" of the male body.[40]

In addition, Skakkebaek had noted a dramatic increase in testicular cancer rates. In follow-ups to the Danish team's original observations, researchers documented in young men an increase of testicular cancer, the most common form of cancer in men age 15–44, with a peak incidence between the ages of 18 and 35. Some studies found that rates of testicular cancer had increased worldwide, with the highest incidence in Denmark, Switzerland, and New Zealand. One research group reexamining the evidence concluded that the evidence was overwhelming that testicular cancer incidence had "increased rapidly" in virtually all countries studied.[41] In the United States, testicular cancer rates among white active-duty servicemen 17–44 increased by 61% from the 1970s to the 1990s.[42] Reports in the *Journal of the National Cancer Institute* confirmed that testicular cancer had increased by 51.2% in white men between 1973 and 1996.[43]

Critics challenged these numbers as well, with scientists such as Stephen Safe arguing that the evidence showed not a comprehensive increase but changing demographic distributions in these disorders before 1985. Rates of hypospadias and cryptorchidism, he argued, had not changed or had actually decreased in some areas since 1985.[44] Although increased rates of testicular cancer appear to be relatively undisputed, critics like Safe suggested that geographical variations in rates remained unexplained and were unlikely to be due to environmental exposures.[45] Despite such criticisms, the evidence seemed fairly clear that these two disorders, as well as rates of testicular cancer, had increased dramatically over a relatively short time period and that these increases were not limited to a single geographical area.

"Bye, Bye, Baby Boys"

Researchers also saw changing birth sex ratios as one indicator that male reproductive health may be affected by environmental toxins.[46] A 1976

explosion at a chemical plant in Seveso, Italy, exposed residents to high levels of dioxin (TCDD). Parents with the highest blood levels of the toxin produced no baby boys for the next seven years. In the general Seveso population in the nine years that followed the explosion, the rate of birth for baby boys dropped to half.[47] Interestingly, the study found that TCDD exposure had a greater impact on men than on women. Females, the study found, were "insensitive to the effects of TCDD" and gave birth to both male and female children if the fathers were non-exposed men. On the other hand, the young men in Seveso who were exposed to relatively low levels of TCDD before or during puberty continued to produce disproportionately female children later in life. For these men, dioxin exposure seemed to permanently affect the sex ratio of the children they fathered.[48]

Initially, following conception, all embryos are female. Between six and nine weeks of gestational age, hormonal stimulation typically begins the process of sexual differentiation. Historically, birth rates are skewed slightly in favor of boys (on average 106 males to 100 females). Little or no androgen stimulation can either stop male development or produce a "feminized" male that may appear female at birth.[49] Estrogen or estrogenic chemicals, if delivered to the developing embryo at this stage, have been shown to disrupt sexual development in clinical animal studies.[50] Incidents like the Seveso accident seemed to suggest that the same process could be produced in humans. Researchers turned to broader studies of sex birth ratios.

Throughout the late 1990s, researchers found a decrease in male births in Denmark, the United States, and Canada. In 1996, researchers in Denmark found statistically significant declines in male births from the 1960s to 1995. Researchers again suggested that toxic exposures in utero may have caused increased miscarriage rates for male fetuses or sex transformation in utero.[51] In 1997, researchers in Canada documented a declining male birth rate from 1970 to 1990, with a loss of 2.2 male births per thousand.[52] Researchers in the United States also found a decline in male births from 1970 to 1990, with a loss of one male birth per thousand. As the U.S. researchers suggested:

Such small changes . . . can have profound implications for large populations, where hundreds of thousands or millions of births occur each year. For example, the reported statistically significant decrease of 2.2 males per 1,000 births in a country the size of Canada with an annual average of 333,159 births represents a cumulative decline of about 8,600 male births since 1970. During the same period, the U.S. decline of 1 male birth per 1,000 corresponds to approximately 38,000 male births.[53]

Studies of male agricultural workers exposed to herbicides and pesticides have shown statistically significant increases in birth abnormalities in their children, and such birth defects seem to disproportionately affect their male children. Additional studies that examined the sex ratio patterns of workers exposed to dioxins have found significant evidence that male birth rates have declined for these workers.[54] And studies of men exposed to the pesticide dibromochloro-propane (DBCP) also found that those men not rendered infertile by the exposure produced three times as many girl children as expected in the years following exposure.[55]

Some researchers argue that the male fetus is more vulnerable to harm from paternal exposures than the female fetus—more likely to be miscarried, more likely to have sexual development disrupted, more likely to have future fertility affected, and more likely to be born with birth defects as a result of in utero exposures. Evidence also appears to indicate that fathers are more vulnerable to toxic harm than mothers in the sense that they are more likely to pass on to the developing fetus damage from such exposures, even if those exposures occur long before conception. As the authors of one comprehensive study concluded, "It appears that the male fetus is more vulnerable to paternal exposures that take place prior to conception and that may be linked with birth defects."[56]

Still, there is no clear causal relationship between environmental toxins and changing sex ratios. Sex ratios can be affected by a wide range of factors, including race (male births are lower in black populations), parental age (older parents produce more girls), use of fertility drugs, and

decreased stillbirth rates (stillbirth rates are typically higher for male babies and so reduced stillbirth rates will produce an increase in male births).[57] In some occupational studies, sample sizes may be limited; in some environmental research, sex ratio effects are significant but small; research on some environmental accidents shows no change in sex ratios in their aftermath; little is known, cross-culturally or historically, about what may be natural fluctuations in human sex ratios.[58] Yet, animal studies clearly indicate that certain chemical exposures can change birth sex ratios. Some argued that the evidence was strong enough to consider sex ratio changes a "sentinel health indicator"—a red flag signaling that an "avoidable" factor is having a significant impact on human health, a flag that shows the need for public intervention.[59] Yet others saw it as one more instance of "environmental hysteria," this time combined with male reproductive panic.

On sperm count rates, male reproductive disorders, reproductive cancers, and sex birth ratios, there seemed to be little agreement and limited human data. But animal research, which documented some of the same problems in wildlife species, provided additional support for those who argued that male reproductive health was in trouble.

Wildlife Studies: Turtles, Panthers, Alligators, and Fish

In the 1980s, prominent scientist John McLachlan and a team of researchers at the University of Texas dramatically demonstrated the estrogenic qualities of the toxin PCB. By painting the outside of turtle egg shells with the chemical, they were able to reverse the sex of neonates developing inside from male to female. Clinical research such as this, as well as evidence from wildlife research on alligators, panthers, birds, and fish, lent support to the thesis that male reproductive health was in trouble and seemed to confirm suspected environmental causes. Many of the disorders of men were also found in animals in the wild.

Since the 1960s, scientists had documented the effects of pesticides on the reproductive systems of wildlife. During the 1970s and 1980s, research on birds and fish in the Great Lakes basin found "male birds growing

ovarian tissue, and female birds growing excessive oviduct tissue; male fish not reaching full sexual maturity; and hermaphroditism in fish."[60] Researchers suspected high levels of chemical pollutants were contributing to poor reproductive outcomes for eagles, herring gulls, and terns living off the lakes. Meanwhile, beginning in the 1980s, British biologists discovered "intersexed" fish downstream from sewage outfall pipes in northern England and suspected that residues of birth control pills were washing into water supplies. One in twenty fish, researchers found, were hermaphrodites—containing the genitals of both sexes.[61] Experiments showed that male fish placed at the mouth of the outfall pipes became hermaphrodites with exposure to the effluent, literally changing their sex.[62] In 2002, scientists continue to report the "feminisation" of fish downstream of sewage plants in England, as one reporter put it, "changing the sex of half the fish in Britain's lowland rivers."[63] They have since discovered hormone-disrupting chemicals in four of every ten samples tested in the rivers of England, reduced fertility, and "widespread sexual disruption" in fish.[64] The source of this disruption remains in dispute, with some arguing that it is due to the sewage "tainted" by hormones excreted through the urine of women using birth control pills, and others that a component of plastics, nonylphenol, might be responsible for the estrogen-like effects.[65]

In 1994, researchers led by Louis Guillette of the University of Florida reported alligators born with dramatically decreased penis size and undescended testes in Lake Apopka, Florida.[66] Lake Apopka had been polluted with DDT by chemical runoff from nearby farms and a chemical spill at an adjacent chemical company in 1980. In the immediate aftermath of the spill, 90% of the alligators disappeared. The remaining alligators survived but showed signs of toxic damage, including reproductive dysfunction. More than ten years later, researchers found female alligators with abnormal ovarian growths, juvenile males with depressed testosterone levels, and adult males with "poorly organized testes and abnormally small phalli."[67] Guillette went on to find similar symptoms in lakes considered to be "non-polluted" in Florida and suspected the cause might be background levels of chemical contaminants.[68]

Animal research suggested that hormonal exposures can have an impact on reproductive development not just in the aftermath of toxic spills but at extremely low dosages. Biological scientist Fredrick vom Saal argued that changes in the functioning of the prostate, glandular development in fetuses, and sperm production can be caused by tiny changes in hormone exposure:

> To most people if I said there's only a millionth of a gram of it here you'd say, "How can it do anything?" A millionth of a gram of estradiol [the female hormone] in blood is toxic. The natural hormone is actually operating at something like a hundred millions times lower than that. . . . We experimentally elevated estradiol levels in mouse fetuses during the period when their reproductive organs were forming. And what we did was we experimentally elevated estradiol by one tenth of one trillionth of a gram of estradiol in a milliliter of blood. We estimate that we're increasing estradiol by about one molecule of estradiol per cell in the body. . . . The consequence of this is that at the end of the first day of development of the prostate in the male fetuses we could see dramatic change in the sprouting of prostate glands. We rendered the prostate abnormally enlarged, and this was detectable within twenty-four hours of the beginning of its embryonic development. And when we looked at these treated animals as adults, that difference had persisted. They had abnormally enlarged prostates that were hyper-responsive to hormones.[69]

In 1995, scientists also reported reproductive disorders in the endangered Florida panther, only thirty to fifty of which survived in the wild. The panthers had been captured and tracked since the 1970s. By the 1990s, studies showed an increase in genital malformations. Researchers found that cryptorchidism (undescended testes) had "increased exponentially in male cubs since 1975," from about 15% to 90% of the population in 1995. Increased rates of sterility were also found among the male panthers. And more than 75% of the male panthers' sperm "exhibited severe deformity,"

compared with 20–25% in other wild cat species.[70] Panther researchers argued that the cats were bioaccumulating mercury and pesticides by eating raccoons as their major source of food. Raccoons ingest a high level of toxins from the aquatic food chain, and according to researchers, such toxins disrupted the endocrine systems of the panthers who ate them.[71]

Animal studies are often problematic as predictors of human risk and as such have been reasonably subject to scientific skepticism. Thalidomide, for instance, is a notorious human reproductive toxin, but animal studies showed few signs of teratogenicity. Yet for reasons of human ethics, experimental studies on animals as well as evidence from wildlife studies often provide the only avenue for predictors of risks to humans. Although animal studies are clearly not definitive of risks to humans, they nevertheless provide invaluable data on potential risks to human health.

By the turn of the twenty-first century, many were convinced that human and animal studies together confirmed symptoms of a deteriorating male reproductive system. They suspected the source lay in environmental exposures of males either in utero or after birth.[72] Debate began over a range of possible causes.

Causes

Researchers theorized a number of causes, with environmental chemicals at the top of the list. But a wide range of other causes were considered as well: the use of plastic diapers on boys, increased rates of sexual activity, the shift from boxer to jockey shorts, the rise of male obesity and dietary changes in men, increased use of drugs and alcohol, the shift from factory to sedentary work, maternal use of drugs during pregnancy, the use of hard bicycle seats, even the advent of feminism and the decline of war!

Some researchers argued that increased levels of sexual activity for young men since the 1960s might have lowered sperm count over the decades. Men who engage in frequent sex have lower sperm counts than other men. But in reexamining past sperm count studies that controlled for frequency of ejaculation, researchers found no association between

increased sexual activity and sustained dropping sperm counts.[73] It seemed that sexual frequency did not increase dramatically enough to change aggregate sperm counts.

Others looked at the shift from boxer shorts to jockey shorts as a potential source of the sperm count drop; snug underwear, by holding the testicles closer to the body, might increase testicular temperature and cause a drop in sperm counts. As one news report put it, "tight pants" and "tight underwear" should be avoided by anyone concerned with his sperm counts.[74] Another warned men that "long hot baths and a fondness for tight trouserings are particularly dangerous."[75] But researchers found no such temperature increase in men tested wearing boxers or briefs.[76]

Attention in the 1990s shifted also to the use of plastic diapers for not only leaching plastics into the environment after use but also increasing scrotal temperature. A team of scientists in Germany found that plastic diapers increased the scrotal temperature in boy babies and possibly damaged their long-term ability to produce healthy sperm. The scientists placed forty-eight babies in disposable diapers and cotton diapers with tiny heat monitors that recorded scrotal temperature every thirty seconds for twenty-four hours. Temperature in the plastic diapers was one degree Celsius higher than in cotton and, because increased temperature can decrease adult male fertility, the scientists speculated that increases in the temperature of male babies might have similar effects.[77] Lending additional credence to the theory, the authors of the report speculated that sperm count drops seemed to correspond with the development and distribution of plastic diapers worldwide after World War II. But the one-degree increase didn't seem to be enough to cause long-term testicular damage. And, as might be expected, the thesis came under immediate attack from the diaper industry: "We believe the study is scientifically flawed and unsound. The conclusions are irresponsible, inappropriate and unreliable."[78] Or as one Australian report put it, "Nappy manufacturers . . . condemned the research's methodology and conclusions."[79]

Other researchers suggested a diet low in folic acid could cause low sperm counts. In studies of rats where folic acid was withdrawn, sperm

counts dropped by 90%.[80] But it was not clear why men's diets, across the world, would have so suddenly changed in the same direction to cause a drop in folic acid and related decrease in sperm production.

The most convincing evidence seemed to lie in environmental causes. Debates over the causes of male reproductive health problems were galvanized in 1996 by the publication of *Our Stolen Future* by Theo Colborn, Dianne Dumanoski, and John Peterson Myers,[81] which argued that many of the reproductive ailments documented since the 1970s could be caused by the introduction of estrogenic chemicals into the environment. Estrogenic chemicals are compounds that are not estrogens but mimic their function and disrupt the endocrine system once introduced into the human body. Colborn, Dumanoski, and Myers argued that pesticides, herbicides, and plastic compounds could have such effects, producing higher rates of cancers in both men and women, increased birth defects, and decreased sperm production. During the 1970s, researchers had examined the estrogenetic effects of a range of pesticides.[82] DDT seemed to have similar effects on reproductive systems, and researchers suspected other pesticides, such as trichloroethylene (TCE) and/or polychlorinated biphenyls (PCBs), as well. Many studies focused on the association of sperm counts with toxic exposures. A study of 225 farmers who attended an infertility clinic in Argentina found associations between sperm count levels and exposure to insecticides, herbicides, and fungicides.[83] A study of 1,001 men in four European cities found associations between sperm defects and stress, "occupational posture," and metal welding.[84]

In the late 1980s, U.S. scientists accidentally discovered the estrogenic qualities of plastics. In unrelated research, researchers noticed that cells stored within sealed plastic tubes were strangely reproducing, as if they had been exposed to estrogens. They discovered that the plastic tubes were the source of the problem.[85] Hormonal effects in the wild or in human populations, some argued, might be produced by the introduction of plastic compounds into the environment since the 1960s. In 1999, a study suggested that phthalates, a solvent used to make plastics flexible, may have estrogenic qualities. Researchers administered the chemical to female rats; their exposed male offspring produced far less testosterone and

developed reproductive abnormalities and testicular tumors, even after very low exposure levels.[86]

Others criticized the focus on environmental causes and argued that men's "lifestyle" factors—drinking, smoking, obesity, and hormonal drug use—might be the cause of the decline. As one researcher put it, "You see all these risk factors, yet men blame some environmental factor when they should blame themselves."[87] But little research focused on these risk factors. One suspects that researchers finding a decline in female fertility might be quick to examine the drug and alcohol use of women, but few studies examined this association in men. Instead, most studies of men focused not on male behavior or even the exposures of men as adults but on maternal transmission of harm to the developing male fetus.

Many researchers found the evidence on the sperm count drop, as well as associations with environmental estrogens, if not decisive, then convincing. Animal studies had been used many times before to justify regulatory action, and animal studies in this case seemed to prove at least the damaging reproductive effects of pesticides, plastics, and solvents on males. But this time it seemed that animal studies and historical evidence were not enough. Again, critics launched sharp, at times virulent, attacks against the arguments that environmental toxins were placing male reproductive health at risk.

Once again, scientist-critic Stephen Safe questioned not just the evidence but the theorized association with environmental estrogens. For one, Safe argued, the presumed timing of the sperm count drop didn't seem to correspond with the introduction of chemicals into the environment. In reanalyzing data from the Danish study, Safe found that most of the sperm count decline had occurred before 1960, with little decline from 1960 to 1990. This seemed counterintuitive, given increasing uses of chemical pesticides during the later period.[88] Safe also argued that exposure to industrial estrogens was minuscule compared with the average intake of estrogens naturally found in foods.[89] As Safe himself colorfully suggested, "Just because Denmark has a problem and a few alligators in a swamp below a Superfund site develop small penises doesn't mean our sperm counts are going down or our reproductive success has declined.

I just don't think we should extrapolate."[90] Safe and others argued that reproductive disorders in the wild, particularly among limited populations of Florida panthers, could be due to simple inbreeding.[91]

Media commentaries supported Safe's research and argued that the sperm count scare could be attributed to "chemophobes' fact-butchering." As commentator John Belau graphically put it, "Whereas man-made chemicals used to be characterized as the Grim Reaper [in cancer scares], they're now a stand-in for Lorena Bobbitt."[92] While scientific debate continued, media coverage of the issue reflected the two extremes of alarm and disbelief. By the 1990s, public discourse on the debate had in large part already been constructed by these two extremes.

Media Coverage: The Emasculation of Men

Male reproductive health concerns broke into the news in 1992, in the aftermath of the publication of the Danish study in the *British Medical Journal*. The report set off a series of alarms and debates in the media, almost exclusively focused on sperm count drops, with relatively little attention to the other disorders reported. The level and intensity of media reports suggested that this was a debate not just about a potential human health problem but about masculinity itself. Sperm were, in essence, "little men" weathering an assault of social, technological, and environmental forces. Sperm counts represented not only a measure of one's manhood but also the symbolic measure of a nation's strength and well-being.

Like the controversies in the scientific and political communities, media coverage swung between alarm on the one hand and vigorous denial on the other. At both extremes were common themes that suggested the representational value of male reproductive health debates.

Personification

Often stories personified sperm as tiny beings with will and intention. Sperm were either "sluggish" or "vigorous" swimmers.[93] Sperm were also

cast as Casanovas who "seduce young women." Many reports reflected the sentiments of a tongue-in-cheek editorial in the *San Francisco Chronicle*, "Dealing with Heir Loss," which proclaimed: "Here's a new crisis that dwarfs all the others into insignificance." Noting the symbolic meaning of sperm counts, Arthur Hoppe noted, "When we approach a pretty young woman, tip our hat and inquire, 'Do you come here often?', it's those 250,000 spermatazoa doing the talking, Yes, sir, it's they who make a man a man."[94] One environmentalist magazine published a story accompanied by a cartoon image of a personified sperm wearing a USA baseball cap turned backward and shedding worried sweat from its brow, as it plummets down a sloping scale of sperm counts over time.[95]

Sperm were sometimes described as warriors in stories like "Sperm under Siege" or "Sperm Wars"—consistent with highly prized ideals of manhood.[96] Masculine characterizations of sperm were reinforced by militaristic language that portrayed them as the tiniest soldiers, fighting off threats from toxic chemical assaults. In a *New Yorker* article on the sperm crisis, Lawrence Wright's characterization of the reproductive process is replete with war images: "It takes a healthy army to achieve conception," he argues. "The head carries the payload—a compressed molecular dollop of DNA—surrounded by a helmet of enzymes that will help it break down the wall of the egg." An early report of low sperm counts, he says, "reads like a casualty report from some devastating battlefront." Sperm are first on the front lines: "Altogether, the sperm is an elegant testament to form following function. It is pure purposefulness—the male animal refined into a single-celled, highly perishable posterity-seeking rocket." Though not a war against women, it is certainly a war against the female hormone estrogen ("the most likely villain"). Sperm may be under siege, but they are heroically fighting the good war—a war in which they have suffered casualties but in which they are sure to prevail.[97]

Other stories employed boxing metaphors to describe sperm's fight for survival. Such language reinforced associations of male reproduction with the physical prowess and aggression of traditional masculinity. An article in *Mother Jones* was titled "Down for the Count," and a Reuters

story reported that "modern living is hitting men right where it hurts the most, with sperm counts falling more quickly than anyone thought."[98]

Ironically, even when sperm are pictured as miniaturized beings, their production over a 72-day period within the male body is never cast as a form of gestation. Rather, the male system is a machine—an industrial production facility, a plant or factory where sperm is "built" on a conveyer belt. As one reporter characterized the spermatic factory, "The toxicants affect sperm production—a conveyor-belt process that takes place in the huge bundles of tubules in the testicles, taking about 10 weeks to manufacture each sperm."[99] Such portrayals deflected the notion that real men were being harmed. Men didn't need care; the male machine needed structural repair.

When not portrayed in human terms, sperm were often referred to as an endangered species. Again recalling associations with traditional masculine roles, hunting metaphors abound in such stories—the "hunt was on" for the causes of the sperm count decline, as if sperm were being tactically stalked by an assailant.[100] Another article jokingly (?) concludes with a recommendation to establish a "Sperm Protection Agency."[101] Whether human or animal, sperm appear to have volition of their own—an independent will separate from their male maker. Like the Florida panther, sperm faced the threat of extinction. If sperm were endangered, it was because the human testis was "an organ at risk."[102]

Feminism

What was apparently placing this organ at risk was not just environmental toxins but, some stories suggested, the feminist movement. Dropping sperm counts were a sign that men were losing the sex wars. One supposedly comical editorial, for instance, suggested that the sperm count decline might be due to a "sinister development in the sex war . . . a sperm strike of epic proportions" launched by men fed up with "the invasion of the cackling sisterhood into every sphere of their lives."[103] In another swipe at feminism, one report of a study of college men suggested that the reduction in male students' sperm counts was proportional to the rise of the

number of women in universities over the past fifty years.[104] As a story titled "That Feminine Touch" put it, women (represented by the female hormone) were apparently responsible not just for invading male workplaces or colleges but for undermining the very procreative power of men.[105]

Even reports of the potential damages done by polyvinyl chlorides (PVCs) were framed as part of a war of women against men. As one piece comically framed it, "Barbie kills sperm dead. . . . The next time you open your wallet and contemplate your credit cards, be aware that you are looking at vinyl. Actually, it's the same stuff that comprises the weird bodies of Barbie and Ken Dolls. It's going to be a long bitter debate."[106]

If feminism was not to blame for the decline in sperm counts, it might be at least partly to blame for the public panic about sperm count evidence. Journalist John Berlau, a critic of the evidence, suggested that feminist activists might welcome the reported associations: "In a twisted way, some in the environmental movement seem to welcome the alleged link between chemicals and male reproductive disorder." Feminist advocates, like former congresswoman Bella Abzug, had been trying to get Congress to ban chlorine for its supposed links with breast cancer, to no avail. "But now that manhood is threatened," Abzug told *New York Magazine*, "We should do much better. I mean, these men don't want to go around with shrinking penises."[107]

This was not just a story about environmental hazards. It was Barbie against Ken, Bella Abzug against the congressmen. It was college girls emasculating college boys. Some even suggested that the "absence of involvement of men in war" might be responsible, presumably because peace might depress testosterone in men.[108] In its most extreme characterizations, it was the pacific androgynous politics of feminism undermining the testosterone-producing war machine. As a result, men were becoming "intersexed."

Maternal Transmission

Research released in 1993 indicating that estrogen exposure during pregnancy might damage male fetal reproductive functions led to a series of

news stories on the issue. Richard Sharpe and Niels Skakkebaek, in an article published in *Lancet,* suggested that the increase in women's consumption of cow milk during pregnancy might be responsible for such exposures because cows had been increasingly treated with the female hormone.[109] In a front-page story, *USA Today* focused primarily on "estrogen passed from pregnant mothers to their sons."[110]

Many news stories stressed the mediation of harm though the maternal body. As Sharpe was quoted as saying, "I have absolutely no doubt that this is the most important time of your life, certainly if you're a male." Reporters emphasized that "if even a small amount of an extraneous synthetic estrogen slips across the mother's placental boundary at a critical moment and invades the body of a developing fetus, it can have a devastating impact on male sexual development."[111] Researchers referred to the "adverse prenatal factors" that later handicap sperm production in the adult male.[112] Others suggested that estrogen-mimicking chemicals "block testosterone in the womb, disrupting sexual development" and "feminizing male fetuses."[113] Men's sperm-producing capacity was "crippled at birth."[114]

It was not men who were at risk but the "male fetus." Encased in the uterus, there was nothing the male fetus could do to avoid chemical emasculation. Men were vulnerable only by virtue of their captive position inside the female body. Such stories shifted focus from the vulnerabilities of the male body to the culpability of the pregnant body. Perhaps mothers were once again responsible, if only by passive transmission, for the problems of men.[115]

Assault on Manhood—The Feminization of Men

The most disturbing effect of exposure to estrogens was often said to be the blurring of the divide between men and women—the production of the "intersexed," the "feminized male," the "hermaphrodite." As men became "more like women," the dissolution of the boundaries between them produced disease and "weakness." It was this presumed feminization of men that had produced testicular cancer, lower sperm counts, and increased rates of "abnormal" development in men.

Men were not just experiencing male-specific reproductive problems but were being *turned into women*. Chemical exposures produced "gender bending," as men with low sperm counts or with genital malformations were somehow cast as deformed women. The feminization of men followed the "feminization" of men's work. As one story in *Esquire* magazine put it, with a play on men's weakened economic position, men were subject not just to downward mobility but now to "downward motility." Reduced sperm counts threatened not only to throw male fertility into jeopardy but also to undermine manhood itself: "Reduce our sperm count? Why in no time we'll be a nation of pallid, Jell-O–spined wimps, watching Wheel of Fortune rather than Monday Night Football and asking strangers for directions."[116]

The theme of feminization was especially evident in stories on wildlife research.[117] Fish and alligators with malformations of the genitals were not called just deformed but "feminized." Penis size was also cast as a measure of one's manhood. As one PBS report, entitled "Teeny Weenies," on the discovery of alligators with reduced penis size reminded men, "In Florida's Lake Apopka, size does matter."[118] Research on fish in Great Britain also reported with alarm that "proportionately, a man now produce [*sic*] only about a third as much sperm as a hamster" and that the world is more likely to end with a "wimp" than with a "bang."[119] In 1993, a BBC documentary depicted the issue as an "assault on the male" and dramatized it by showing film of scientists skulking through the Florida swamps in search of baby alligators with tiny penises and images of hermaphrodite fish.[120]

With titles like "That Feminine Touch" and "The Gender Benders" throughout 1994 and 1995, news stories suggested that environmental toxins were "emasculating" both men and wildlife.[121] The well-regarded science publication *Nature* titled a story "Masculinity at Risk" and called "urgently" for more research on the subject.[122] News reports of studies on the association between plastics and sperm counts were reported with headlines like "Common Pollutants Undermine Masculinity."

Some stories declared, "You're only half the man you used to be" with sperm counts lower than those of your grandfathers.[123] Others

warned of impending male "impotence" (wrongly named because impotence does not refer to potency but to erectile function). Stories suggested men were threatened with "chemical castration" or "sterilization" (also wrongly named, because sterilization implied a zero sperm count).[124]

The disorders of the male reproductive system were characterized not as male disorders but as forms of feminization. One might expect this sort of language if males were growing ovarian tissue or men were developing breasts (but even in this case wouldn't they still be *men* with ovarian tissue, *men* with developed mammary glands?). But the language of feminization and emasculation was frequently used not just when males developed "female" organs but when men experienced male reproductive disorders—when sperm counts were dropping, when men were reported to have increased rates of testicular cancer or genital malformation.

Stories of impending crisis were followed quickly by speculation about the possible causes of such a drop. Most stories suggested that chemical pollutants were the prime suspect, but other themes seemed to suggest that the "softening" of the world had led to a weakening of men. Stories speculated about a possible link of male health problems to "too much drinking," "tight pants," or an increase in male stress.[125] Others suggested that the decline might be due to too much TV watching resulting in cathode-ray tube radiation and could correspond to the rise in television viewing. As one letter to an editor suggested, "I would venture to suggest that, among the small percentage of people who forgo television will be found many families that enjoy a higher-than-average birth rate."[126] Or perhaps the modern comfort of indoor heating was to blame, with some suggesting that the higher indoor temperatures might depress sperm production.[127] News stories reported that "sperm cells are the most delicate in the male body" and subject to damage from toxins at fairly low levels of exposure.[128] Men, no longer invincible, were failing in the manufacture of their most important product.

Others suggested "desk work" was to blame or work in which men spent long periods of time sitting—airline pilots, taxicab drivers, or bus

drivers. Sitting presumably increases the temperature of the testis, and heat may cause reduced sperm production, the speculation went. Perhaps the drop was a consequence of the decline of the industrial economy and rise of the service industry—the "feminization" of men's work. Perhaps men were biologically unfit to perform sedentary service jobs. The male reproductive system, often likened to industrial production, perhaps was revolting at the shift to desk work. Yet others suggested the toxins of industrial employment might be equally hazardous. Men exposed to pesticides in chemical production, men exposed to car exhaust in indoor parking garages, or men working in tunnels might also be at risk.[129] Shame still accompanied stories on men's loss of fertility from environmental toxins. A personal account of a Hispanic male worker in California, presumably rendered infertile by chemical exposures at work, reported: "He doesn't want his name used. 'I don't want people to know,' he says in Spanish, 'that I am not a man.'"[130] Low sperm counts produced not just health problems but "pathetic male ineffectuality."[131]

Nationhood

Manhood was also tied to nationhood. A nation's sperm count was a measure of its national virility. Stories compared the sperm counts of various nations in Olympic competition terms. Finnish men could "stand tall," while American men "faced extinction." Western sperm counts could "plummet" as Third World sperm counts remained unchanged.

Sperm were often given nationalist status. In the United States, men were facing "The Gelding of America."[132] An article in *The Futurist* included a pull-quote that "developing countries may see widespread infertility, falling birthrates." A "sperm count chart" illustrated the threat with two sharp lines in dramatic decline, one marked "Americans" and one marked "Europeans."[133] Soon, developed countries might be outpopulated by more virile Third World nations. A 2000 study by University of Southern California scholars finding no change in U.S. sperm counts brought welcome headlines in newspapers. As the *New York Times* reported, "American Sperm, as Hardy as Ever."[134]

Reports of falling sperm counts and birth rates in Scotland led to panicked reports that "there is something rotten in the state of the nation" and that a "draining life force" had produced a "lack of national virility."[135] By contrast, three stories reported the results of a study published in the *British Medical Journal* that found Finnish men "way above average" in their sperm counts. As news stories recounted, "the mighty men of Finland are walking tall these days" and "the men of Kuopio [Finland] are the spermiest in the world."[136] In apparent international sperm rivalry, Glasgow's *Herald* reported the "first ever" survey of sperm counts in a random study of healthy young men that found that 43% of Danish army recruits have sperm count levels low enough to lead to decreased fertility. "Paradoxically," the report went on, "scientists at Glasgow Royal Infirmary's test tube baby clinic turned to Denmark for sperm donors last autumn when confronted with insufficient domestic supply to meet demand."[137] Perhaps the Danes should be turning to the Scots.

Representing their nation, men who retained high sperm counts were truly men—the "spermiest" Finnish men could "walk tall" because they had superior sperm counts, while man-made chemicals were threatening not just men but "American manhood."

Global Doom

The loss of masculinity and decline of worldwide sperm counts led in some quarters to predictions of catastrophe and global doom—not just reduction of male fertility (for which there was still very weak evidence) but the end of the human race. As one story put it, "Imagine a future in which the male sperm count drops, universally, to zero. The sap runs out for Homo sapiens." Religious revelations laced through such reports suggested dropping sperm counts as the beginning of worldwide apocalypse: "The revelation of a striking decline in human sperm number and quality has rung alarm bells world wide. Could the Western male become sterile in the next century?" Or perhaps, as one editorial jested: "It's the Good Lord trying to tell us something."[138] One prominent British mys-

tery novelist, P. D. James, was inspired to write a futuristic novel in which all men had become sterile.[139]

Many stories cautioned of a "disaster" in the making or of "terror on the trouser front."[140] The *USA Today*'s front-page headline, "Sperm Count Slide," suggested that such a decline might continue down that slippery slope toward extinction.[141] More general accounts of spreading alarm over the possibility that environmental chemicals might be damaging male health were presented with headlines like "Scientist reveals nightmare vision of infertile race," with images of a "barren planet" whose inhabitants become extinct and "it could be all over for the male of the species."[142] In advocacy pieces, environmental organizations declared: "The sperm count of our species is in serious decline!"[143] and "U.S. men face extinction" as a result of "chemical castration." "If current trends continue," one report cautioned, "U.S. males will be sterile by 2020."[144]

News reports painted a picture of an "infertile race," a "barren planet," a species in decline. It "could all be over for the male of the species" and for the human race as well. The end of manhood apparently meant the end of the human race. The world was ending with a "wimper" and not a bang. As one story entitled "Goodbye Macho Man?" put it: "A dramatic fall in sperm count has triggered a hunt for causes—and fears for all humankind."[145]

Others reported the drop in sperm counts as an "impending catastrophe." "It is not a good time to be a sperm," reported one journalist. "Most reproductive scientists now agree: Western men's sperm counts are falling—and fast. With the quality of sperm also in rapid decline, and with sperm defects already responsible for a quarter of all cases of infertility, some even expect that male infertility will become the norm by the end of the next century."[146] The commentator concluded that "any man who suspects he has a fertility problem should not consider it a shameful reflection on his manhood." Rather, men can follow a twelve-step plan to increase their fertility, including avoidance of cigarettes, alcohol, and drugs; reducing hazardous exposures at work; exercising regularly; eating more fruit and vegetables; and reducing stress.

Taken together, these themes strike the note of panic for modern manhood. With manhood already in crisis from loss of jobs and the rise of the feminist movement, stories like these were made easy to believe. In this context of a crisis in masculinity, government agencies sought to respond to the sense of panic created by the evidence that male reproductive health was at risk. Although the themes in the popular press did not determine the policy response or the response of the scientific community, they more explicitly expressed the underlying anxieties and concerns that informed these. Representations in the media give us a window into the symbolic meaning of these debates for broader questions of masculinity.

Regulating Men

What has been the political response to controversies over evidence that male reproductive health was in trouble? In the political process, male reproductive health concerns were subsumed, and sometimes eclipsed, by broader concerns about the impact of endocrine disruptors on human health. Activists raised concerns about increasing rates of breast cancer, birth defects, and other human cancers presumably produced by environmental estrogens. The earliest attention to the issue in the U.S. Congress came as a result of activism on two fronts. First, advocates focused political efforts on representatives from districts where research showed pollutants had had a significant impact on wildlife, most notably in the Great Lakes states. In 1991, the senators from Michigan and Wisconsin held hearings on the question of endocrine disruptors, with the prompting of Theo Colborn, who had headed most of the research in this area.[147] Colborn focused on the association of PCBs with birth defects, as well as the "feminization" of the offspring of pregnant rats exposed to dioxin.

On a second front, advocates focused on the possible links between endocrine disruptors and the rise in breast cancer rates. In 1993, the U.S. House of Representatives sponsored hearings primarily on breast cancer as a possible outcome of endocrine disruption, with secondary atten-

tion to the sperm count drop. In 1993 and 1994, eight bills were introduced into the House and Senate related to endocrine disruptions, all of which focused on further research on the question and testing of chemicals for their broad hormonal effects. In 1996, Congress mandated that the EPA report on the impact of environmental estrogens on women's health. The political drive behind this and other bills was concern about breast cancer. The two senators (Alfonse D'Amato and Daniel Patrick Moynihan) who were chief sponsors of major legislation were from New York, where research showed clusters of breast cancer in communities on Long Island. As political scientist Krimsky has noted, "The activism of Long Island women organized around the issue of breast cancer was a key factor in focusing D'Amato's attention on the issue of estrogenic chemicals and ultimately in winning his support for the screening program." Advocacy by women's organizations produced an increase in funding for breast cancer research from $5 million in 1990 to $500 million in 1995.[148]

In 1996, Congress passed two major acts that addressed the issue and set the framework for future policy developments. The Food Quality Protection Act (FQPA), passed unanimously in 1996, gave the Environmental Protection Agency the authority to require data from chemical companies on the endocrine effects of the pesticides they produced.[149] Congress also passed an amendment to the Safe Drinking Water Act that required the EPA and the Department of Health and Human Services to develop a screening program to determine whether chemicals found in drinking water had estrogenic effects on humans. At the time, the pesticide industry was deeply engaged in more threatening battles with environmental organizations attempting to ban all pesticide residues from food products. To the industry, the provisions of the act were fairly moderate, giving the EPA three years to determine whether certain substances have "an effect on humans that is similar to an effect produced by naturally occurring estrogen[s]."[150]

The FQPA had mandated that the EPA develop a screening program to determine whether chemical substances had an effect on the hormonal system. Of the 87,000 compounds the EPA estimated to be in use, few

had been studied for their hormonal effects. By 1998, the EPA estimated that for only 50 to 100 chemicals were there sufficient data for the EPA to proceed to formal hazard assessment. The EPA recommended that another 500 to 600 compounds "proceed directly to testing." The rest lacked sufficient data for the EPA to make a formal assessment of risk.[151] Initial screening of these compounds would lead to sorting chemicals up through a tiered testing system. Compounds would be tested for their effects not just to estrogen but to androgen and thyroid hormones. But testing systems themselves were still not yet developed. By the year 2000, the EPA reported that there were still "no adequately validated routine screens or tests for determining whether a substance may produce an effect in humans similar to an effect produced by a naturally occurring estrogen or any other naturally occurring hormone."[152]

Of great political significance was a report released in 1999 that had been commissioned by the EPA to assess the state of the knowledge on endocrine disruptors. In 1995 the EPA had sponsored a workshop to identify a research program to address risk assessments and environmental effects of endocrine disruptors. The majority of the more than ninety scientists and environmental health professionals present agreed that the "endocrine disruptor hypothesis was of sufficient concern to warrant a concerted research effort."[153] Through the National Academy of Science, a board of experts was commissioned by the EPA and the Department of Interior in 1995:

> To review critically the literature on hormone-related toxicants in the environment; identify the known and suspected toxicological mechanisms, and impacts on fish, wildlife, and humans; identify significant uncertainties, limitations of knowledge, and weaknesses in the available evidence; develop a science-based conceptual framework for assessing observed phenomena; and recommend research, monitoring, and testing priorities.[154]

The committee was composed of seventeen members, many of whom had been active in research on the issue. It included, for instance, Stephen

Safe of Texas A&M, one of the most vocal critics of the evidence, as well as Louis Guillette, who had directed much of the research on Florida alligators. The intent of the committee was to provide a consensus statement on evidence. Yet years of internal disagreement delayed the committee's work. As reports in the media observed, the committee was "dogged by . . . deep disagreements."[155] The committee could hardly agree on the definition of the term *endocrine disruptor* itself, finally settling on the more neutral term *hormonally active agent* (HAA). Neither could it agree on the significance of wildlife studies, the agents that might be causing visible effects, or the possible associations between laboratory studies on animals and human health problems. Such fundamental disagreements produced a committee that could come to consensus on very little. As the committee's final report, *Hormonally Active Agents in the Environment* (HAAE), stated:

> It became clear as the work of the committee progressed that limitations and uncertainties in the data could lead to different judgments among committee members with regard to interpreting the general hypothesis, determining appropriate sources of information, evaluating the evidence, defining the agents of concern, and evaluating environmental and biologic variables.[156]

Specifically on the question of a sperm count decline, the evidence, the report concluded, was simply unclear: "With respect to the end point most closely studied, sperm concentration, retrospective analysis of trends over the past half-century remain controversial."[157] In such studies, the committee argued, "it was impossible to control for all confounding factors . . . due to limitations in the original data sets." The failure of past studies to control for such confounding factors and geographical variation made knowledge of sperm counts uncertain.

"In fact," the committee concluded, "within single study centers and populations, considerable local variation has been demonstrated, with some studies suggesting a decline, and others no change, or even a possible increase in sperm concentration over the past 20 years." Given the

limitations of past data and the lack of current data, the report concluded, "No analysis to date can prove or disprove a uniform global trend in sperm concentration." Perhaps, the report suggested, studies of sperm concentration "may not be the appropriate question for study."[158]

The report confirmed that laboratory studies of animals exposed to a range of pesticides and other chemicals clearly showed that such exposures could cause "reproductive and developmental abnormalities."[159] These effects had been shown across animal populations and appeared to be dose-responsive. But some committee members challenged their significance for human health. As the report put it, "Although it was clear that exposures to HAAs at high concentrations can affect wildlife and human health, the extent of harm caused by exposure to these compounds in concentrations that are common in the environment is debated."[160] What was missing, it argued, was conclusive "low dose" human data.

The report confirmed increases in rates of hypospadias, cryptorchidism, and testicular cancer in men. Increasing rates of testicular cancer had been found in the United States, Canada, and six European countries, particularly for men born after 1950. In the United States, testicular cancer in white men, for instance, had increased by 2.4% each year from 1973 to 1994. This increase, the report suggested, could be related to growing rates of hypospadias or cryptorchidism in boys, both of which elevate risks of testicular cancer. But it concluded that none of these conditions could be definitively "linked to exposures to environmental HAAs at this time."[161] It also affirmed significant studies of changing birth sex ratios, particularly in the aftermath of accidental exposures to TCDD, but noted that "the causes of the declines in sex ratio is [sic] yet unknown."[162]

Internal disagreements within the committee were, in part, produced by the nature and complexity of the problem. The end points to examine were wide-ranging, from birth defects to childhood neurological problems, adult fertility issues, and cancers and other medical disorders. Scientists were brought together from a wide range of disciplines, often with different research regimens. Yet research on other environmental

toxins seemed to face the same complexities with less internal conflict and more success, which suggests that additional cultural forces were at work in this environmental debate.

Released in 1999, two years after its planned completion date, the report called for prospective studies and recommended only that "wildlife and human populations continue to be monitored for adverse developmental and reproductive effects."[163] Such prospective studies would take years to complete. Media critics of the endocrine disruptor thesis used the report to dismiss all concerns about their effect on the environment. As commentator Michael Fumento, writing for *American Spectator*, put it, the report contained "enough scientific conclusions to box the ears of the endocrine alarmists."[164]

Within the scientific committee, debates over the evidence appeared to go beyond simple lack of data. So deep were the disagreements that they seemed to throw into question accepted scientific methods of evidence, observation, and extrapolation. Committee members could not agree on the methodologies underlying such research: "of the value of different kinds of evidence obtained by experiments, observations, weight-of-evidence approaches, and extrapolation of results from one compound or organism to others, as well as allowable sources of information and criteria for arriving at meaningful conclusions and recommendations."[165] Resistance to evidence of male vulnerability came in the form not only of questioning the data but also of doubting the very scientific methods that produced the evidence in the first place.

What standard is used to judge the causality of an association? In general, scientific causality is judged by "the strength of the association, the presence of a dose-response relationship, specificity of the association, consistency across studies, biological plausibility, and coherence of the evidence."[166] It appeared that most of these conditions were met through studies conducted on animals in the lab, yet these studies didn't seem to meet the criteria for affirming significant risks to the human population.

Almost ten years after Skakkebaek's original observations, there was no agreement on whether human fertility rates were in decline, what the

cause of wildlife abnormalities might be, whether there might be an association between environmental toxins and breast or testicular cancers, or whether sperm counts had fallen or were continuing to fall. It seemed that a higher level of proof would be needed to justify public recognition of male reproductive disorders, as well as any governmental interventions to "protect" men. In the meantime, there were hardly any men's organizations publicly demanding action on falling sperm counts or rising rates of male reproductive disorders. And such debates were politically loaded, implicating not just the profits of the plastics and chemical industries and the reputations of competing scientists, but dominant norms of masculinity.

Paradoxes of Reproductive Masculinity

Some might say that the skepticism about claims of male reproductive risks was similar to that facing all environmental struggles—no more divisive, say, than debates over global warming. But an additional set of cultural meanings appears to be attached to this debate. This was a debate not just about the evidence but about manhood. Assumptions of masculinity were implicated in the belief or rejection of the evidence that male reproductive health was at risk. Gendered norms of manhood intensified the response in both directions, with sharply critical attacks at one extreme and predictions of global doom at the other. Indeed, in the end, the question was not whether male reproductive health was at risk at all, but how the perception of risk was obscured by these norms of masculinity.

Evidence of reproductive risk was deeply entangled with the second presumption of reproductive masculinity—the idea that men are less vulnerable than women to the harms of the outside world. The male body has been codified as relatively invulnerable to risk. The evidence suggested that this was no longer assured. The male reproductive system was cast as a machine, a factory that produced the goods necessary for human reproduction. As a machine, not an organic biological unit, the male body was presumably steeled against harm. Evidence of men suffering the "as-

saults" of environmental chemicals threw this presumption into question. The fact that this assault was not just on the male body but on the reproductive functions of men added insult to the injury. Men who were fragile or weakened were "more like women," with bodies vulnerable to external dangers.

Two stages of response characterized the social reaction to evidence of male weakness and vulnerability. First, evidence that threatens to disrupt presumptions of masculinity was met with highly charged responses of *panic* and *denial*. Overreaction to the evidence suggests that signs of male risk socially implicate deeper norms of masculinity. Assumptions of male risk potentially throw into question not just gender but all of social order, producing predictions of global doom. If the strength and virility of the male body was no longer assured, if we could not count on the biological distinctions between men and women to hold firm, if the protectors of the nation needed protection, then where was the foundation of social order? If men presumably protected the vulnerable, then who would be left to protect the men? Evidence so loaded with meaning for broader understandings of masculinity (and by implication femininity) elicited reactions of social denial—subjecting evidence of risk to inordinately high standards of scientific proof.

When evidence of male risk and vulnerability was strong enough to overcome this social and scientific resistance, it was met with social responses of *deflection* and *reinstatement*. Arguments that the risk to men was transmitted through the maternal body during gestational development helped to shift attention away from the vulnerabilities of men. Threats to the male body were seen as transmitted through the maternal body, which mediated and delivered toxic risks to the male fetus, men "crippled at birth."[167] Men were at risk not because the male body was inherently vulnerable but by virtue of their captive position inside the female body. In this way, assumptions about the nature of men's vulnerability were qualified by the mediation of harm through the maternal body.

The social processes of deflection functioned to reinstate the idea that men were neither needy nor dependent, nor were they the appropriate

subject of state protection or surveillance. To publicly acknowledge the risks of the male body was to suggest that perhaps men were the ones in need of state protection, perhaps even more so than women. Male fetuses might be at greater risk than female fetuses—more likely to be lost during pregnancy, to be born with significant birth defects, or to eventually pass along defects to their own children. The harm that men suffered in utero or as adults might be more severe and long-lasting than that suffered by women. Perhaps men would need to be subject to the surveillance of the state—tracking rates of diseases and disorder, monitoring sperm counts for signs of illness or decline. The social risks of acknowledging male vulnerability to harm seem to eclipse the real health risks suffered by men.

Politically, masculinity faced a catch-22. To recognize the risks of men and the vulnerabilities of the male reproductive body was to threaten presumptions of male domination, yet to fail to recognize them was to put real men at further risk of real damages to their health and their ability to father children. Where were the men's organizations demanding attention to these issues and regulatory action by the state, or at least clarification of the nature and extent of the risks? As long as male reproductive function was symbolic of manhood and male vulnerability was a source of shame, few men would stand up to demand public attention to the issue. Scientists, physicians, and politicians fed this reservoir of shame by their reluctance to adequately examine questions of male reproductive health.

In the end, this is a story not about the "gender wars" but about the price men pay for gender privilege. Do we *know* whether men's reproductive health is at risk? We know only that the question will be forever clouded in a social order reluctant to face the vulnerabilities of men or determined to deny them.

The paradox of masculine privilege would also frame discussions of male virility as social and economic forces pushed questions of male infertility into the public light. The development of technologies of artificial insemination would make it possible (and in the U.S. context, profitable) to address the health needs of men suffering from infertil-

ity. Yet the growth of a multimillion-dollar industry in sperm banking would threaten to disrupt the third presumption of reproductive masculinity—the assumption of male virility—and would be met with similar social resistance.

Male fertility and, specifically, the quality of a man's sperm would come to define manhood and supersede the identity of the man. Like a production line turning out widgets that are, of course, more important than the machine, men in the sperm banking industry, representing in microcosm the ideal qualities of all men, would be measured by the "quality" of their sperm.

COMMODIFYING MEN

4

The Science and Politics of Male Infertility and Sperm Banking

Within home-run distance of Boston's Fenway Park sits one of the largest sperm banks in the world—Northeastern Cryobank. In the bank's cryopreservation room are stored 165,000 vials of sperm in giant stainless-steel canisters. Tens of thousands of these vials wait to be purchased by reproductive consumers. In its fine categorization of human traits, the room has the feel of a eugenic fantasy; vials are etched with numerical codes and categorized by the height, weight, eye color, facial structure, skin tone, hair texture, religion, IQ, hobbies, talents, and interests of their donors—traits presumed to be genetically transmitted through sperm. This is a practice common to most U.S. sperm banks. Vials are also color-coded by race: predictably, white caps for Caucasian, black for African American, yellow for Asian, red for "all others."[1] And at the largest bank in the world, donors are "hand printed" with a biometric identification device that records a three-dimensional measurement of the donor's hand.[2] Like the product they produce, donors have become "consumables"—screened for physical and social traits most desired by prospective reproductive consumers, stocked, packaged, and sold like Wal-Mart products.

Only men meeting standards of ideal masculinity are "hired" by the bank to "donate." Donors may be rejected if they are too young (under twenty-one) or too old (over thirty-five), too short (under 5'8") or too tall (over 6'2"), or if they weigh too little or too much. They may be rejected if they are of a race, religion, or ethnic group that is not in demand by consumers. They may be rejected if they are not heterosexual—if they've ever had sex with a man or had sex with a woman who has had sex with a bisexual man. They may be rejected if they've spent more than thirty days in prison. Reaching back three generations, they may be rejected if anyone in their family has ever had one of a hundred different diseases or physical disorders.[3] Only men with no hint of history of human frailty or disease, no question about their sexuality, and a physical stature not too different from the ideal fit man are accepted as sperm donors. Sperm banks sell their germinal product through catalogs that feature glossy photos of strapping, handsome male models (in a range of "colors"), presumably selling not just potent sperm, but the masculine ideals represented by such images.

What are we to make of this public trade in men and the sperm they produce? What impact does this public marketing of sperm have for understandings of reproductive masculinity? In a social system that places male virility at the heart of ideal masculinity, how do we understand the development of a public market dependent for its success on public exposure of male infertility? This chapter explores the third element of reproductive masculinity—the presumption of male virility— through the history and current practices of sperm banking. It analyzes the social, technological, and economic forces that pushed male infertility into public light at the end of the twentieth century and led to the commodification of sperm. It traces the processes of social deflection that come into play to reinstate ideals of masculinity in the face of the public exposure of male infertility. And it assesses the paradoxical nature of masculine privilege that valorizes sperm as the carrier of ideal human traits but still measures a man by his fertility.

Seminal Merchants and Proxy Fathers:
A Social History of Artificial Insemination

Like other body parts that have entered into human exchange, sperm has a social history. The first documented account of artificial insemination is attributed to the Italian priest and physiologist Lazzaro Spallanzani, who successfully impregnated a spaniel with the semen taken from a male dog in 1779.[4] As Spallanzani reported in 1784:

> Sixty-two days after the injection of the seed, the bitch
> brought forth three lively whelps, two male and one female,
> resembling in colour and shape not the bitch only, but the
> dog also from which the seed had been taken. Thus did I
> succeed in fecundating this quadruped; and I can truly say,
> that I never received greater pleasure upon any occasion,
> since I first cultivated experimental philosophy.[5]

The earliest documented case of human artificial insemination was reported at the end of the eighteenth century in Great Britain, when John Hunter reportedly impregnated "the wife of a linen draper" by injecting her husband's sperm into her vagina, producing a "normal pregnancy."

In the United States, artificial insemination developed along two tracks. One involved the treatment of female infertility in married women through the placement of her husband's sperm into her cervix —a procedure today referred to as "artificial insemination homologous" (by husband) or AIH. The other track used donated sperm for the treatment of male infertility, or artificial insemination donor (AID). AIH occurred first and, although controversial because it involved a violation of Victorian female modesty, was nonetheless reported in the medical literature.[6]

AID developed as a response to male infertility. First used in 1884, it was not described in the medical literature until twenty-five years later, and then by an observer rather than the physician who undertook the procedure. Addison Davis Hard (who is suspected as the sperm donor) wrote

that Philadelphia physician William Pancoast administered donated semen to a wealthy, anesthetized Quaker woman who had been under his care for the treatment of sterility. Upon discovering the husband to be azoospermic, Pancoast arranged for the wife to be chloroformed under the pretext of undergoing some minor surgery and inseminated her with the sperm of the allegedly "best-looking member" of his medical class. The insemination proved successful, and the woman was never told how she became pregnant. The fact that the procedure was kept secret suggests that despite Hard's advocacy (in part on eugenic grounds), practitioners were reluctant to tread on the shaky moral and legal grounds on which such a procedure rested.[7]

By the early twentieth century, AIH and to some extent AID found greater acceptance. Scientific advances made inseminations easier and more successful. Thanks to the microscope, doctors could easily diagnose azoospermia; thanks to growing knowledge about the menstrual cycle, they could better determine the period of peak fertility; thanks to the syringe, they could apply fresh donor sperm into the willing (or perhaps anesthetized and unknowing) patient; and thanks to medical research, they would learn how to conduct and interpret postcoital examinations. Prior to the 1930s, few cases of AID were reported in the medical literature. Duluth, Minnesota, physician R. T. Seashore found only twenty-four articles when he reviewed the literature before reporting his own case. Seashore's discussion of AID included the observation that it offered an opportunity to "practice good eugenics," and he encouraged use of the procedure "only in those who are apt to improve society."[8] Other physicians writing about AID in the 1930s eschewed eugenics in favor of a discussion of the most effective techniques or the legal issues involved in the process.[9] Whatever their emphasis, the authors all implicitly argued that AID was a therapeutic option that had to be carefully controlled by the physician. Doctors had to use careful judgment in determining who required the treatment and could endure the strains it produced within the family. And too, doctors had to procure the sperm and place it in the recipient—performing an act that was, at that time, legally uncertain and morally suspect. Secrecy, it was argued, thus benefited the

physician, the woman receiving the sperm, any resulting child (who were called artificial bastards by some critics), and the husband whose infertility remained hidden from view.[10]

The commonplace assumption that children resembled their parents became, in the hands of early practitioners of AID, a mandate to match the social as well as the physical characteristics of sperm donors with those of the men they would make into fathers. New York physician and eugenics advocate Frances Seymour, for example, attempted to match the men by temperament and background. As a 1936 *Literary Digest* article about Seymour's work explained, "This is to avoid the tension which might develop later when the growing child, if of mercurial Italian heredity, might clash with a eugenic father of phlegmatic German stock."[11]

Another physician, following the policies of Seymour and her medical collaborator Alfred Koerner, chose donors between ages thirty and thirty-five and of proven fertility, and similarly argued for careful matching to avoid embarrassment for the parents "who are both sandy-haired Scots to present to the world a dark-eyed Spanish brunette."[12] The popular belief that "racial" identities involved both physical characteristics and personality types was fed by the eugenic beliefs of those considered to be the pioneers in reproductive medicine.

Eugenics rested on the unproven scientific claim that by controlling the breeding of those deemed unfit or genetically defective and by encouraging the breeding of the fit, the quality of the population could be improved. Embedded in this belief were a strict hierarchy of race (and often ethnicity) and a presumption that physical, mental, and behavioral characteristics were linked and heritable. As a political movement, eugenics reached the public through "Fitter Families" contests at state fairs in the 1920s, held to instruct people in the Mendelian laws of inheritance and to gain support for positive eugenics. Contestants submitted eugenic histories, underwent medical examinations, and took an IQ test as part of the competition.[13]

Negative eugenics also flourished in this era, with the passage of the 1924 Immigration Act, which restricted the admission of immigrants from southern and eastern Europe; with the enactment of state laws preventing

the unfit (those deemed insane, idiotic, and epileptic, for example) from marrying; and with the 1927 Supreme Court ruling in *Buck v. Bell*, which upheld state-based compulsory sterilization laws for the "unfit."[14] Despite growing social and scientific criticism, in the 1930s and 1940s many remained convinced that when it came to selecting sperm to be used for artificial insemination, it was wise, or even morally imperative, to choose the seed of the smartest, fittest, and most successful of men, even as it was also deemed critical to find a donor who matched the husband in physical characteristics and temperament.

Despite the scientific and cultural challenges to eugenics, Seymour and Koerner remained outspoken supporters of AID and touted its eugenic potential. Seymour, the leader of the National Research Foundation for the Eugenic Alleviation of Sterility, Inc., received much acclaim for her work and published, alone and with Koerner, articles about the eugenics possibilities of AID.[15] In one article, she noted, "The ideals, from the ethical and scientific standpoint, of eugenics may actually be carried out in a group of offspring which are as near humanly perfect as our scientific knowledge can produce."[16] By selecting the best sperm donors— men who might ordinarily contribute few children to the nation's pool of superior citizens—a social good was achieved even as individual couples fulfilled their desire for a child. Other physicians apparently shared the view that AID needed to be practiced from a eugenic standpoint. An Oregon practitioner, for example, noted that the couple receiving the sperm should be "of a high moral and intellectual type, and financially able to give the child the educational advantages demanded of their social station." He reported approvingly that the "Seymour group requires a minimum I.Q. of 120 in all receptive mothers."[17]

An alternative view of the uses and practice of AID came from Alan Guttmacher, famed Johns Hopkins obstetrician who, along with some allies, challenged the claims and findings of Seymour and Koerner, as well as their motives. At a time when there were few effective treatments for most causes of infertility and AID failed more often than it succeeded, Guttmacher found that helping infertile couples become parents was "among my most satisfying medical experiences."[18] Elsewhere he argued

for keeping the fees low and performing inseminations as a "personal medical service, the contribution of an aesculapiad to the happiness of some wretched, worthy, sterile couple."[19] But to the degree that doctors saved AID for the "worthy," they were at least tacitly following the eugenic ideal.

In the midst of the Great Depression, with marriage rates falling, birth rates in steep decline, and couples seeking effective techniques of birth control or illegal abortions, Americans began to openly contemplate new ways of overcoming infertility. The media began paying attention to AID in ways that made it seem more common than many might have thought —portraying it as a modern scientific procedure, albeit one that danced on the edge of moral and legal legitimacy. Woven into these reports were periodic discussions of the eugenic benefits of AID. A 1934 *Newsweek* article described how Seymour helped her mechanic's wife, Mrs. Lillian Lauricella, have twins through AID.[20]

In 1938, *Time* profiled a sperm donation center established at George-town University School of Medicine. Public doubts about the process may have ebbed with the report that its founder, physician Ivy Albert Pelzman, carefully assessed the heredity and background of his donors. He maintained a list of fifteen drawn "mostly from medical students and interns who are glad to get the $25 fee per insemination." Pelzman, like his peers, was pleased when AID succeeded and when, thanks to successful matching, the child had the appropriate physical characteristics. He proudly reported that in one instance a Chicago woman who bore two children conceived with AID heard from her friends that they "look just like their father."[21] The article concluded with a description of the donor list that mentioned Pelzman offered sperm not only from blonds, brunettes, and redheads but also from Jews, Catholics, and Protestants. The fact that Pelzman bowed to his clients' interest in matching donor and husband by religion suggested that the public and the press, as well as medical professionals, understood inheritance more broadly than scientists would define it.[22]

The confusion of heritable characteristics with individual traits not genetically transmitted occurred frequently in popular accounts of AID. A *Literary Digest* article summarizing the medicolegal arguments of

Seymour and Koerner and titled "Eugenic Babies" described how the two rejected professional donors as semen salesmen and relied instead on educated, middle-aged male donors with good health and family history and "an interest in genetics." Embracing the idea that personality was a heritable trait, the author of the article concluded with an explicit comparison to the breeding of thoroughbred horses: "Thus the pure racial strain of the desirable sires is perpetuated."[23] But breeding humans for "personality" was a more questionable project than selective breeding for a single physical trait—speed—in race horses.

A more jocular tone and a more skeptical approach to the eugenic theories of some of the leading supporters of AID came in an *American Mercury* piece in which the author questioned whether "Lucy Stoners" would be using artificial insemination to bypass "Dame Nature." Referring to the work of Seymour and Koerner, the author asked, perhaps facetiously, whether the wife who hesitated to "bear an heir for a lord and master whose I.Q. is low may choose to conceive by implantation from Genius Vial 70703-B, double strength." However, the article also employed the language of eugenics: "It would be difficult to imagine a greater medical error than to allow a couple of dark-skinned Mediterraneans to become the ostensible parents of a Nordic blond."[24]

As the medical and popular literature of the 1930s and 1940s made clear, AID was shaped by consumer demands and political ideologies, as well as by medical findings regarding its clinical applications. Families no longer accepted barrenness as an "act of God" but instead sought medical intervention for sterility. When AID was the designated treatment, other factors came into play, including the need to match the characteristics of donors and husbands in order to conceal the presence of the one and the barrenness of the other. Until laws conferred paternity upon the husband and kept the wife from being charged with adultery in cases of divorce or in requests for child support, physicians sometimes obtained signatures from all the parties involved.

Finally, new clinical applications for AID also propelled its use. The discovery of Rh incompatibility, which women who were Rh-negative and conceived an Rh-positive child with an Rh-positive partner devel-

oped, meant that donor sperm could be substituted for the sperm of the husband so that the problem could be avoided. Other genetically transmissible diseases could also be avoided this way.

Donor insemination would not reach its full medical or market potential until the development of technologies to freeze human sperm. Cryopreservation of sperm had first been developed in 1866 by Mantegazza in the field of animal husbandry. Sperm freezing came into popular use in the cattle industry during the 1950s (producing, by 1972, more than 100 million calves from frozen bull sperm).[25] From the 1930s through the 1950s, scientists had experimented with various methods of preserving human sperm through freezing, including dry ice and liquid nitrogen. But human sperm proved more fragile than that of bulls, often losing its fertility in the cold storage process. By the 1950s, however, U.S. scientists had conquered the preliminary challenges of human semen cryopreservation, and in 1953 reproductive physicians R. G. Bunge and J. K. Sherman reported the births of four children conceived with frozen semen. With the safety and potency of frozen human sperm now assured, the opportunity to create human sperm banks arose.[26] And the practices these sperm banks developed reflected what had become the long-standing pillars of sperm selection: matching the husband and donor by particular traits and attempting to create babies with particularly valued characteristics.

Like their eugenic predecessors, some reproductive and genetic scientists perceived the tremendous potential of the technology for purposes of "positive eugenics." In 1965, Nobel Prize–winning geneticist Hermann Muller, who viewed traditional eugenics as reactionary and flawed, promoted the use of frozen sperm as one element of what he coined "parental choice." Techniques of donor insemination could be used to "rationalize" human reproduction. Muller argued that "the means exist right now of achieving a much greater, speedier, and more significant genetic improvement of the population." The obstacles to such improvement, he said, were purely "psychological ones, based on antiquated traditions from which we can emancipate ourselves." Anticipating the future, Muller advocated the establishment of banks "of stored spermatozoa . . . derived from persons of very diverse types, but including as far as possible those whose

lives have given evidence of outstanding gifts of mind, merits of disposition and character, and physical fitness."[27]

After the dawn of the atomic era, Muller, who discovered that radiation caused heritable changes in reproductive cells, questioned whether sperm banking might permit society to "preserve the genetic character of the human race in the event of an atomic war."[28] Arguing that modern medicine was keeping alive the "bearers of defective genes," he proposed the creation of a "seminal Fort Knox" to store the semen of men about to be exposed to radiation. From there, the next step would be "completely planned fatherhood" as a means of avoiding paternity by those with a "dubious genetic endowment."[29] By 1966, there was talk of creating a sperm bank for geniuses.[30] With such advances, it seemed that all Americans might come to resemble those who live in the fictional town of Lake Woebegon, where all the children are above average. Indeed, an early account of children born through AID had made just such a claim.[31]

By 1968, S. J. Behrman, a leading physician and pioneer in the field of cryopreservation, was favorably quoting Muller and advocating cryopreservation for purposes of positive eugenics in a lecture delivered at the annual meeting of the American Association of Obstetricians and Gynecologists.[32] As one listening physician affirmed in response, "We need shed no tear over the lost lineage of the azoospermic husband,"[33] one presumably rendered infertile by processes of "natural selection." The human race would thus replace aristocratic lineage and hereditary monarchy with the new lineage of positive genetic planning—guided by "thoughtful scientists and clinicians" willing to develop "semen freezing" to the full extent of its potential.[34]

Despite the enthusiasm of sperm banking progenitors, most medical practitioners continued to use "fresh" semen for artificial inseminations during the 1960s and early 1970s. Thawed semen still produced lower rates of conception, and the general public viewed the practice with suspicion, despite claims that children so produced were not only healthy but also of superior stock to those conceived naturally.[35] Articles in medical journals and the popular press raised a variety of public health and social concerns about the use of frozen sperm. Some addressed the risks

of birth defects, but studies proved that such concerns were unfounded. Others continued to question the psychological and legal impact of AID, as well as its social meaning.[36]

By 1972, almost twenty years after Bunge and Sherman opened the first sperm bank, only 300 children were reported born from frozen sperm. By 1974, that number had risen to 500 and by 1977 to 1,000 children.[37] While witnessing slow but steady growth, a 1978 article in the American Fertility Society's journal, *Fertility and Sterility*, noted that "the early enthusiasm for using frozen semen has been tempered. . . . The ideal method for freezing gametes has not yet been found, and the commercialization of sperm banking has not developed."[38]

The slow growth of the industry was due not only to technical difficulties but also to social concerns about the impact of sperm banking on the masculinity of those infertile husbands in need of the seminal services of other men. A 1976 article in *Fertility and Sterility* reported the findings of a study of forty-four couples who had conceived using AID. Psychological interviews with the husbands indicated that "80% had guilt feelings. They felt that they could not give proof of their manhood or act as real fathers." Researchers, noting an increase in marital conflict, speculated that "the growing abdomen may be a reminder to the husband of his 'incapacity' and of a rival father."[39] Husbands who resolved this challenge to their masculinity apparently did so through a kind of reproductive narcissism, where the services of the donor were cast as an extension of the prospective father's will. Payment to the donor was essential to this process: "They regarded the semen of the donor as a mere fertilizing agent whose product in conception imparted nothing alien to the marriage. By paying the donor, indirectly, they had no resentment or other feeling toward him." The masculinity of the father thereby rested on the commodification of the donor and his reduction to "one function" as the "agent of fertilization"—in essence, an extension of the will of the infertile husband.[40]

The role of the medical technician also seemed critical to reinstating the masculinity of the husband. As long as a gynecologist performed the insemination, neither husbands nor courts considered AID to be a

form of adultery.[41] The medical technician thus provided a physical and social barrier between the conceiving woman with her husband, on the one side, and the "rival father" on the other. Concerns about the husband's loss of masculinity also led some to mix the sperm of the husband with the sperm of the anonymous donor before insemination. But studies showed that the mixing of husbands' sperm seemed to weaken donor sperm and significantly reduce rates of conception.[42]

Through the 1970s, reproductive scientists continued to work on alternative methods of freezing and thawing sperm to improve rates of conception and make frozen sperm more competitive with fresh. In the mid-1970s, reproductive physicians Joseph Barkay and Henryk Zuckerman (in Israel) developed their "cryofreezer"—an "easy-to-operate, precise, sperm-freezing instrument" that could freeze "pellets" of sperm in a mere twenty minutes.[43] By the end of the 1970s, techniques had been developed to successfully cool semen with liquid nitrogen down to a temperature of -196 degrees centigrade. In medical journals, leaders in the field of cryopreservation declared: "Thawed semen produces babies" and that "instances of conception occurring from semen preserved longer than 10 years have been recorded."[44] In addition, they argued, "the safety of thawed semen for clinical insemination exceeds that of fresh semen. The literature indicates that abnormal spermatozoa are killed by the freezing-thawing process. Thus, only the fit and healthy sperm survive." As a result, they argued, of 530 pregnancies produced by frozen semen by 1977, there were lower rates of spontaneous abortion (less than 8%, compared with the norm of 10–15%) and dramatically lower rates of birth defects (less than 1%, compared with the norm of 6%).[45] Indeed, the medical and genetic promise of AID seemed to be proven in part by the growing and successful use of the procedure with lower rates of birth defects than occurred naturally, but the misapplied eugenic faith—that AID could create "phlegmatic Germans" or "mercurial Italians"—remained unfulfilled. Nevertheless, the sperm bank industry that developed in the wake of the successful application of cryopreserved sperm played to these hopes, as well as on a scientific understanding of heredity.

The technological ability to freeze and market sperm was not sufficient to produce a mass market in semen. Only certain conditions made it possible to commodify and market "male seed." The following section suggests the historical conditions under which human body parts and human body products have come into market exchange, as well as the specific conditions that made it possible to market human sperm.

Commodification of the Human Body

Commodification refers to the process by which an item comes to have market value, which depends on a number of social and economic conditions. First, the ability of an item to be subject to market forces depends in part on the cultural distinction between the sacred and the profane.[46] That which is sacred is presumed to be unique—to have no equivalent value—and therefore to be inappropriate for market exchange. This principle has historically underlain prohibitions on the selling of human beings, human organs, and human body parts, which are considered to be "priceless."[47] Human slavery, as such, has depended on the dehumanization of the slave as a necessary prerequisite to the market exchange of human beings. Items can be "priced," therefore, only if they are understood to have a value equivalent and thus register on some common matrix of exchange (either "like items" or money).

While generally exempt from market exchange, human beings or human body parts may be subject to social exchange (for instance, through marriage, adoption, or organ donation). These social exchanges are characterized as "gifts" that help to solidify bonds between individuals in a community. Such gifts both rest on and produce obligatory relations between giver and recipient, which are presumably absent in exchange relations between producers and consumers of market-based commodities.[48] Indeed, it is the absence of monetary exchange that produces the social obligation in gift giving.

Second, to enter into exchange, an item must also be "alienable," that is, separable from its holder. Reproductive technologies have multiplied the opportunities for the alienation of reproductive assets (sperm, eggs,

and embryos). But these technologies are only necessary, not sufficient, conditions for commodification. The separation of male seed from its male maker may be scripted by nature as a necessary part of the reproductive process, but alienation of male seed—that is, its exchange on the market—may only be produced by cultural practices in the reproductive political economy. The ability to alienate an item from its holder is thus dependent on both physical and cultural conditions of separation.

A number of body parts and body products have moved back and forth across the divide from the sacred (priceless) to the exchangeable (priced). The exchange of blood and milk are good examples. Blood went from being a product delivered by paid live donors to a donated substance, in part because of the call for volunteer donors during World War II. In the postwar years, there were both paid and volunteer producers, with a strong emphasis on recruitment of the latter, so that today blood is largely a donated product, although blood plasma is obtained from paid producers, and some blood is still purchased overseas for U.S. use.[49] Like blood, breast milk was transformed from a commodity to a donated item, and similarly, its pool of producers shifted from a lower-class to a middle-class base.

Other body products have different culturally or nationally specific commodity histories. Hair is privately sold (or donated), and this marketplace is unregulated. Organs from living donors—kidneys and parts of the liver—as well as cadaver organs are donated in the United States and Western Europe. Historically and cross-culturally, the potential of a body part (or body product) to be commodified has less to do with the inherent nature of the item (i.e., how easy it is to be removed from the human body or how necessary for human survival) than with the cultural meanings ascribed to it at a given historical moment.[50] Particular cultural practices may permit some kinds of assets to be commodified while others remain "sacred" and beyond the reach of market forces. Historically, body products are more easily offered for exchange than are body parts, in part because they are renewable, but not all body products are considered to be appropriate for market exchange.

Ova have been more difficult to commodify for a number of reasons. They are more difficult to separate from the human body, requiring

hormonal stimulation of the female body and surgical retrieval, both of which involve risks to human health not incurred in the same way by the "retrieving" of sperm. Because females are born with all of the eggs they will produce in a lifetime and sperm is continuously produced, ova are more likely to be considered body parts and sperm to be renewable body products. As such, ova are often perceived as more valuable than sperm because of their limited number, even though women carry a vastly larger supply of eggs than they could ever use in a lifetime.

Even when profit is a powerful motive, commodification may be constrained by a number of intersecting cultural practices: accepted business conventions, religious beliefs, ethical norms, and gender and racial relations. Such constraints may produce processes of "incomplete commodification."[51] Reproductive commodities appear to be subject to such processes, as the social meanings attributed to ova, sperm, and embryos have shifted over time, allowing increasingly for their public transfer but not their full monetary exchange. Processes in sperm banking have made sperm the subject of a more extensive form of commodification than eggs, even though neither are completely commodified, that is, bought and sold on the market without pretext of "donation."

Some body items carry meanings associated with maleness and femaleness, and their exchange, therefore, may also be constrained by gender norms. Commodification of such items may disrupt or reinforce gender dualities or gender power relations. Like breast milk, ova clearly have gendered significance and have been less subject to commodification in part because ova are more likely to be considered more humanly precious than sperm. The presumption, explored in previous chapters, that women are more central to human reproduction than men is reflected in the disproportionate social value, and human attribution, given to egg and sperm.

The exchange of sperm has historically been constrained by norms of masculinity, which first delayed the scientific examination of semen (as a body fluid improper to look at), deflected attention away from male infertility, and cast sperm as a substance inappropriate for public exchange. Once made "public" by a variety of social, economic, and technological

forces, sperm became available for processes of commodification. But what happens to norms of masculinity when sperm enters into market trade? The evolution and current practices of sperm banking as an industry illustrate the paradoxical nature of such processes for reproductive manhood.

"Like Bird's Eye Peas": Current Practices of the Sperm Banking Industry

Cryopreservation of sperm provided the technological landscape upon which commodification could flourish. It contributed to the geographical and temporal distance between donor and client. Freezing eliminated the need to coordinate the delivery of "fresh" sperm with the peak of a female client's fertility cycle. No longer was it necessary to house the willing medical student in the room next door to the ovulating woman. As such, cryopreservation reduced the possibility that sperm donation might be construed as gift giving from the man to the waiting woman by further eroding the social relations between donor and recipient. As one social commentator in the late 1960s put it, in poetic form:

> What kind of worm
> Would chill his sperm
> And, like a demon
> Save his semen,
> Refrigerated,
> Labeled, dated
> 'Til time is free
> For progeny?

> What human weed
> Would freeze his seed,
> Packaged, please
> Like Bird's Eye Peas. . . .[52]

Like frozen peas, critics charged that sperm was now "cheapened" as a market "product."

Cryopreservation also had tremendously important consequences for the expansion of the sperm banking industry. Practically, it became possible to store thousands of specimens in a single location to be preserved indefinitely.[53] The ability to reliably freeze semen also expanded the potential clientele of the industry to men wishing to deposit "insurance sperm" before undergoing chemotherapy or vasectomies or before going off to war. Freezing also made possible greater safety precautions, allowing for more reliable testing for infectious diseases, such as AIDS, both at the point of deposit and six months later.[54] Frozen sperm offered access to the same donor for repeated inseminations.[55] Most important, cryopreservation meant that production could be centralized in corporate banks, to be marketed nationally or internationally.

Although business practices and medical advances shaped cryobanking services, cultural expectations and consumer demand also played a significant role. The marketing and sale of semen kept alive eugenic ideals—by promoting particular traits—and they obscured from public understanding the function of genetics and meaning of heritability. To a significant degree, the selling of sperm was like the selling of any other commercially marketed product, in that the advertised goods were swathed in imagery that promised what could not be bought. In this regard, the Corvette convertible sold with reference to the sex appeal of the driver, the beer marketed as a way to have a good time with members of the opposite sex, the clothing that promised to attract a good-looking partner, and the sperm hawked as having come from a Harvard man were similar. However, while few consumers may have believed that dressing right or owning the swiftest vehicle would deliver what the advertisements promised, the eugenic message of sperm banks was transmitted to buyers who may not have understood (or wanted to know) that human beings were more than the sum of their genetic parts. One telling example of this was the use of positive eugenics to create a sperm bank for Nobel laureates and other designated men of genius: the Repository for Germinal Choice created in 1971 by millionaire entrepreneur Robert Clark Graham.[56]

Clients of more ordinary sperm banks could now custom-order the exact characteristics of the germinal product, whether seeking to match

the color and characteristics of husbands or seeking an improved version of him, guided by some social ideal. Sperm banks made available thousands of stored donor samples from which to choose. Marketing techniques employed by sperm banks sold what they perceived to be the characteristics most in demand by clients.

Profile of the Sperm Banking Industry

In 1969, there were ten sperm banks in the United States.[57] Twenty years later, the number had grown to 135.[58] A Congressional Office of Technology Assessment report in 1988 noted that about 11,000 physicians were practicing artificial insemination on their patients, with most physicians buying "fresh" donor sperm from medical students, residents, and other physicians.[59] The move away from AID by individual physicians and toward the development of a private sperm banking industry had come between 1986 and 1989, when reports surfaced that six U.S. women had been infected with the HIV virus as a result of artificial insemination.[60] By the mid-1990s, physicians in Canada and Australia had also reported such cases.[61] Fears of infection spurred a demand for cryopreserved sperm—sperm that could be held "on ice" until donors tested clean for HIV and other infectious diseases. By the end of the 1980s, these fears, combined with the development of relatively simple equipment for sperm freezing and storage in liquid nitrogen tanks, produced the growth of the sperm banking industry.

In 1995, a survey conducted by the American Association of Tissue Banks (AATB) found sperm banks in all fifty states, with more than ten each in Texas and California. In 1998, researcher John K. Critser estimated that "between 50 and 150" sperm banks were in operation (depending on how broadly one defined sperm banking services).[62]

A number of problems made such estimates difficult to confirm. Some studies defined *sperm bank* as any facility that collects and stores sperm. Others included banks that provide insemination services but import sperm from other storage facilities. Sperm banks of any sort are not required to register, nor are they inspected by the federal government.

Although total figures are difficult to confirm, interviews with leading sperm bank directors indicate that the industry underwent a process of increasing corporate concentration from 1995 to 2001. Those in the industry indicate that the expense of recruiting donors and screening them for HIV and hereditary diseases has increased the cost of banking and driven smaller operators, like individual physicians' offices, out of the market.[63] By 2001, only twenty-eight sperm banks operating nationally (defined as facilities that collect, store, and offer sperm for sale) could be located in the United States.

In the summer of 2001, information was collected from all twenty-eight sperm banks to construct a profile of industry practices and available semen donors. These banks were located in sixteen different states, concentrated on the east and west coasts and in the upper Midwest.[64] All shipped specimens nationally, with some requiring shipment to physicians only and others shipping to private individuals (for home insemination) as well. Only one sperm bank was nonprofit (the Sperm Bank of California, founded in 1982 as an offshoot of the Oakland Feminist Women's Health Center). Three sperm banks, all in California, explicitly stated that they served "nontraditional" families and lesbian couples. A fourth bank, Heredity Choice in California, specialized in "genius sperm."

Donor lists were solicited from all of these sperm banks, and all but one provided the requested list.[65] Of the twenty-seven banks providing donor lists, specimens from a total of 1,298 donors were available nationwide. Three of these banks had more than 100 donors, and two others had 90 or more donors available.[66] These five banks together supplied almost half (46%) of all donors available nationally (593 of 1,298).

Semen is subject to the same sales practices as other market commodities. As a commodified product, semen comes with fully articulated product liability and return policies: no returns for unused product; credit issued to buyers if semen falls below minimum sperm counts. Semen can be FedExed, with extra charges for shipping on weekends or holidays. Semen may be purchased by credit card, but billing discounts are often offered for advance payment. Two sperm banks offer sex preselection

services.[67] Fourteen sperm banks provide "matching" services, selecting donors who appear to look like the father-to-be or members of the extended recipient family.

Through some banks, donors are paid only in checks made out to "cash." No 1099 tax forms are issued, presumably to protect donor anonymity. Like a new Chevy, donors come with time limit and vial limit warranties: at most banks, "five years, or . . . fifteen hundred (1,500) acceptable vials," whichever comes first.[68]

The commodification of sperm at the beginning of the twenty-first century depends not only on a number of technological conditions but also on social conditions. As noted earlier, commodification requires that an item have equivalent value so that it may be "priced" and that the item be alienable from its human source. Cryopreservation contributed to the alienation of sperm—essential to its development as a marketable product. The ability to freeze sperm made it possible to physically separate not only semen from donor but also donor from recipient. Donor semen could thus be abstracted from its human origins and more readily treated, by all concerned, like a market product and so priced. These processes of commodification (and some might argue dehumanization) extended not only to donor semen but also to donors themselves.

Donor Physical Traits

Corporate business practices spawned by the growing sperm banking industry contributed not just to the commodification of sperm but to the commodification of sperm donors as well. Donor catalogs categorize donors by a range of traits, some of which are clearly heritable and many others that are not. All donor catalogs listed descriptive traits such as height, weight, hair color, eye color, and blood type. In addition, twenty-three banks provided information about "skin tone" (dark, olive, medium, light, or fair or, in some instances, "tanability"). Nineteen banks provided information about "hair texture" (wavy, straight, curly). Such traits are, at least in some part, heritable, although, as siblings attest, even eye color and hair texture can range dramatically within the same genetic family.

In a process reminiscent of the discredited science of phrenology, Fairfax Cryobank in Virginia provides a detailed analysis of the "facial features" of donors, compartmentalizing the face into eyes (set, size, shape, and shade), the nose (size, width, length), the chin (prominence, cleft), the forehead (high or low hairline), and the overall shape of the face (square, oval, or round). Some categorize body type as "ectomorphic (thin), endomorphic (heavy) or mesomorphic (muscular)."[69] Some banks provide information about the "dentition" of donors, with reports of impacted teeth or the donor's need for braces as a child. Some provide video or voice recordings or "baby files"—pictures of donors themselves as babies. One sperm bank even provides information about donors' hat sizes.[70]

Donor lists also categorized donors by a range of other traits of more questionable genetic origin. Chief among these were race, ethnicity, and/or "ancestry." Sperm banks used a wide variety of categorizations under the broad terms of race and ethnic origin: standard racial categories such as Caucasian, African American, or Asian; the country or region of origin of the donor's family (Germany, Europe); ethnic identifications (such as Italian American). Some conflated religion (primarily Jewish) with race and/or ethnicity. In donors of mixed ethnicity or race, donor charts often indicated the relative proportion of such mixing (e.g., 50% Japanese, 50% English).[71]

As might be expected, donors were disproportionately Caucasian. Of all donors listed in the twenty-seven catalogs, 80% were so identified, 8% as Asian, 5% as African American, 5% as "other" or mixed race, and 2% as Hispanic.[72]

These percentages are not reflective of the general population in the United States. Caucasians and Asians are overrepresented, and African Americans and Latinos are underrepresented. For instance, African Americans make up approximately 12% of the population yet represent only 5% of all donors. Asian donors make up 4% of the total population yet are 8% of the donor list. In addition, population statistics by age suggest that the Hispanic and African American U.S. populations have a greater proportion of people of childbearing age, with mean population ages of 30 and 33, respectively, compared with the Caucasian mean age of 39.[73] One

might think that these rates reflect disproportionate rates of infertility among different racial groups, but infertility rates are similar across racial groups. Rather, sperm bank directors report that they reflect consumer demand.[74]

Donor Social Traits

Of even more questionable genetic origin is the information sperm banks provide about a range of social traits. Ten of the twenty-seven banks list the religious affiliation of donors (Christian, Catholic, Jewish, Baptist, Hindu, Muslim, Mormon, and even Christian Science), suggesting one can purchase "Muslim" or "Catholic" sperm.[75] As a presumed measure of inherent intelligence, twenty-three sperm banks provide information about the donor's education (years in college, highest degree), sometimes including college major, college grade point average, or SAT scores. To maximize marketability, some of the largest banks require that donors be college students or have completed a college degree at a four-year major university. For instance, California Cryobank reported that the majority of their donors come from UCLA, USC, Stanford, Harvard, and MIT.[76] Two banks sell specimens specifically designated as "doctorate donors" from donors with advanced degrees (JD, PhD, MD) and charge more for such semen than for "ordinary" sperm (at Fairfax Cryo $265 versus $195 per straw of semen from "ordinary" donors).[77] Heredity Choice, specializing in high-IQ sperm, provides detailed reports of SAT and GRE scores, musical ability, academic achievement, and social characteristics of donors (distinguished professor of chemistry at major university; editor of major international journal; quietly charismatic; college track star).[78]

Fairfax Cryobank in Virginia provides consumers with a list of donors' "favorites": favorite pet, car, movie, song, play, food, and color. Some provide detailed character profiles, including extrovert-introvert scales of behavior. Others provide handwriting samples from donors.[79] At the University of Utah Medical Center's Adopt-a-Sperm program, donors are required to have a "pleasant personality," as judged by the center's staff.

All but one sperm bank prohibit donations from gay donors because of the presumed risk of transmitting HIV through donor semen (even though all specimens are held in quarantine for six months while donors are repeatedly tested). Even a single "protected" sexual contact with another male or with a woman who has been with a bisexual male can rule out a donor for his entire lifetime. Sperm bank directors report that the belief in the possible transmission of a gay gene limits the heterosexual market in "gay" sperm. Only one bank, which caters to "alternative" couples and families, provides information about the sexual orientation of donors, because it is the only bank to accept semen from gay men.[80]

In these selection and marketing processes, we see at work the intermingling of commodification with norms of idealized masculinity. Donors considered to be desirable, by both banks and consumers, are those that most closely match not just abstract idealized *human* traits but abstract ideals of Western *masculinity*.[81] These processes function at two levels: in donor selection by banks and in donor "consumption." It is not just health and potency that drive donor selection but the ability to match cultural ideals of masculinity (except, of course, for the willingness of donors to sell their sperm). Tall donors are preferred over short. With men under 5'8" rejected out of hand by most banks, donors generally are well over the average adult male height of 5'9".[82] Gay donors are turned away not just because of the risk of HIV transmission, for which they are thoroughly screened, but because they fail to meet heterosexual cultural ideals and thus are not "marketable." Those who most closely match the mythical masculine standard—like "Paul," the slender, blond-haired, blue-eyed, college graduate with a history of military service (and time in the Boy Scouts), who estimates that he has fathered forty children—are most highly prized by both commercial banks and potential recipients.[83] Not unlike the ubiquitous glossy images of women in "girlie" magazines, portraits of donors in the promotional literature of commercial sperm banks sell not just sperm but "manhood," in a full range of "colors." Male models posing as donors represent various mixtures of the most prized traits of masculinity: tall, handsome, well educated, athletic, and most important, virile.

These processes also function at the level of consumption. Consumers prefer donors who reflect idealized masculinity in the questionable eugenic faith that their sperm will produce healthy and sound, or even superior, children. One could reasonably argue that these processes of compartmentalization of human traits are driven not by sperm banks but by consumer demand; indeed, sperm bank directors report that they are simply responding to consumer requests when they provide detailed information about donors, such as SAT scores, hobbies, hat size, or "tanability."[84]

The director of Biogenetics in New Jersey, Albert Anouna, characterized the selection process of consumers in this way:

> If I have someone who is 4'7", chances that this donor will be picked is very rare because the majority of people would like people who are tall. There are very few people who call here and say "I want to make sure the donor is under five feet because my family is under five feet." If he's overweight, people will reject that automatically as well, even if the husband is overweight. They also want someone who's educated. You could have a non-college graduate who is very bright, but that's not going to be their choice.[85]

This process of "upward selection" both reflects and perpetuates the stratification of certain human—and specifically masculine—traits.

How do donors compare with the average man? To take one physical measure, in body mass and height, donors are well above average. Body mass index (BMI) is a calculation used by the Centers for Disease Control (CDC) to determine if an individual is a healthy weight, underweight, or overweight, based on proportions of height to weight.[86] According to a CDC analysis using BMI as a measure, in 1988–1994, 24% of all U.S. males between the ages of twenty and thirty-four were obese, while only 6% of all sperm donors were obese.[87] In general, donors appear to be selected from men "above average" on body mass index scales, with the predisposition of donors to be of healthier weight than the average male and with significantly lower rates of underweight, overweight, and obesity than the average young man.[88]

Sperm donors are also disproportionately taller than the average young male. Sperm donors are twice as likely as their nondonor counterparts to be six feet tall or taller. While 38% of all sperm donors were six feet tall or taller, fewer than 20% of the general population of twenty-year-old men were of this height.[89]

Educational attributes also provide a contrast between donors and the average male. Data taken from the U.S. Census Bureau for U.S. males 25–34 years of age (as of 1995) indicate that 29% of Caucasian males and 16% of African American males had achieved a bachelor's or higher educational degree. But more than half of all sperm donors had, with 55% holding completed a bachelor's degree or better.[90] If we look at only African American donors, we see that the gap is even more striking, with more than 33% holding bachelor's or higher degrees, compared with only 16% of the general young African American population of men.

Statistics on the educational achievement of Hispanic men are not available. If we look at the limited average statistics available on both male and female U.S. Hispanics (between the ages of 25 and 29), we find that 11% of Hispanics had only a high school education, 37% had high school with some college, and only 15% had a bachelor's or higher degree, again much lower than levels of education for sperm donors at 55%. Given that women overall tend to have higher levels of educational attainment than men as a group, one could expect these figures on college education to be even lower for Hispanic males. Banks' requirements for donors to have college educations function to exclude the great majority of Hispanic and African American males, even if overt racial selection does not.

The "talents and hobbies" of donors indicate a preference for traditional male social behaviors. The vast majority of donors indicated "masculine" hobbies such as baseball, bodybuilding, carpentry, hunting, fishing, rowing, soccer, weight lifting, and model building. Fewer than 20% of all the hobbies mentioned (donors could list more than one hobby) were "feminine," such as cooking, aerobics, caring for children, crafts, drawing, gardening, poetry, folk dancing, or yoga, and these were usually listed in combination with more "masculine" hobbies, like contact sports.

Donors are clearly screened not just for their health and virility but for their ability to match a particular physical and social profile of masculinity. It is a profile that reflects intertwined social hierarchies of class, race, and masculinity, with a tall and slender Anglo frame preferred over other "stocks" of human beings. Assuming that reproductive consumers are more likely to meet U.S. averages for height and weight, donor selection appears to reflect not just a search for fertile sperm but a search for the more perfect male.

Regulating Sperm Banks: "Not Just a Hot Dog Cart on the Street"

Governments around the world have responded in various ways to these issues. Some prohibit AID entirely. Most Muslim countries, for instance, consider AID to be a form of adultery and prohibit it.[91] Other countries permit AID but heavily regulate it, with restrictions on access for cohabiting heterosexual couples, older women, unmarried women, or lesbian women.[92] In the United States, sperm banks are virtually unregulated, permitting nontraditional families access to such services but at the same time allowing the unlimited marketing and commodification of sperm donation. Sperm banks are not even required to register with the federal government before opening their doors to business, except for complying with basic standards in effect for any medical "lab." As an industry, health and safety standards have evolved informally over the past two decades through two professional associations and through standards set by some state health departments, such as New York and California.[93] Public health regulations evolved in response to concerns in the 1980s about the transmission of AIDS through donor semen and to a scandal involving the surreptitious use of one sperm bank director's semen to "father" his clients' progeny.[94]

Though not set into law, professional guidelines recommend excluding from donation men who have a history of homosexual activity, prisoners, IV drug users, men who have engaged in sex for money, and men who have undergone acupuncture, body piercing, or tattooing.[95] Because

it's possible for HIV and sexually transmitted diseases to be transmitted through semen, professional guidelines also recommend against inseminations using fresh semen so that specimens can be frozen and quarantined for at least 180 days while donors are tested for the antibodies of HIV and other STDs.[96]

Interestingly, the American Society for Reproductive Medicine (ASRM), the professional association that establishes standards for the industry, recommends mental health screening for egg donors but no such screening for sperm donors. Egg donors should be screened, they recommend, for emotional stability, history of personality disorders, current interpersonal relationships, traumatic reproductive histories, current life stressors and coping skills, legal history, psychopathology, history of sexual abuse, marital instability, and evidence of financial or emotional coercion.[97] No such psychosocial screening procedures are recommended for sperm donors, whose motivations, presumably, are simpler and who give up their genetic material with less risk of psychological trauma to themselves.[98]

The American Association of Tissue Banks (AATB) has put forth "ethical guidelines" for commercial activities related to tissue banking, guided by the principles they recommend for donation of human organs. For members that advertise services, AATB advises, it is important to "consider carefully the public perception of the advertisement and avoid terms that cheapen the concept of the 'gift of life.'"[99] In addition, businesses should "honor and treat with respect the gifts that have been donated and to reflect this in all activities related to cell and tissue procurement, processing, and distribution by maximizing the usefulness of the gifts while minimizing risk and waste."[100] Despite these stated standards, even those sperm banks accredited by the AATB (which provides professional accreditation of sperm banks for a fee), most sperm banks use aggressive marketing techniques to recruit sperm donors and sell their product.[101]

Federal and State Regulations

Some states, such as New York, California, and Maryland, license, regulate, and inspect sperm banks. Since 1989, New York State has barred gay

men and intravenous drug users from donating sperm and has required at least two HIV tests on donors before sperm is used.[102] New York State regulations also exclude donors who have had more than one sexual partner within the previous six months or who have "a history of behavior or factors which place the donor at increased risk for human immunodeficiency virus (HIV) infection," including injected drug use, men who have engaged in anal intercourse or oral sex with another man in the preceding five years, men who have been prison inmates for longer than seventy-two consecutive hours, men who have been tattooed or had skin piercing, or heterosexual partners of anyone who fits any of these categories.[103] The only exceptions permitted to these rules are "directed donors," when recipients have specifically requested a donation from a particular individual.[104]

Although the U.S. Food and Drug Administration (FDA) has regulated tissue banks dealing in blood, bone, skin, cornea, and organ donation since the early 1990s, reproductive tissues, such as sperm, eggs, and embryos, have been virtually exempt from federal regulation. In 1988, the FDA and the CDC recommended, but did not require, that all sperm be frozen and quarantined for six months so that donors could be tested for antibodies to the AIDS virus.[105]

In 1995, the FDA announced that it would begin developing regulations to cover reproductive tissues and cells. In 1999, the FDA had already found, "based on recent conversations with sperm banking industry experts," that the twenty largest sperm banks in the country, which reportedly account for "approximately 95% of the commercial production of donor sperm," already follow the standards set by tissue banking associations.[106]

Some in the industry welcomed public regulation, as it potentially "legitimized" an industry still regarded with some suspicion. As Albert Anouna, director of Biogenetics in New Jersey, put it, federal regulations provide "public support and public awareness that this is not just a hot dog cart on the street. There is an actual science to it. We're not doing it just because we want to put a sign up and all you need is a city license. It's an actual clinical medical facility."[107]

It was not until 2004 that the FDA released its final standards for the industry, which ban from donating sperm men considered to be at high risk of HIV transmission, including men who have sex with men.[108] Representatives of gay rights organizations protested the FDA's ban on donations by all "men who have had sex with men," arguing that such bans are discriminatory and unnecessarily broad. They argued that it's possible to identify "a reliable and safe" subset of gay men with a prevalence rate of HIV infection similar to those outside the excluded groups.[109] But the FDA remains skeptical that such a subgroup could be identified.[110]

There are significant differences in government regulation of male and female reproduction. The sale of ova has received much more public attention than the sale of sperm, not only because the retrieval of eggs involves substantial health risks for women but also because the donation of ova is perceived as more like the sale of human babies. Although the marketing of sperm has provided increased reproductive opportunities for women, this is more a by-product of state reluctance to restrict the reproductive labor and opportunities of men than any commitment to reproductive choice, as evidenced by its increasing restrictions on the right to abortion, limited support of access to contraception (particularly for women on public assistance), and minimal support for the development of male contraceptives.[111]

State action is most evident in efforts to restrict access to both gay men and other men considered to be at "high risk" of transmission of HIV—for instance, men in prison or men who have had tattoos. These exclusions are not just the product of health-based risk reduction strategies, although it might be reasonable to subject men at "high risk" to health screenings, rather than outright prohibitions. These restrictions are made possible by (and in turn perpetuate) a hierarchy of masculinity that makes it easier for the state to target certain classes of men for exclusion from the sperm banking industry. No doubt, if such blanket health exclusions had a disproportionate impact on wealthy white men, they would be more difficult to sustain.

The Paradoxes of Reproductive Masculinity

When scientific or medical evidence conflicts with ideals of reproductive masculinity by suggesting the weaknesses or vulnerabilities of men, such evidence is often met with a great deal of social and political resistance. In terms of the presumption of male virility, this resistance has come in the form of a denial of male infertility (the presumption that reproductive failure is of female origin) and limited medical research on the dysfunctions of the male reproductive system. This lack of historical attention was not a product of the simple limits of science. Early medical pioneers, for instance, demonstrated the viability of artificial insemination in the early nineteenth century, long before performing these services became socially acceptable. Rather, cultural resistance was produced by a reluctance to publicly discuss and medically treat male infertility, which potentially undermined presumptions of the strength and virility of the male body. Male infertility was, and remains, an embarrassment for most men—a source of personal shame.

Yet despite this reluctance, a number of social forces have pushed male reproductive vulnerabilities into public light, including the American eugenics movement's questionable desire to use artificial insemination as a tool for "human betterment," the development of more effective artificial insemination techniques, the ability of markets to profit off that technology, and the demands by social movements, particularly the women's movement, to increase access to all reproductive technologies.

Once in the public arena, and left relatively unrestrained by public regulation, sperm banking turned into an industry dependent on the commodification of both sperm and sperm donors for its success. Indeed, critics like conservative author David Blankenhorn have argued that sperm banking turns both men and fatherhood into a cheap commodity. As Blankenhorn has put it:

> The Sperm Father is marketplace father: a father of the cash
> nexus and of short-term exchanges. His is a fatherhood that
> can be bought and sold as a commercial product, or some-
> times obtained for free, no strings attached. It is a fatherhood

that can fit in a vial and be purchased off the shelf, like aspirin
... the Sperm Father also perfectly embodies the modernist
aspiration of paternity without masculinity. No gender roles,
no "mascupathology," no "splitting." Here is a fatherhood
that certainly transcends gender. Here is the perfect father for
people who believe that men in families are either unneces-
sary or part of the problem.[112]

In part, Blankenhorn is right. The compartmentalization of human traits
in the marketing of sperm turns not only semen but also the young men
who produce semen into priced objects, subject to market forces driven
by promises of masculine social attainment in intelligence, physical prowess, and virility. They are objects sold through the use of these masculine
ideals. Such marketing is not unlike the "selling" of young women in girlie
magazines, this time with masculine virility as the lure. Donors themselves have become products, with sperm banking relying on their marketable traits to produce business profits. The sperm donor is reduced
to the set of his eyes, the bridge of his nose, the turn of his lips, the cleft
of his chin, and only those social human traits that can be weighed and
measured. His reduction to a set of compartmentalized traits is necessary to the sale.

 Despite the language of donation, men who sell their sperm are the
ultimate "pieceworkers." At any time in the production process, they
may be rejected by their "employers" with no compensation for the
personal screening, blood and urine testing, or abstinence requirements
if their "product" falls below acceptable production levels. Although
they may receive $75 for each "acceptable" donation, one donation can
produce four times that much profit in marketable vials sold. Stripped
of the donation veneer, such young men are clearly selling their bodies' products.

 The abstraction of the sperm donor through this process also perpetuates the belief that the traits of sperm donors are genetically and not
socially produced. Marketing practices encourage the belief that consumers can purchase ideal human beings in some pure form, captured within

the genetic heart of the male seed. What is erased in the commodification of sperm donors is the social context that produced the traits on the donor spreadsheets. What can we know about a donor from his "dentition"? Certainly there is a genetic component to good teeth, but we can also see through the teeth the social relations that produced the donor—the quality of life of the boy, the social system that produces, for some boys, high-quality medical and dental care and, for others, little or none. This social system is made invisible by donor catalogs. With the social system so erased, donor qualities—both assets and deficits—are assumed to be genetic in origin and to reflect the inherent value of the sperm donor.

Not all fertile men are equally valuable in the sperm banking marketplace. Reproductive value reflects predictable patterns of masculinity, intertwined with class and race. Sperm donors who are tall are literally more valuable to the industry than those who are short; the privately educated are privileged over those who attend public and vocational institutions; the fair-skinned are privileged over the dark; the fine-haired over the nappy. One never buys just sperm, but "Caucasian" or "Hispanic," "Muslim" or "Jewish" sperm. In allowing consumers to special-order the race, ethnicity, and religion of its donors, the sperm bank also perpetuates the notion that race, ethnicity, and religion are immutably part of the genetic landscape. This form of commodified masculinity perpetuates an ideal human standard reflective of the tastes, habits, and physical stature of the Western, white middle class.

Regardless of his value as a human being, or even the value of his "genetic material," the young man presenting himself at the door of the sperm bank who is too fat, too short, or too "gay," the donor who has had limited access to economic or educational opportunity, the donor of the wrong color or educational stature, will surely be dismissed as someone who has little value in the reproductive marketplace. Reproductive consumers participate in this process. No stocky, balding man presents himself, with his wife, to a sperm bank looking for a donor with a family history of endomorphic baldness. Vials of sperm contain, figuratively, the cultural expression of what is socially valued and desired. It expresses an ideal of masculinity that few men, in reality, can meet.

If the economic trade in sperm potentially undermines the masculinity of those who must buy other men's sperm to achieve fatherhood or the masculine status of those men who sell their sperm to make a living, it has elicited countervailing forces that attempt to reinstate ideals of masculinity in their light. Much of the literature produced by sperm banks portrays the act of selling as a form of gift giving and not market exchange. Sperm donation is presented not as waged labor but as an act of male reproductive benevolence. Such linguistic constructions deflect the commodification of donors as subjects of economic exploitation. Women, either alone or with their infertile husbands, are not purchasing men but the life-giving substance that men uniquely possess and most generously offer for donation. Commodification is thus transformed from a type of self-alienation into an expression of male altruism. The language of donation itself obscures the profits of the industry, as well as the wages earned by sperm workers. In doing so, it elevates the social status of men who sell their sperm for profit and potentially reinstates sperm into the realm of the "sacred."

Yet as the language of masculine gift giving frames the marketing of sperm and deflects associations with the "cheapening" of men, this language can only obscure, not unmake, the reality that the commodification of sperm, however incomplete, has profoundly changed reproductive relations. In reality, sperm is not a gift. Women buy it with their credit cards with as little obligation to its maker as the Gucci bag they buy at Bloomingdale's. Sperm can be bought on the open market, ordered and shipped on the Internet with as much contact with its producer as the authors of the books one buys on Amazon.com. As long as this industry profits from the "donations" of men, it will continue the belittlement of men.

While these services make public the infertility of male reproductive consumers, the infertility of men continues to be masked by attempts to match the traits of donors with male reproductive consumers and thus hide their infertility. Most heterosexual couples seek to mimic the traits of the husband in order to keep male reproductive "disability" secret. A man's wish to see himself mirrored in his offspring is driven by a desire

to mask the infertility that may undermine his standing as a man. Although the "likeness" of the child to the mother is presumably assured through her contribution of a genetic egg, as well as her work of gestation, his "likeness" must be socially produced. His search, metaphorically, for a genetic "relative" or sperm of common social ancestry functions to reestablish his masculine status in the face of masculine "failure."

Yet in searching for such a match, he perpetuates the idea that the ability of a man to transmit such traits by impregnating a woman is essential to manhood. Like no time before, the public trade in sperm—advertisements in subway cars, on billboards, on Web sites, and in newspapers—makes visible the inability of some men to father their own children. Ironically, masculine virility is promoted by donor catalogs at the same time that the very existence of such catalogs makes visible the infertility of those men who must purchase the seed of other men to fulfill their ideal role as "father." Sperm banking practices serve to reify ideals of masculinity, even as (or precisely because) the act performed by donors potentially undermines these same ideals.

The diminution of sperm as a simple market product and men as mere reproductive "servicemen" is countered by elevating the significance of sperm over eggs through the notion that "superior" human traits are transmitted primarily through sperm. Donor categorizations in sperm banking catalogs perpetuate the notion that differential human rankings are genetically embedded in the male seed, ready to be activated by both checkbook and ova. Implicitly, if not explicitly, sperm banking practices hark back to ancient assumptions that male seed is responsible for the quality of the human being produced through gestation.[113] As historian Daniel Kevles has noted of the eugenics movement at the beginning of the twentieth century, eugenicists sought to improve the quality of the human race through "eutelegenesis"—production of pregnancies from afar.[114] In this dream, Kevles notes, "women were noticeably absent. . . . The role of women in eutelegenesis amounted to little more than that of conceptual vessels for the sperm of admirable men." This vision magnified "the reproductive power of a 'few superior men.'"[115] Current sperm banking practices continue,

in modified form, this presumption of sperm as superior in reproductive value.

Yet it is women, with their husbands or lesbian partners or as individuals, who are very much present in the sperm banking industry. Sperm banking practices do not just reaffirm traditional heterosexual family structures but make possible a whole range of alternative forms of parenting where *men* are often absent. The valorization of sperm does little to shift that balance of reproductive power back in favor of traditional paternal authority.

As reproductive anthropologist Marilyn Strathern has observed, this process of revealing the social production of biological relationships is irreversible: "The displacement effect of uncovering assumptions, of making the implicit explicit, sets off an irreversible process. The implicit can never be recovered, and there is no return to old assumptions; displacement becomes radical."[116] In significant ways, the "marketplace father," bemoaned by conservatives like Blankenhorn and celebrated by others, has permanently displaced the paternal father of the past, despite linguistic efforts to reinstate traditional reproductive manhood.

What would be a more equitable way of addressing the problem of male infertility? It might include imposing limits on the marketing practices that promote the commodification of sperm and sperm donors, such as restrictions on the information made available to consumers about the social traits of donors, like religion or personal habits, that help to perpetuate notions that such traits are transmitted genetically. Or there might be restrictions on the profits made from the trade in sperm, or limits on the income earned through donation, like the established restrictions on the trade in other human body parts and products.

Such restrictions on the marketing of sperm come with some social risks as well, by limiting the choices of reproductive consumers. Such restrictions might reduce, or drive up the cost of, reproductive options by decreasing the supply of male gametes on the market. State surveillance of sperm industry practices might reduce the eugenic potential of the industry by limiting the kind of donor information made available to potential consumers but come at the cost of reducing reproductive

choice for infertile men and their partners, as well as for those seeking to start nontraditional families. But the choices now offered to reproductive consumers are in large part illusory, based as they are on the highly questionable assumption that ideal human traits are transmitted genetically through sperm.

In the end, a more equitable approach to the problem of male infertility might also include greater medical attention to the male reproductive health problems that produce the inability to biologically father children in the first place. It would address the risks to male reproductive health posed by the toxins of work, war, and environmental exposures, which increase not only rates of male infertility but also a whole host of male reproductive health problems. It would require recognition of the vulnerabilities of the male reproductive system to the harms of the outside world. But these risks are not possible to address in a social system intent on denying the vulnerabilities and weaknesses of the male reproductive body.

THE CHILDREN MEN FATHER 5

The Science and Politics of Male-Mediated Fetal Harm

It was the late 1960s, and Gladys Friedler was just finishing her PhD dissertation in the medical sciences at Boston University. She was studying drug addiction to opiates, trying to understand the biological mechanisms that produced increasing levels of tolerance to the drug. In humans, this tolerance was the earliest stage of addiction before physical, and then psychological, dependence developed. Researchers suspected that some mechanism in the immune system, perhaps evidenced in the blood, produced this response. If so, Friedler thought, it might be transferred from mother to fetus in pregnancy. To test for this mechanism, Friedler decided to expose female rats to morphine before they became pregnant and then see if their offspring would be born more tolerant to drugs. As Friedler reports, "That was a leap, but then I was always leaping off into the blue."[1]

Disappointed, she found no change in drug tolerance in the offspring but noticed instead that the babies of these mothers were consistently smaller. Although previous researchers had noted the effects of drug exposures in gestation, no one had imagined that exposing a female before conception could lead to effects on offspring like retarded growth. Intrigued by the results, she set off to search for a mechanism.

On a hunch, she eliminated the maternal exposure to drugs altogether and exposed only fathers to morphine before conception. Perhaps

a similar mechanism might be at work through the male system that might tell her something about how this mechanism worked. "You know, when I first started looking at the male, I thought I would find nothing. In a way, I hoped I didn't because I thought, 'What are we going to do with *that*?'" In the dead of night in her lab, out of sight of her skeptical advisor ("he really thought it was a waste"), she began her work on male rats. What she found was more than she expected. When she used mother rats who were never exposed to drugs, paternal exposures to opiates produced effects on growth not only in the first-generation offspring of the males but also in the second generation. "It was really very strange because there was no evidence then, nor is there now, that opiates are mutagenic; therefore, how could this happen? . . . No clue."[2]

Thirty years later, Friedler reflects on the combination of "serendipity and stubbornness" that led her down this path. "To me, what's interesting is the stuff that doesn't fit. I don't think people do it consciously, but I think when people work in science sometimes the stuff that doesn't fit you assume is a fluke and you let it go. And I can never let go."[3] Friedler's work was met with great skepticism. She had difficulty publishing her work, and research funding was sporadic. Friedler surmised, "Because it's the father, I'm sure there was reluctance to look at it. . . . It's easier to see and easier to understand the female effects."[4] Although her papers at professional conferences generated a great deal of interest, few followed in her path. As she recalls, "I heard both kinds of comments. Several men said, 'Why are you picking on the male? Once the baby is conceived that's mommy's problem.' Yet on the other hand, I heard comments from women saying, 'Why are you focusing so much attention on men?' There was resistance on both sides."[5] Cultural assumptions about male and female reproduction made Friedler's work difficult to believe.

Funding waned, and by the early 1980s, Friedler had given up her paternal research. For nearly twenty years after Friedler's first experiments on rats, few scientists followed up on her work, as public attention focused almost exclusively on the transmission of harm through

the mother: in the 1950s and 1960s on the thalidomide tragedy, in the 1970s and 1980s on women's use of alcohol, in the 1980s and 1990s on "crack babies." When it came to research on fetal harm, children were treated as *filius nullius*—as if they had no fathers. It was not until a series of wars and environmental disasters dramatized the damage that could be done to men's reproductive health—and through men, to fetal health—that public attention shifted back toward men.

By the mid-1980s, Vietnam veterans struggling to care for children born with spina bifida, Gulf War veterans whose children were born with strange birth defects, and men rendered sterile by their exposures to toxic chemicals at work had all voiced demands that both science and government explore the connections first observed by Friedler. They were supported by labor union activists and a small number of rogue researchers who had tried, with limited success, to raise scientific and public attention about paternally mediated harm throughout the late 1970s and early 1980s.

By the year 2000, hundreds of studies had been conducted on the effects of drugs, alcohol, nicotine, and occupational, wartime, and environmental hazards on both male reproduction and the health of men's children. Studies have shown significant associations between male toxic exposures and increased rates of infertility, miscarriage, stillbirth, and childhood health problems. Although the science of male-mediated fetal risks leaves many questions unanswered, there is growing evidence that the exposures of men can affect the health of the children men father. Yet there has been no public outcry demanding either the protection of men or an outpouring of funding for research in this area.

How are we to explain the relative silence on this issue? The answer lies, in part, in understanding how the third presumption of reproductive masculinity—the idea that men are distant from the children they father—has influenced both the kinds of questions we ask and the answers we find acceptable in the science and politics of male-mediated reproductive harm.

Early Barriers to Research

The "All or Nothing" Theory (or "Only the Virile Survive")

There is a long tradition of scientific and social suspicion that the exposures of men can affect the children they father. Plato had warned that "when drunk . . . a man is likely to beget unstable and untrusty offspring, crooked in form and character,"[6] and laws in both Carthage and Sparta prohibited the use of alcohol by newlyweds, presumably for fear of conceiving damaged children on drunken wedding nights.[7] The 1700s "gin epidemic" in England focused social concern on the impact of both men's and women's drinking on the quality of their offspring.[8] In the 1800s, temperance movement activists raised similar concerns about the drinking of Irish immigrant men in the United States.[9]

Some of the earliest accounts of reproductive disease caused by workplace toxins were reported by those in the field of occupational medicine who examined male reproductive health. In 1775, an English physician, Percival Potts, reported a high level of cancer in the skin covering the scrotums of young chimney sweeps.[10] In the mid-1800s, occupational health researchers in England documented increased risks of miscarriages, stillbirths, and birth defects among both men and women who worked in industries using heavy lead.[11] In the 1930s and 1940s, researchers found that the workplace chemical glycol ether could cause deformities in sperm.[12]

Although researchers in earlier times suspected biological links between paternal exposures and fetal health, these suspicions were muted in the second half of the twentieth century.[13] Standard scientific literature on reproductive toxicity dismissed the links between paternal exposure to toxic substances and harm to fetal health, because it was assumed that damaged sperm were incapable of fertilizing eggs. Indeed, the singular measure of sperm health was egg penetration: Sperm that succeeded in fertilizing an egg were assumed to be healthy and free from defect. The male reproductive system was assumed to "repair" itself every 72 days, as new sperm were produced in the male body from the stem

cells from which sperm were generated.[14] In the field of andrology, measures of male reproductive health centered on men's "ejaculatory performance": sperm volume, sperm concentration and number, sperm velocity and motility, sperm swimming characteristics, sperm shape and size.[15] Based on the all-or-nothing theory, damaged sperm were assumed to be incapable of fertilization and to simply drop out of the race before crossing the reproductive starting line.

The all-or-nothing theory was based on certain culturally imbued assumptions about the reproductive process. Scientists characterized the egg as the passive recipient and the sperm as conqueror in the process of fertilization.[16] Scientists also proposed two distinct kinds of sperm: abnormal "kamikaze" sperm, incapable of fertilization, and "egg-getters."[17] In the kamikaze sperm model, British scientists Robin Baker and Mark Bellis claim that in studies of rats "some sperm sacrifice themselves on a kamikaze mission to further the success of their brothers."[18] Baker and Bellis suggest that abnormal sperm thus play a useful process in reproduction, explaining why approximately 40% of all sperm produced by the average man are abnormal. As Baker explains, "Abnormal sperm put their misshapen heads together and entwine their deformed tails to form a barrier that keeps out sperm from other males." This "sperm plug," located at the entrance to the cervix, presumably forms after their normal comrades, what they call the egg-getters, have entered, allowing them to pursue fertilization upstream undeterred by "rival sperm."[19] The kamikaze sperm theory helped to distance men from fetal harm by reinforcing the presumption that abnormal sperm are functionally incapable of fertilizing an egg.

The kamikaze thesis also reinforced the idea that sperm competition was an essential element of procreation. Proponents of sperm competition suggested that the sperm of one male engaged in "search and destroy" missions of the sperm of enemy males with enzymes "loaded" on sperm heads in acts of "tactical chemical warfare."[20] Sperm competition implied that weakened abnormal sperm would be destroyed in this process and that only the most virile would survive.

The theory of sperm competition is also predicated on the idea that female infidelity is biologically founded and that only the healthiest sperm

survive the competition initiated by the female: "Females mate with several males because this allows them to pit the sperm of different males against each other in their reproductive tracts. In this way, they ensure that they are fertilized by the best-quality sperm."[21]

Articles on male infertility in popular science magazines, such as *Discover*, also characterized the process of fertilization as a heroic achievement for the sperm and an act of passivity for the egg. Sperm require a distinct kind of virility to make it on this trip: "During the final moment of ejaculation, when catapulted forward at speeds up to 200 inches per second, sperm undergo intense shearing forces that could rip them apart," reports a 1991 story titled "Sperm Wars."[22]

War metaphors abound in descriptions of sexual reproduction.[23] Sperm "navigate" toward the cervix and "speed through the fallopian tubes" to pursue the "waiting egg." They then "fire their penetrating enzymes" into the outer layers of the egg in preparation for fertilization. The sperm "bores in," and the egg "slams shut to all further intruders." As the caption exclaims under one photo of a sperm at the moment of penetration, "After an exhausting journey, this could be the winner."[24] This is surely not a mission for the weak, misshapen, damaged, or otherwise feeble sperm. Abnormal sperm are simply "inadequate for conception."[25] As such, most scientific studies on the effects of toxins on male reproductive health focused almost exclusively on infertility as the primary outcome of hazardous exposures and dismissed the possibility that damaged sperm could transmit harm to the fetus.

As a result of these assumptions, maternal transmission dominated research on fetal harm. As Ernest Abel, an early researcher on the paternal effects of alcohol, put it, this was "original sin biologized . . . the view that women were responsible for all the evils of the world."[26] Abel had noted Friedler's work on opiates and tried to pursue a similar line of research on alcohol.[27] But he found the same barriers to research as Friedler: "Nobody believed there was anything there and so it was hard to get funded. . . . There were just too many skeptics because there wasn't any mechanism that readily came to mind." He "eked out" research studies from departmental funds. Such lack of funding presented serious barri-

ers not only to him but also to young scholars looking for new areas of research on which to build careers. As Abel characterized it, "If you're looking for cost-benefit ratios, it's a long payoff for . . . paternal research. The mechanisms are much clearer and the effects are much more dramatic through the mother. . . . So if you're starting out and you want to forge a career, you're not going to look at fathers."[28] Abel pursued the research only after he had tenure. But he, too, was eventually discouraged by the continued lack of funding for this research.[29]

Medical researchers Barbara Hales and Bernard Robaire, working in Montreal in the early 1980s, report similar barriers to their research on the effects of chemotherapeutic drugs on sperm. Robaire had been working in the field of andrology and had been approached by clinicians treating men with cancer. More effective chemotherapeutic treatments meant that cancer patients were surviving longer, and patients wanted to know what effects such treatment might have on their ability to father healthy children. Robaire researched the literature, thinking that surely someone had asked this question before, and found that there was "absolutely nothing."[30] He joined with Barbara Hales, working in the field of teratology, to conduct animal research on one common chemotherapeutic drug, cyclophosphamide. Their first research proposal was "totally rejected" by the Medical Research Council in Canada (equivalent to the U.S. National Institutes of Health) as "completely implausible."[31] Hales and Robaire eventually received a research grant from the March of Dimes and published reports of significant effects on sperm from the drug, but with little fanfare.

Similar was the experience of Ellen Silbergeld, also working in the mid-1980s on the male-mediated effects of lead exposure. As Silbergeld reports:

> We actually didn't get funding for this area of research. We had funding to look at the effects of lead on pregnancy and we piggybacked on that grant. In addition to exposing pregnant animals, we also exposed some males to see the effects on neurodevelopment. When we had the neurologic data out of

that research, we did write up a grant in which we proposed to look at the male mechanisms and I must say I got the most scathing review I've ever received. The review said, "This is the most ridiculous set of hypotheses we've ever heard of. There is absolutely no reason to believe this could ever happen. . . . Don't come back."[32]

Like Friedler and Abel before them, Hales, Robaire, and Silbergeld eventually published their findings, but as Silbergeld put it, "It fell on deaf ears."[33]

Sea Urchins and the "Aggressive Egg" Theory

By the early 1990s, the all-or-nothing theory of male reproduction, which kept many from seeing any possible connection between fathers and fetal harm, was about to undergo a (literal) sea change. Marine biologists had been puzzling over the sea urchin's ability to engage in "external fertilization," where sperm is released and must locate eggs free-floating in the sea. In the late 1980s, scientists explained sperm's ability to find eggs of the same species by postulating that sea urchin eggs release a chemical substance that attracts sperm.[34] In the early 1990s, this theory of sperm "chemotaxis" was extended to research on human reproduction.

In 1991, research confirmed that when isolated in test tubes, human sperm swam toward the fluid surrounding the egg.[35] Major science magazines reported the news with titles such as "Does Egg Beckon Sperm When Time Is Right?" (*Science*, April 1991), "Eggs Urge Sperm to Swim Up and See Them" (*New Scientist*, April 1991), and "Do Sperm Find Eggs Attractive?" (*Nature*, May 1991). As *Science News* newly characterized the process of fertilization:

> A human egg cell does not idle languidly in the female reproductive tract, like some Sleeping Beauty waiting for a sperm Prince Charming to come along and awaken it for fertilization. Instead, new research indicates that most eggs

actively beckon to would-be partners, releasing an as-yet-unidentified chemical to lure sperm cells.[36]

Newspapers such as the *New York Times* carried this characterization further, reporting that "fertile eggs secrete a compound that in test-tube experiments proved irresistible to sperm."[37] These so-called seductive molecules send "alluring chemical cues" to sperm. In addition, research suggested that "tiny hairs in the female reproductive tract move sperm along whether they are healthy or defective."[38]

Scientists confronted with this new evidence vacillated between a model that emphasized the egg as seductress and the more mutual paradigm of sperm-egg fusion.[39] In either case, the sperm take on a less aggressive role in the process of fertilization. In 1992, the *Los Angeles Times* reported the sperm-egg fusion model in this way:

> Fertilization is a delicate process that requires several distinct steps, many of them involving the zona pellucida, a protective coating that surrounds the egg. The sperm first binds to a protein on that coating, then a thin sac on the head of the sperm—called the acrosome—breaks open, releasing enzymes that dissolve the coating. The sperm wiggles through the coating to come into contact with the egg membrane. There, PH-30 causes the sperm membrane to fuse with the egg membrane and, in the key step in fertilization, the sperm's contents are inserted into the egg.[40]

This is a far cry from the perception of sperm at war and one that had implications for more general arguments about the links between "weak" or "damaged" sperm and fetal health. These changing characterizations of the process of fertilization produced a new twist in thinking about the connection between paternal exposures to toxins and fetal harm.[41] Only virile sperm can "bore in," but even weak sperm can "wiggle" enough to fertilize an egg. Sperm damaged by reproductive toxins might thus be capable of fertilization.[42]

The "aggressive egg" theory allowed for the possibility that sperm damaged in shape, size, or speed could still be actively "captured" by the egg. Indeed, sperm so weakened might be even more vulnerable to such ovist aggressions. And if damaged sperm were capable of fertilization, then the health problems of a child so produced might be traced back in etiology to the father.

Indeed, some argued that sperm were potentially more vulnerable to damage from toxins than were human eggs. Because adult males continuously produce sperm throughout their lives, the germ cells from which sperm originate are continuously dividing and developing. Sperm take approximately seventy-two days to develop to maturity and then move for another twelve days through the epididymis, where they acquire the ability to fertilize an egg. Because cells that are dividing are more vulnerable to toxicity than cells that are at rest (as are eggs in the female reproductive system), sperm may be more vulnerable than eggs to damage from toxins during this developmental process.

The failure to examine male mediation might explain, in part, the extraordinarily high rates of couple infertility, miscarriage, birth defects, and congenital childhood illnesses and diseases whose causes remain unknown. Between 5% and 8% of all babies born in the United States have defects detectible at birth. Sixty percent of all birth defects are of unknown origin.[43] Perhaps some of these origins might be traced to the exposures of men. Beginning in the late 1970s, a series of events pushed male reproductive health and male-mediated harm into the public spotlight. These events generated renewed research in three primary areas: men's exposures at work, men's exposures at war, and the effects of men's drinking, smoking, and drug use on fetal health.

The Search for Evidence

Men at Work

We meet the workers in various locales: as they leave work, at the union hall, in bars, playing softball. They are big men, into

muscle shirts, Peterbilt caps and physical boisterousness. On
the basis of their size and vigor alone, they seem healthy. They
are not. Their noses bleed inexplicably. Some of them can no
longer smell at all. Headaches and nausea are facts of their
daily lives. Spots appear on their bodies. Some never have
children. (Ben-Horin, 1979, commenting on men working at
the Occidental Chemical Plant in California)

In 1977, a worker at an Occidental Chemical plant in Lathrop, California, who had been trying to father a child with his wife without success,
decided to go to his doctor to be tested. His fertility test showed that he
was sterile. He reluctantly shared this information with a coworker, who
confessed that he, too, had had trouble conceiving a child. The wives of
workers began to talk, and soon word spread among the workers at the
plant, as worker after worker discovered their common problem and all
began to suspect the chemicals they worked with as a cause of their problem. At Occidental, they handled hundreds of chemicals, mixing inert
and active ingredients in the final production and packaging of pesticides.
Alarmed at what seemed to be a widespread problem, they went to their
union, the Oil, Chemical and Atomic Workers Union (OCAW). OCAW
officials requested a complete health evaluation by the National Institute
for Occupational Safety and Health (NIOSH), and the workers agreed
to be tested. Nine had sperm counts of zero. Altogether, fourteen were
sterile, and thirty-four had reduced fertility. Although some would regain their fertility after exposure to the chemical had ended, others
would remain sterile for the rest of their lives.[44] The pesticide DBCP
(dibromochloropropane) was identified as the chemical sterilant.

DBCP (a halogenated hydrocarbon) was first produced by Shell and
Dow Chemical corporations in the 1950s. The thick yellow liquid had been
widely used in orchards, vineyards, and banana plantations as a soil fu-
migant to kill the worms that attack the roots of plants. In the late 1950s,
Dow Chemical had funded research on the carcinogenicity of DBCP and
found associations between DBCP and testicular atrophy.[45] Despite recommendations by the researchers who conducted the study that occupational

exposure be limited to one part per million (ppm) airborne, Dow quietly shelved the research, never reporting the results to U.S. regulatory agencies.[46]

Occupational safety and health activists had known of the potential reproductive effects of DBCP after the researchers funded by Dow published their results in 1961.[47] But with no regulatory standards set on the chemical and no "right to know" laws, they had no way of knowing what chemicals were handled by workers or what effect these might have on workers' health.[48] More than 12 million pounds of DBCP were being produced each year, exposing nearly 3,000 U.S. workers to the hazard.[49]

With the dramatic effect on men's fertility in the national news, the response from the Occupational Safety and Health Administration (OSHA) was swift. In July 1977, the workers had discovered the problem. By August, OSHA had established an emergency temporary standard, and by March of 1978 OSHA had instituted a permanent standard so restrictive that it virtually prohibited its production in the United States. By contrast, it would take eleven years for OSHA to establish a standard for the carcinogen benzene. Word about the sterility effects of DBCP spread internationally, and the pesticide was suspended from use in Japan, Mexico, Israel, the Netherlands, Finland, and Sweden.[50]

As Rafael Moure, who worked as the industrial hygiene director at the national OCAW office at the time, observed:

> When you can show that DBCP has a direct effect on men, that made it . . . dramatic and real. There were some who did defend the use of it [DBCP], like the American Peach Growers Association who argued that it was the only nematode that works on peaches. They would say "If you want beautiful peaches, you have to use DBCP." . . . There were others who even argued that lots of workers want vasectomies and they could agree to work with the stuff and get a free "chemical vasectomy." But you know DBCP is also a carcinogen and, needless to say, the union didn't think that was such a hot idea.[51]

The DBCP restrictions passed with little opposition from the chemical companies who produced it. As Moure commented, "Corporations are given the power to stop the [regulatory] process in its tracks and they often exercise that power. But on DBCP they knew they couldn't take the public relations fallout."[52] Both Dow and Shell pulled pesticides containing DBCP off the market.[53]

During 1977–1978, seven studies were done with men working with DBCP. Of the 440 men examined, 75 men were sterile, and 103 men had sperm counts low enough to render them infertile. In an average group of men, these numbers might be, respectively, 4 and 35.[54] By 1980, researchers had documented not only sterility but also increases in spontaneous abortion resulting from paternal exposure to DBCP.[55] Twenty years later, paternal exposure to the pesticide was associated with birth defects, retarded fetal growth, some childhood cancers, and chromosome damage in a number of human studies, although none of these associations has been conclusively proven.[56]

Just one year after the DBCP scandal, a case of workplace hazards and female sterilization provided a dramatic lesson in gender politics. In January 1978, management at the American Cyanamid's Willow Island, Virginia, plant informed female employees that they would be excluded from work in eight of the plant's ten departments unless they could prove to the company that they had been surgically sterilized. This left only two departments and janitorial jobs open to the women. The company justified the policy based on evidence that the lead used in the company's production of paint posed a potential risk to fetal health, should any of the women become pregnant. Some women offered to sign waivers, releasing the company from liability. Others argued that their husbands had had vasectomies or that they had no plans to have children. But the company refused to revise its policy. Five women, ranging in age from twenty-six to forty-three, were surgically sterilized to retain their higher-paying jobs at the plant.[57]

The same union that had represented the male workers involved in the DBCP case, OCAW, also represented the workers of American Cyanamid. The union immediately protested the policy, with organizer

Anthony Mazzocchi arguing that the company "has an obligation to bring the lead [exposure] to the level where it is safe for men and women."[58] Like Mazzocchi, occupational health physician Jeanne Stellman, who also worked for OCAW at the time, was incensed by policies such as American Cyanamid's, which were based on what she called the "perpetual pregnancy myth—the idea that women are assumed pregnant until proven otherwise."[59] Such exclusionary policies protected neither women nor men, she argued. Stellman and Mazzocchi helped found a coalition of more than forty-four feminist, labor, civil rights, and civil liberties organizations, the Coalition for the Reproductive Rights of Workers (CRROW), whose 1978 statement of purpose called for the elimination of reproductive hazards "affecting all workers, regardless of sex" and the provision of leaves or transfers with full pay and benefits "for both female and male workers in jobs where hazards still exist."[60]

In response to organized demands, OSHA inspected the plant at Willow Island and found that the company did not meet even minimal standards for lead safety. In 1975, even before the DBCP scandal, a Romanian study had shown that lead decreased sperm counts in workers and increased levels of abnormal sperm.[61] In the midst of the American Cyanamid case in 1978, the proactive OSHA director, Eula Bingham, had flown the Romanian researchers to the United States to talk to U.S. researchers and labor activists about their results.[62] In October 1979, Bingham issued a violation against the company under the "general duty clause" of the Occupational Safety and Health Act of 1970, which requires "each employer to . . . furnish . . . a place of employment which is free from recognized hazards."[63]

American Cyanamid immediately challenged the citation. As Robert Clyne of American Cyanamid tellingly argued: "The ideal is that the workplace has to be safe for everyone—the man, the woman and the child. In the real world that's totally unachievable without emasculating the chemical industry."[64] The violation was overturned by the independent board, the Occupational Safety and Health Review Commission, as an unreasonable extension of the powers of OSHA under the general duty clause, and the sterilization policy continued. Just one year later, Ameri-

can Cyanamid closed down its paint production facility for unrelated market reasons, putting all five sterilized women out of work.[65] It would be thirteen years after American Cyanamid first instituted its policy before the U.S. Supreme Court would strike down, as a form of gender discrimination, an identical policy at the Johnson Controls company in 1991.[66]

Although clearly there are differences between the "involuntary" sterilization of men from DBCP and the "voluntary" sterilization of women at American Cyanamid, these cases demonstrate the difference in thinking about men's and women's relationship to work. For men, the price of sterilization was completely unacceptable as a condition of men's employment. For women, especially those women seeking to enter the masculine world of industrial chemical work, it was not.

Both the DBCP case and controversy over American Cyanamid's policies generated increased public and scientific attention to the reproductive effects of workplace toxins on both men and women through the late 1980s and the 1990s.[67] The DBCP incident, combined with attention brought to the issue by Vietnam vets suffering from the consequences of chemical exposure at war (as discussed shortly), generated new scientific and social attention on the issue of male reproductive health and male-mediated fetal harm.

Occupational health researchers approached these questions from a number of different angles. Some examined particular toxic substances (pesticides, solvents, and heavy metals) and looked for related health outcomes (low birth weight, infertility, miscarriages, birth defects, and childhood cancers and illnesses).[68] Others examined particular occupations, such as "painters" or "pesticide appliers," and looked for correlations to specific reproductive disorders or childhood diseases, such as cancers. Since 1980, more than seventy studies have found positive associations (although not all have been statistically significant) between paternal exposures to occupational hazards and fetal health problems.[69]

Some of the earliest epidemiological research studied the effects of radiation exposures on the children born to men who survived the atomic bombs at Nagasaki and Hiroshima.[70] However, few associations were

found between paternal exposures and childhood health problems, possibly because so few men conceived children in the six months after the bombing, when the exposure effects of radiation were at their strongest.[71]

In 1990, researchers in England reported a six- to eightfold increase in leukemia rates for children born to fathers exposed to low-level radiation at a nuclear power plant.[72] Associations have also been found between paternal preconception irradiation and stillbirth rates.[73] But such findings remain controversial because, as Helen Inskip comments, "There is no obvious mechanism for the association," and researchers took no account of maternal age or smoking behavior.[74]

At least forty-eight chemicals are known or strongly suspected to have adverse effects on male or female reproduction. Of these, eighteen have been found to produce either male infertility or abnormal sperm.[75] Positive associations have been found between increased rates of spontaneous abortion and exposures to toluene, xylene, benzene, TCE, vinyl chloride, lead, and mercury. Paints, solvents, metals, dyes, and hydrocarbons have been associated with childhood leukemia and childhood brain tumors.[76] In the aftermath of the American Cyanamid case, studies have shown that elevated blood lead levels can produce abnormal sperm in men with significant dose-response ratios.[77]

Dozens of studies have further evaluated the impact of pesticides and herbicides on male reproduction and paternal-fetal health.[78] Following the DBCP incident in 1977, studies confirmed a dose-response relation between duration of employment and effects on sperm quality and testicular function.[79] Studies also found positive associations between childhood leukemia and maternal or paternal occupational exposure to pesticides.[80] A study conducted in India of men working in cotton fields found statistically significant increases in rates of spontaneous abortion and stillbirth among the wives of male workers exposed to pesticides.[81] A Minnesota study found statistically significant increases in birth defects in the children of men employed as "pesticide appliers," with their children also more likely to experience circulatory problems or respiratory illnesses.[82]

Studies of dentists, operating room technicians, and male anesthesiologists have shown associations between men's exposures to anesthetic

gases that escape during surgical procedures and increased rates of spontaneous abortion in their female partners.[83] Janitors, mechanics, farm workers, and metal workers have been reported to have an excessive number of children with Down syndrome.[84] One study of 727 children born with anencephaly found correlations for paternal employment as painters.[85] Painters and workers exposed to hydrocarbons have also been shown to have higher rates of children with leukemia and brain cancer.[86]

More than fifty studies have examined the relationship between paternal occupation and childhood cancer.[87] Two comprehensive studies have affirmed an association between certain paternal occupations and childhood cancers, although the specific agents of harm have yet to be identified because there has been no systematic study of a single type of exposure.[88] Occupations that appear to experience significant effects include work in the chemical and petroleum industries, hydrocarbon work, and work in the paint and pigment industry.[89] But elevated effects for most of these epidemiological studies are often just slightly above the norm. None have shown a dramatic association between exposure to a single toxin and a specific childhood cancer.

Although these studies raise suspicions that fetal health can be damaged through paternal exposures at work, few are conclusive. Often little is known about the levels of exposures individuals experience at work. Workers often don't know what they are exposed to at work, and interviews with workers are subject to recall bias. Companies are not eager to share such information with either workers or researchers. Occupational categories like "painter" are too broad to be very predictive of toxic exposures, and without individual monitoring, workplace exposures for the same worker in the same job can vary from day to day or week to week. In addition, studies are complicated by questions about confounding factors, like men's cigarette smoking, drug or alcohol use, or the exposures of the female partners of male workers, factors often not included in occupational studies of men. One leading researcher in this area, David Savitz, assesses the bulk of these studies as "limited in quality and quantity" and "methodologically weak." Without the "biologic plausibility" of a "pathway that makes sense," funding agencies,

particularly in the United States, are unlikely to keep funding such studies.[90] Or as Andrew Olshan puts it, because of methodological problems, the absence of dramatic effects, and continuing disbelief about the nature of the male mechanism, "there is no way any agency is going to fund another epidemiological study on male occupational exposures and childhood cancer."[91] "Good" studies would be both too time-consuming and too expensive for an area of research where the biological mechanisms still appear "implausible" to many funders.

Most promising are studies being conducted outside the United States. In Denmark, researchers are collecting sperm samples from 1,100 men working as stainless-steel welders, monitoring exposures to the chromium fumes produced by the welding, taking urine samples from the female partners of these men to monitor early and otherwise undetectable pregnancy loss, and collecting information as well about paternal and maternal smoking, caffeine use, and alcohol use. To date, the study has shown that stainless-steel welders have increased rates of abnormal sperm and that their female partners have higher rates of miscarriage. In addition, high caffeine use and alcohol use by these men also produced higher rates of spontaneous abortions in their partners.[92]

Beyond human studies, animal studies have also shown significant male-mediated effects from toxic workplace exposures. For instance, for more than thirty years, studies on lead's effects on mice have shown that male mice exposed to relatively low levels of lead, comparable to levels permitted in U.S. workplaces, produce decreased litter size, increased miscarriage rates, and abnormal neurological development in offspring in both the first and second generations of exposed males.[93] But such animal research is often viewed with skepticism in terms of its implications for occupational exposures, despite the fact that many human hazard standards are based solely on animal studies.

In the United States, what has been the regulatory response to evidence of male-mediated reproductive risks? OSHA remains woefully inactive on questions of reproductive risks to men or women. The DBCP incident in 1977 led to the establishment of OSHA limits that virtually banned the chemical from production in the United States based on its

male reproductive effects. But the DBCP standard has been one of only three OSHA standards based primarily on evidence of reproductive problems, despite the fact that OSHA estimates that workers are regularly exposed to more than 1,000 chemicals that have been identified as reproductive hazards.[94] OSHA has established no general standard governing reproductive hazards in the workplace.

It is not always for lack of evidence that no standards are set. The first toxic effects of glycol ethers—a solvent commonly used in industrial work—to the male reproductive system were reported in the 1930s and 1940s by scientists who reported testicular atrophy in animals exposed to the chemical. In 1983, NIOSH held an international conference to examine the research on glycol ethers. It took another ten years for OSHA to issue a proposed ruling for its regulation. And to date, almost two decades after the federal government began its investigation, there is still no final standard set for its safe use in the workplace.[95]

The workers' compensation system, established state by state, still provides no relief for workers whose reproductive systems are damaged by workplace toxins. Workers who lose reproductive capacity because of workplace exposures may not receive compensation for the damage, for financial relief is provided only for harm that prevents a worker from performing his or her job. In addition, workers are prohibited from suing their employers for damages because employers are protected from such suits by workers' compensation law, even in cases of gross negligence.[96]

Throughout the 1980s, no amount of labor pressure could break the regulatory atrophy of OSHA under the Reagan and Bush administrations. As one occupational health and safety activist put it: "Standard-setting came to a dead halt."[97] Labor union organizers, hopeful that the Clinton administration would be more active on these issues, were "woefully disappointed." According to health and safety advocate Daryl Alexander:

There was very little progress on a whole series of regulations. At least for the first six years of the Clinton Administration very little was done. The agency took an overly defensive posture. They were getting bombarded by Republicans in

Congress and the usual suspects, like the U.S. Chamber [of Commerce] and the National Association of Manufacturers. They behaved more as an advocacy organization for employers than they did for workers. . . . It was an administration that didn't really understand how important a good regulatory agency is to the health of working people. It was really sad.[98]

NIOSH, the research arm of OSHA, has operated with a minuscule budget since dramatic cuts under the Reagan and Bush administrations. According to Theresa Schnorr, the director of a NIOSH research team on "fertility and pregnancy abnormalities," research on reproductive problems, for both men and women, is also seriously limited because of the lack of national surveillance systems, such as a national birth defect registry, and so "we simply have no way to know the extent of the health problem we're facing."[99] In addition, most workers, as well as most physicians, are unaware of the reproductive problems that might result from occupational exposures. As long-time labor advocate Tony Mazzocchi has observed:

If someone's got a reproductive problem, the first thing they're going to do is think that there's something wrong with them. If you have a problem reproducing today and you go to your clinician, that doc probably wouldn't know from bones about an environmentally caused problem. We try to say, what's the first thing you should ask a person? "Where do they work, what do they work with and under what conditions do they work with it?" We don't currently train people to do that.[100]

While toxicologists and epidemiologists studied occupational exposures from many angles, another set of researchers worked to untangle the even more complicated questions involved in men's toxic exposures at war. If occupational studies seemed burdened with problems, when it came to men and war, such problems would grow exponentially.

VIETNAM AND AGENT ORANGE

We have drafted the unborn and the unborn are now going to war with their fathers and mothers. (Vietnam Veteran activist Michael Ryan)[101]

Dioxin still kills Vets and their children. (NJ Agent Orange Commission Web site, banner headline, 5/30/01)

The government ought to treat these children as if they had been shot in Vietnam. (Rep. Lane Evans, D-IL)[102]

From 1962 to 1971, the U.S. military sprayed 19 million gallons of Agent Orange and other herbicides from Air Force planes over the forests in Vietnam. The herbicide killed the vegetation that provided cover for enemy troops.[103] Strange illnesses, birth defects, and cancers began to appear in the early 1960s among the Vietnamese farm families and mountain people who lived under the toxic rain. Suspicions that these were caused by Agent Orange were reinforced in 1969 by a U.S. study showing that exposure to dioxin, one ingredient in Agent Orange, produced cancer and birth defects in lab animals. By 1971, with concerns over health effects rising, the U.S. military halted the spraying.[104]

It was not until five years after the war's end, in 1978, that a Veterans Administration (VA) caseworker began to notice a similar pattern of illnesses among the Vietnam veterans she was seeing in Chicago.[105] She suspected that their strange symptoms—chronic rashes, nerve disorders, cancers, and problems with their children—were due to their toxic exposures in war, and she brought her concerns to the VA. The VA and military officials dismissed her concerns, arguing that any residue of dioxin sprayed from the air would have quickly dissipated in the sunlight, posing little risk to American troops. Almost 3 million troops had served in Vietnam, and no one knew how many had been exposed to Agent Orange.

Frustrated by the lack of response by the military, Vietnam vets turned to both Congress and the courts. Based on the early studies of

dioxin, some of which had shown serious health effects on workers who produced it from the early 1950s, 15,000 vets filed suit against the seven companies that had manufactured Agent Orange. In addition, they demanded funding from Congress for further research. In 1979, Congress authorized $100 million for the Department of Veterans Affairs to conduct a study of the health effects of Agent Orange.

In the meantime, collaborations began between occupational health physicians Steven and Jeanne Stellman and a number of Vietnam veteran organizations.[106] A name familiar from the 1977 DBCP pesticide incident, Jeanne Stellman had already been involved in studies on the impact of pesticide exposures on male reproductive health. The Stellmans helped a vets' organization, Citizen Soldier, conduct a survey of 500 Vietnam vets in 1980 and found that men who showed physical symptoms of toxic exposure to dioxin had twice the incidence rate of children with congenital anomalies than men without symptoms.[107] Too small for findings of any significance, the survey nevertheless suggested that something was going on that warranted more research. Jeanne Stellman approached the American Legion, then active in lobbying for better investigations into Agent Orange exposure, and the Legion commissioned the Stellmans to conduct more research.[108]

In 1982, the Air Force decided to begin its own study. It would compare the health of soldiers who had flown Agent Orange spraying missions over Vietnam—known as Ranch Hands—to the health of unexposed vets. Although limited in size to only 1,000 men, it was the only group of soldiers for whom exposure information could at that time be confirmed. The Air Force assigned Lieutenant General Murphy Chesney to head the study—the man who had been in charge of health and safety for Air Force personnel during the Vietnam War, including assessments of the safety of Agent Orange spraying.[109]

By 1983, the $100 million study Congress had ordered the VA to conduct in 1979 had not even been started. As one *Washington Post* reporter put it: "The VA foresaw to its horror a multibillion-dollar drain on its budget should medical care and/or compensation be granted."[110] Congress pulled the project from the VA and turned it over to the Centers

for Disease Control (CDC).[111] The first phase of the CDC study focused on birth defects, examining 4,800 babies born with birth defects in the Atlanta area from 1968 to 1980 and comparing them with a control group of 3,000 healthy children born in Atlanta. In 1984, the CDC released its findings: no positive associations were found between Agent Orange exposure and birth defects in general. But when controlling for possible levels of exposure, based on the places and times of service in Vietnam (information provided by the Army), the study found statistically significant associations between Agent Orange exposure and slightly increased rates of spina bifida, cleft palate, and certain tumors for children of Vietnam vets.[112] Few inferences could be drawn, the CDC argued, because the increases were so slight and the study so small. Of the nearly 8,000 babies in the study, only 696 had fathers who had served in Vietnam. Of these, perhaps a fourth had been exposed to Agent Orange. Unless exposure to Agent Orange produced astoundingly high rates of birth defects, finding statistical significance in these small numbers (given how seldom such birth defects occur) was difficult at best. The birth defect spina bifida, for instance, normally occurred in about 5 of 10,000 births.[113]

Growing scientific evidence linking dioxin exposure not only to birth defects but also to a range of cancers pushed the manufacturers of Agent Orange to seek a settlement in their case with the vets. In 1984, just hours before jury selection was to begin, the chemical companies decided to settle the vets' class action suit for $180 million. As part of the settlement agreement, the benefits were to be shared with all vets who were exposed to Agent Orange. By 1989, 250,000 vets had applied to be included in that settlement class.[114]

In 1987, after $50 million and five years of study, the CDC decided to end its Agent Orange study. Limited information about levels of exposures, the CDC argued, made it impossible to conduct reliable scientific research.

In the meantime, Vietnam vets with illnesses they suspected were caused by Agent Orange exposure continued to seek disability compensation through the Department of Veterans Affairs. For ten years after the war, they were turned away on the grounds that there was insufficient

evidence of a causal association. The political irony was not lost on the vets. As one investigative reporter put it, "The shameful truth is the VA has gone to great lengths to make sure there would be no scientific evidence."[115] Or as Jeanne Stellman put it, "It was a studied, purposeful effort not to ask or answer any of the right questions."[116] In addition to delays at the VA, by the end of the 1980s, the Air Force had been accused of delaying and withholding "damaging" data from their study, particularly on reproductive effects, of political manipulation of the study design, and of failure to provide adequate representation of vets on the study's review board, as required by the study protocol.[117]

Turning again to the courts, the vets sued the VA over what they considered to be unreasonable denial of their claims. In 1989, a federal court in California ruled in their favor, agreeing that the VA's standard for assessing compensation claims had been too restrictive. The court ordered a reexamination of every Vietnam vet claim denied since 1985. Diseases with a proven "positive association" with a wartime exposure were to be compensated. "Positive association" was to be legally defined as when "the credible evidence for the association is equal to or outweighs the credible evidence against the association." Where evidence was mixed, vets were to be given the benefit of the doubt.[118]

By the late 1980s, the Vietnam vets were joined by a key political ally. Retired Navy Admiral Elmo Zumwalt had been chief of naval operations in Vietnam and had himself ordered Agent Orange spraying in the Mekong Delta. His son, Elmo Zumwalt Jr., had commanded a Navy boat in the same area. In 1988, his son died of cancer, and his grandson, Russell Zumwalt, was diagnosed with a "sensory integration dysfunction," the same communication disorder that exposed vets had complained of in their own children. Zumwalt was convinced that both were caused by his son's herbicide exposure during the war.[119] Zumwalt became an advocate for research and compensation for the vets.

In addition, a number of key Congressional actors, including Vietnam vet Senator John F. Kerry (D-MA), also joined the fight. Until 1990, the only disease for which the VA provided disability payments from Agent Orange exposure was chloracne, a severe skin disorder long known

to be common among workers in plants that produced dioxin. Cosponsored by Senators Kerry and Alan Cranston (D-CA) and Rep. Lane Evans (D-IL), the Agent Orange bill would order the VA to extend benefits to Vietnam vets disabled by either of two forms of cancer: soft-tissue sarcoma and non-Hodgkin's lymphoma. In addition, it would mandate that the National Academy of Sciences review all scientific evidence on the possible health effects of exposure to Agent Orange, to be updated every two years, and that these reviews inform VA judgments about disability claims.[120] In an act whose irony would only later become apparent, the Senate passed the Agent Orange bill the same day U.S. Marines led the first major ground battle of the Persian Gulf War—January 30, 1991. Eager to appear supportive of veterans in the midst of the emerging military conflict in the Persian Gulf, President George H. W. Bush signed the Agent Orange bill into law.[121]

As mandated by the act, in 1993 the National Academy of Sciences (NAS) released its first review. It classified evidence of the health effects of dioxin exposure into five categories: "health outcomes with sufficient evidence of association," "limited/suggestive evidence of association," "inadequate/insufficient evidence of association," "limited/suggestive evidence of no association," or "sufficient evidence of no association."[122] The report confirmed "sufficient evidence" of an association between Agent Orange exposure and soft-tissue sarcoma, non-Hodgkin's lymphoma, Hodgkin's disease, chloracne, and the liver disease known as PCT. The NAS also found "limited/suggestive" evidence of associations between Agent Orange exposure and respiratory cancers, multiple myeloma, and prostate cancer. The VA extended disability compensation to all these illnesses except prostate cancer.[123] All soldiers who served in Vietnam and who were disabled by any of these illnesses would be eligible for disability payments, regardless of their individual proof of exposure to Agent Orange. Depending on their level of disability, disability payments would range from $90 to $1,800 per month.

On reproductive effects, the review found only "inadequate evidence" of associations with reproductive disorders, including birth defects, spontaneous abortion, infertility, testicular cancer, childhood

cancer, and female reproductive problems. There would be no compensation for the children of vets.

In March 1996, NAS released its second report, this time finding "limited/suggestive evidence" of a link between paternal exposure and spina bifida in the children of exposed men. It based this assessment on a re-examination of the portion of the Air Force's Ranch Hand study that appraised reproductive outcomes, as well as two additional nongovernmental studies. Although the Ranch Hand study had been conducted in 1984, the Air Force had delayed its release for eight years by claiming they needed to verify data from birth records and "perform additional data analyses."[124] Indeed, a Government Accounting Office examination of the Ranch Hand study (conducted in response to complaints of delays) found that the level of verification required in Ranch Hand was "highly unusual and virtually unprecedented for a study of its size."[125] Nevertheless, the evidence, now combined with two additional studies, was enough to justify bumping spina bifida up from the "insufficient" into the "limited/ suggestive" category of association. Secretary of Veterans Affairs Jesse Brown reported that he was "deeply concerned" about the report.[126]

President Clinton found political opportunity in the 1996 NAS report. At the time the report was released, Clinton's legitimacy with the military was flagging. In the midst of one of many sexual harassment scandals, Clinton had attempted to shield himself against legal charges by appealing to a 1940 law that exempted "military personnel" from damage suits while in "military service." His attempt was met with derision by both the public and the military. Publicly embarrassed, on May 27 he withdrew his request for exemption.

Just one day later, May 28, Clinton called a press conference flanked by Retired Navy Admiral Elmo Zumwalt and dozens of Vietnam vets. In an apparent attempt to restore military favor, Clinton ordered the VA to extend disability coverage to Vietnam vets disabled by two additional diseases, prostate cancer and the nerve disorder peripheral neuropathy. In a remarkable move, he proposed legislation to extend benefits to the children of Vietnam vets for spina bifida. It would be the first time in U.S. history that the children of veterans would be compensated for ill-

nesses traced to the exposures of their fathers. Extending veterans' benefits beyond vets themselves required the approval of Congress.[127]

In Congress, Senator John Kerry introduced, with Senators Jay Rockefeller (D-WV) and Thomas Daschle (D-SD), legislation to extend VA benefits to the approximately 3,000 children of vets with spina bifida.[128] The resistance to the "children-of-war" measure was substantial. Some estimated the cost to support children with spina bifida at $326 million in the first five years, and some argued the move was motivated more by politics than by science. As Veterans Affairs Committee Chairman Senator Alan Simpson (R-WY) put it, "Few words are more effective in evoking an emotional response from us all than the words 'veterans' or 'innocent children.' However, I sincerely believe that the creation of new and precedent-setting entitlements should be decided on the basis of sound medicine and sound science, rather than on the basis of emotion."[129] But such resistance couldn't outweigh the pressure from veterans' organizations representing the millions of men who had fought in war. By September the bill was signed into law.

By the year 2001, nine diseases were on the VA's list of compensated diseases, and diabetes would soon be added.[130] The 2001 NAS report had also suggested that childhood leukemia could also be traced to paternal Agent Orange exposure, and the secretary of veterans affairs had asked Congress for permission to extend benefits to the children who had survived the disease, though most had already died.[131] Of the 2.3 million surviving Vietnam vets, 8,600 veterans and 850 of their children have received disability benefits as a result of their Agent Orange exposure.[132]

More than thirty years after the end of the Vietnam War, plagued by problems and at an estimated total cost of $200 million, the Air Force's Ranch Hand study continues, scheduled to be completed in the year 2006.[133] With only 1,000 "exposed" men in the study, matched up against 1,300 "unexposed" soldiers, many believe the study's small size will seriously limit any of its conclusions.

In the meantime, the Stellmans, like other independent researchers, continued their research, developing databases of information tracking Agent Orange spraying in Vietnam, as well as data on troop locations and

movements during the war. In the late 1980s, the judge in the vets' class action suit against the chemical producers of Agent Orange had asked the Stellmans to become "exposure consultants" in the case to help determine which soldiers were eligible to be part of the settlement class. The court had asked the White House to provide information about spraying and troop movements during the war, and the White House refused, informing all executive agencies not to cooperate with the inquiry.[134] The court then filed a freedom of information inquiry requesting access to the information. As Jeanne Stellman recalls, "Suddenly, one day, there appeared 42 reels of computer tape at our office." It was the record of troop and battalion movements in the most heavily sprayed areas of Vietnam. "We had the underlying data that in a million years, we didn't think we would ever see."[135] In 1989 they began processing the data in order to conduct their assessments for the class action suit.

The Stellmans have since supplemented that data with information from the National Archives. In 1996, they received a major grant from the NAS's Institute of Medicine to clean and process the data, providing the first major database specifying both spraying activities and troop placements during the war. When completed, the project will provide the first reliable database, now more than twenty-five years after the war's end. In the meantime, the Vietnam Veterans of America have initiated a joint research project on the effects of Agent Orange on the South Vietnamese soldiers and families who were—and continue to be—affected by residues of dioxin that remain in the land and water in Vietnam.[136]

Recognition of the harms done by Agent Orange exposure, both to soldiers and to their children, had taken nearly three decades. It came only with the fierce lobbying of organizations representing millions of vets, political alliances with members of Congress and prominent military officials, and the support of scientific researchers who had spent years piecing together information about exposures and veterans' health problems. Recognition of the male-mediated effects of dioxin on the children of vets had in part also been produced by political opportunism: first, in George H. W. Bush's efforts to win support for a new war in the Persian Gulf—a war that would itself produce similar claims of war-induced

harms—and then in Bill Clinton's attempts to win favor with the military by offering benefits.

When Clinton extended benefits to spina bifida children, it was the first time the federal government had publicly recognized the possibility that the exposures of men could transmit harm to the children men fathered. The extension of benefits to children so harmed was implicit recognition that men's bodies were both vulnerable and deeply connected to the children they fathered. Consciousness of this vulnerability would not be lost on the soldiers who fought in the Persian Gulf War.

GULF WAR BABIES

It is 1993, and thirteen of the fifteen babies born to male Gulf War veterans in the small town of Waynesboro, Mississippi, have been born with unexplained health defects: rare blood disorders; underdeveloped lungs, fingers missing or fused together, club feet. In Fayetteville, North Carolina, ten children of vets have died of rare disorders: liver cancers, heart defects, children born with no spleen. In Yorba Linda, California, a child of a Gulf War soldier prepares for surgery after being born with a deformed heart on the wrong side of his chest.[137] Like the Vietnam veterans before them, the soldiers of the Persian Gulf War suspected that their wartime exposures to toxins might have damaged the health of the children they fathered.[138] It would seem a cruel irony if in fulfilling their role as soldiers they had lost their capacity to father healthy children.

Gulf War soldiers heading to war were exposed to a remarkable mix of toxins. Required to take a string of vaccines against plague, typhoid, anthrax, and cholera before leaving for war, they were also ordered to swallow tablets to protect against nerve gas attacks once they arrived in Kuwait. In their encampments, they might inhale diesel mist from fuel used to damp down blowing sand dust, smoke from the fuel oil used to burn human waste, or petroleum fumes from oil-well fires in the field. On the war field, they might be exposed to chemical or biological weapons used by Iraqis or uranium in the armor plating of their own tanks or the uranium-tipped ammunition they carried. At the end of the day, they might shower with water contaminated with fuel, climb into sleeping bags

dried by the leaded exhaust of army vehicles, and then bunk in tents sprayed with pesticides to control sand flies and scorpions. This was truly a war saturated by the products of the petrochemical industry.

In 1994, the U.S. Government Accounting Office reported that Gulf War soldiers were potentially exposed to twenty-one toxins that have been identified by the U.S. government as reproductive hazards, including arsenic, benzene, cadmium, lead, mercury, nickel, toluene, xylene, and ethanol. No one knows how many soldiers were exposed to these hazards, the extent of their exposures, or the combinations of their exposures. No one knows what happens when one person is simultaneously exposed to viruses, pesticides, solvents, and heavy metals all at the same time. It was not until 1994, three years after the war ended, that the federal government began to fund the bulk of research on the health effects of the war. Of the earliest studies, most focused on stress or posttraumatic stress disorder as a cause of Gulf War veterans' health problems. Prior to 1996, only one study was funded to examine the effects of chemical warfare agents. The study of reproductive effects came late in the game. By 1997, only four of the ninety-one studies funded by the U.S. government on Gulf War illnesses examined the possible reproductive effects of Gulf War exposures.[139]

As a result of newspaper reports of birth defect clusters in Waynesboro, Mississippi, researchers from the federal government initiated a number of studies, focusing primarily on rates of congenital birth defects in children fathered by Gulf War soldiers. No definitive link could be found. There were substantial problems with all of the studies: Some included only veterans still on active duty, when by 1993, 44% of those who had served in the war were out of service. Others studied small groups of veterans, although birth defects, because they are so rare, require large studies. In addition, most studies examined only those birth defects classified as "structural congenital malformations" diagnosed in the first year after birth. Birth defects that might become apparent as a child grew older were not assessed. Studies on birth defects could not pick up increased rates of miscarriage or difficulties conceiving. In addition, given that soldiers tend to be in better health than the average American—the

"healthy warrior" effect—one might expect rates of health problems in the veteran population to be lower than the average for the United States as a whole. Studies found that rates of birth defects for Gulf War soldiers were the same as the U.S. average. A more accurate measure would compare rates of birth defects for Gulf War veterans against the rate of birth defects for veterans as a whole.[140]

One significant area of research has focused on the effects of depleted uranium (DU) exposure on soldiers' health. DU is a low-level radioactive heavy metal that is a by-product of the process used to enrich uranium. Because of its extreme density, it is used on the cap or tip of armor-piercing munitions to better penetrate hard targets, like armored tanks. DU is also incorporated into U.S. tank armor to protect against penetration by enemy strikes. When DU munitions strike an object, it "breaks into fragments and fine particles that ignite easily, and it produces uranium dust particles that can be inhaled or ingested."[141] During the Gulf War, a number of these DU munitions were mistakenly used against U.S. tanks, exposing more than 100 U.S. soldiers on or within those tanks to depleted uranium, as well as those soldiers sent to rescue them. In addition, hundreds of soldiers may have been exposed as they "passed through and inhaled smoke from burning DU, handled spent DU munitions, or entered DU-contaminated vehicles on the battlefield or in salvage yards."[142] A study conducted by the Veterans Administration released in the year 2000 found that men with fragments of DU still embedded in their bodies continue, ten years later, to excrete elevated levels of uranium in their urine and that these elevated levels were related to "subtle perturbations" in the reproductive and central nervous systems.[143]

Studies on the possible reproductive effects of Gulf War exposures continue. Some of these focus on populations of veterans exposed to specific toxic substances during the war, like DU or sarin. Others examine medical records from civilian hospitals where the children of veterans who have left active duty have been born. Others expand the scope of reproductive problems examined, such as higher rates of miscarriage or subtler birth defects.[144] Scientists continue to study the

reported clusters of "Gulf War babies" with high levels of skepticism after early studies could prove no link between birth defects and wartime exposures.

Like the problems faced by Vietnam vets, for both technical and political reasons, accurate information about Gulf War exposures has been nearly impossible to obtain. It was not until June 1996, after years of evasion and denial, that the Department of Defense acknowledged that some veterans may have been exposed to the nerve gas sarin after the demolition of an Iraqi ammunition facility during the war. Exposure information has been collected by researchers from veterans themselves, but the first of these studies was not initiated until six years after the war's end. Recall problems plague such studies, and of course it is impossible to collect information from soldiers who have died.[145]

By the year 2000, more than 100,000 of the 700,000 soldiers who served in the war had registered with the Department of Defense and Veterans Administration programs as having a range of health problems that they suspected resulted from their Gulf War service. About 90% of these 100,000 soldiers are symptomatic, suffering from a wide variety of health problems and disabilities.[146]

Scientific and political controversy continues over the very existence of Gulf War syndrome, let alone the causal connections between Gulf War service and birth defects or reproductive health problems. In assessing the state of knowledge about Gulf War syndrome in general, Howard Kipen and Nancy Fiedler, two leading researchers in the field, have observed:

> At least in the case of Gulf War symptoms, careful epidemiology has been done to show us that compared with soldiers who did not deploy to the Persian Gulf, those who deployed had two- to threefold increase in symptoms, without apparent medical explanation. What we still do not have agreement on is what lies beneath these symptoms. . . . There is a problem out there. We still do not know what it is.[147]

It had taken more than twenty-five years for Vietnam vets to gain recognition of their own and their children's illnesses. Gulf War vets face even more considerable barriers. So far, the Gulf War studies have been inconclusive. And compared with Vietnam, questions of epidemiology are far more complicated, given the multiple exposures soldiers experienced over a relatively short period of time. As Jeanne Stellman has observed, "Epidemiology is largely a statistical game and you have to be able to sort out normal background events from abnormal rates. I'm sorry to say, from an epidemiological point of view, the [Gulf] War wasn't big enough or long enough to be able to answer many of these questions."[148]

Men at Home: Drugs, Alcohol, and Cigarettes

The germ plasm itself—that vital spark which continues on through countless centuries—is so affected by alcohol that the children for generations to come suffer from the sins of the fathers. (from poster issued by U.S. National Education Association in the 1920s)[149]

Can it be too gross to suppose that the organs of generation must equally suffer in both sexes, from frequent intoxication; and if offspring should unfortunately be derived from such a parentage, can we doubt that it must be diseased and puny in its corporeal parts; and beneath the standard of a rational being in its intellectual facilities? (Thomas Trotter, English physician campaigning against alcohol consumption, 1813)[150]

Although most research on paternally mediated harm has focused on occupational, environmental, and wartime exposures, a significant body of literature now exists on the effects of men's drinking, smoking, and drug use on fetal health.[151] Research has long shown that excessive drinking can cause sterility in men and that chronic alcoholism can reduce sperm motility and increase defects in the shape and size of sperm. The concentration of alcohol in sperm is almost identical to that in blood.[152]

Men, as a class, are more than three times more likely than women to be heavy drinkers (defined as two or more drinks per day). Additionally, alcoholic women are more likely to be married to alcoholic men than alcoholic men are to be married to alcoholic women.[153] Given these patterns, it would seem that paternal alcohol use should be of major concern to those studying the potential fetal effects of alcohol.

Research conducted in the 1980s and 1990s has correlated paternal alcoholism with low birth weight and an increased risk of birth defects. Savitz and others found a twofold increase in risk of ventricular septal defect in the children of men who consumed more than five drinks per week, but the same study found that paternal alcohol consumption reduced the risk of other birth defects. It is possible that alcohol offers some kind of protective effect, so that the conceptus carrying defects from male alcohol consumption might be at increased risk of fetal loss.[154] Case reports suggest an association between paternal drinking and malformations and cognitive deficiencies in children of alcoholic men, and animal studies have linked paternal alcohol exposure to behavioral abnormalities and higher fetal mortality. Other confounding reports have found no adverse associations for animals exposed to alcohol.[155]

Regarding cigarette smoking, researchers have found associations between paternal smoking and various birth defects, including cleft lip, cleft palate, and hydrocephalus (in a study of more than 14,000 birth records in San Francisco).[156] Significant associations also have been found between paternal smoking and low birth weight.[157] In one study, babies weighed 8.4 ounces below average if a father smoked two packs a day.[158]

One of the most interesting research projects studied the fetal effects of paternal smoking among men in Shanghai, China. In Shanghai, more than 60% of all men smoke, but paternal alcohol consumption is low. In addition, maternal rates of alcohol consumption and cigarette smoking are low, and race and socioeconomic status are relatively homogeneous.[159] This study found that paternal smoking was associated with an increased risk of multiple birth defects, including an increase that was almost twofold in spina bifida, twofold in anencephalus, and threefold in pigmentary anomalies of the skin.[160] With all of these epidemiological studies, it is difficult to

determine whether effects are from maternal exposure to passive smoke or from the effect of smoking on the paternal germ cell. In addition to epidemiological research, lab studies have shown that cotinine, a metabolite of nicotine, has been found in seminal fluid, although researchers are unsure what effect this might have on fetal health.

One researcher has suggested that the link between smoking and birth defects could be due to smokers' low levels of vitamin C. Vitamin C, an antioxidant, helps to protect sperm from the genetic damage caused by oxidants in the body, but the vitamin is depleted in the body of cigarette smokers. This research found that men with low levels of the vitamin experienced double the oxidation damage to the DNA in their sperm.[161]

Regarding illicit drugs, research has found that cocaine increases the number of abnormal sperm and decreases sperm motility in men.[162] Cocaine could also bind to sperm and thereby be transmitted to the egg during fertilization. Reports of cocaine piggybacking on sperm have led to controversy in the scientific community over whether this could contribute to birth defects.[163] As noted earlier, Friedler's studies found that in animal studies, morphine and methadone administered to fathers, but not to mothers, have produced birth defects and behavioral abnormalities in the first and second generations of the father's offspring.[164] Drug addiction in men using hashish, opium, and heroin has also been shown to cause structural defects in sperm.[165]

Despite the scientific research that has shown potentially damaging effects of men's cigarette smoking and drug and alcohol use, public attention has focused almost exclusively on the toxic effects of pregnant women's behavior, with little or no attention to the risks posed by men. For instance, from 1985 to 2000, the nine U.S. national daily newspapers published fewer than a dozen stories on associations between men's drug use, alcohol use, or cigarette smoking and fetal health problems.[166] By contrast, during the same period these papers ran 197 stories on pregnant women and cocaine addiction alone. There has been no *New York Times* coverage of the links between paternal alcohol consumption and fetal health. By contrast, the *New York Times* alone has run at least twenty-seven stories on pregnant women and crack.[167]

While images of crack babies and irresponsible mothers prevail in stories about maternal exposures to drugs, visual images in popular science magazines and news stories about male-mediated harm often place sperm in the center of focus as the tiniest victims of toxicity, somehow without marking male users as the source of the harm.[168] The personified sperm as victim acts as a shield for men—deflecting the blame that might otherwise be placed on the father. One news story titled "Sperm under Siege" presents an image of sperm at the center of a target, menaced by bottles of alcohol and chemicals.[169] Another presents a cartoon image of a man and his sperm huddled under an umbrella while packs of cigarettes, martini glasses, and canisters of toxins rain down upon them.[170] One might expect men and their sperm to be characterized as victims when men were involuntarily exposed to toxins at work, but both of these stories focused on men's (presumably voluntary) use of drugs and alcohol. Indeed, in newspapers the only images to accompany stories about the potential hazards of men's use of drugs, alcohol, and cigarettes for fetal health were photographs or cartoon images of sperm—never of fathers. Yet of the 853 column inches dedicated to pregnancy, alcohol, and drug abuse by the New York Times in one two-year period, almost 200 column inches were taken up by photographic images of crack babies and their drug-addicted mothers.[171]

Even researchers who accept the validity of evidence on male-mediated fetal risks are led to quite different social and political conclusions than those typically recommended for women. The most direct recommendation came from Bruce Ames, who recommended that the U.S. government raise the standard for minimum daily requirements for vitamin C for all Americans to account for the reproductive effects of paternal smoking.[172] There has been no discussion in public health agencies about adding warning labels to cigarette packs or posting public health notices in restaurants and bars to warn men of the potential damage done to fetal health by their excessive use of drugs, alcohol, or nicotine.

Perhaps most troubling is the evidence on the effects of chemotherapeutic drugs and radiation treatment on the children fathered by treated men and the lack of public response to such evidence. At the first major

medical meeting on male-mediated toxicology at the University of Pittsburgh in 1992, men were given "conflicting advice" about whether to postpone procreation during cancer treatment (or "bank" sperm before treatment). In 1992, the journal *Human Reproduction* published a recommendation that sperm saved in the early stages of chemotherapy was safe, "based on the belief that since the drugs did not kill sperm . . . the sperm were healthy." Yet others argued that sperm that survive therapy may be more likely to carry genetic defects.[173]

More than nine years later, at the second International Meeting on Male-Mediated Developmental Toxicity (MMDT), researchers and clinicians still disagreed about the need to bank sperm before cancer treatment, even though animal research has clearly shown that both chemotherapeutic and radiation therapies can cause genetic defects and abnormalities in sperm years after exposures have ended. Hales and Robaire found such effects in the 1980s with one cancer treatment, and they have since demonstrated increased rates of low birth weight, death, and malformation of the limbs and head, as well as up to 80% postimplantation loss in the offspring of male mice treated with one chemotherapeutic drug. British researchers found the same in lab animals in the 1990s, with effects like late fetal deaths, abnormal fetuses, and skull abnormalities from male animals receiving low doses of one antitumor drug. In Great Britain, research has found that male mice exposed to radiation treatments produce "highly statistically significant" levels of mutations in both the first and second generations of offspring, produced at the same magnitude of effect in both generations. And most troubling, such studies have consistently shown that male animals, including humans, regain their fertility long before rates of abnormal sperm decrease.[174]

Yet clinicians remain reluctant to warn patients of these risks. As one Canadian physician, Jan Friedman, put it at the 2001 MMDT meeting, "The advice that I give to my patients is 'If an exposed man remains fertile, the risk to his children is unlikely to be measurably increased.'" Friedman argues that increased rates of chromosomal abnormalities in sperm do not necessarily translate into increased rates of birth defects in children and that the human evidence of male-mediated harm is lacking.

Likewise, Marvin Meistriech at the M. D. Anderson Cancer Center in Houston, Texas, works to speed the restoration of fertility in men after radiation treatment or toxic exposures, based on studies that male mice with restored fertility have experienced "no reduction in litter size" and no increase in defects "obvious at birth" in offspring.[175] Fifteen years after Hales and Robaire's suggestive studies on animals, there have been remarkably few studies on the actual men who have undergone such treatments.[176]

Another equally troubling medical area relates to men's use of a new technique in infertility clinics hailed as the ultimate "cure" for male infertility. Intra cytoplasmic sperm injection (ICSI) is a procedure in which sperm are taken from a man who is infertile because of a low sperm count and injected by syringe directly into his female partner's egg in vitro. Approved for use in clinics without any animal testing, studies have shown that ICSI children have experienced twice the normal rate of birth defects compared with children naturally conceived. Yet practitioners and regulators continue to use the procedure and dismiss the risks to children so fathered.[177]

Like Gladys Fiedler's experience thirty years earlier, scientists engaged in research on men's "personal" behaviors continue to be met with profound skepticism by funding sources, regulators, clinicians, colleagues, journal editors, and newspaper reporters alike.

Uncertain Knowledge

Given the limitations of the research, how are we to assess the evidence on male-mediated reproductive harm? What can we say we know with any level of certainty? There is no doubt that toxic exposures can produce testicular atrophy, infertility, or sterility in men. These can be measured and seen in clinics and lab studies, in animals and in humans. There is no doubt that such exposures can produce deformations in the shape and size of sperm. These, too, can be clearly observed and traced directly to toxic exposures in lab studies. And there is no doubt that toxins can bind to seminal fluid and be transferred directly to the woman, concep-

tus, or fetus through intercourse. Semen studies also clearly show that toxins can produce genetic damage or chromosomal abnormalities in sperm. We know that men can pass on inherited genetic defects to their children. The paternal germ cell is responsible for transmitting the vast majority of genetic defects to children, such as Down syndrome and Prader Willi syndrome. What remains unknown is whether similar harm can be passed along when toxic exposures cause genetic mutations in sperm.[178] There is little reason to think that they cannot. As Ellen Silbergeld bluntly assesses the state of the knowledge: "If you are exposed to something that's going to kill a lot of sperm, it's possible that some damaged sperm might escape and cause problems. End of story. That is what's known, there's very little more."[179]

Despite the hundreds of studies that have been completed, the human evidence remains problematic—producing sometimes positive and sometimes negative results and plagued with seemingly endless methodological problems. Unlike studies of carcinogens or other health risks, human studies on reproductive toxins involve effects on two parents, impacting on a third developing human being. At work, at war, or even in one's community, we often still know little about the multiple toxins to which people are exposed. It's difficult to control for the biases of memory in retrospective studies or for underreporting, particularly of drug and alcohol use, in prospective studies. Without a national birth defect registry, it's difficult to track even the most obvious possible effects of reproductive toxins, let alone the subtler effects, like increased miscarriage rates. Even in the largest studies of veterans, it's difficult to get a sample size large enough to prove conclusive for conditions that are typically rare in children. And it's difficult to control for confounding factors when a man, for instance, has a history of service in war, may be exposed to a dozen toxins at work, and may smoke cigarettes, use drugs, or drink alcohol. Of course, once all of these factors are taken into account for men, they must also be considered for the woman with whom the man has conceived a child.

In addition to the difficulties of the human research, studies of male-mediated effects have been subject to a more critical level of scrutiny than

have studies on female-mediated effects. For instance, while studies on men are criticized for not controlling for maternal exposures, studies on women virtually never control for, or even acknowledge the need to control for, paternal exposures. Studies of men's occupational and environmental exposures are criticized for rarely controlling for men's use of drugs or alcohol, but when women are the subjects, these equally valid critiques are absent. Studies of male "lifestyle" factors, like drug use, are criticized for failing to control for workplace exposures, but studies of women's drug use rarely control for women's workplace exposures. Indeed, questions of causality are exceedingly complex, but they are as complex for women as they are for men. Although these questions of complexity have been muted for women, they have been exaggerated for men.[180] Without dramatic human effects, like the sterility of men exposed to DBCP in the 1970s, the evidence of male-mediated harm that does exist is not likely to be believed.

As Jack Bishop, a research geneticist with more than twenty-five years of involvement in MMDT research put it, "There is no 'male thalidomide.' If we had a male thalidomide, you'd see some action."[181] But perhaps the effects through men will not be as dramatic as a male thalidomide. Perhaps, as Bernard Robaire has put it, the male teratogen will not result in:

> The "monster being born." . . . We don't have the abnormal
> progeny, we don't have the thalidomide babies . . . but in fact
> we do have a high incidence of infertility. . . . If there are
> problems very early in development, then most of our studies
> show that the biggest effect we have is low fertility because the
> female will miscarry so early in the pregnancy. . . . So that
> may be the equivalent.[182]

And as Barbara Hales observes, "It's a small window to actually see the aberrations because there's a fine line between fetal death and fetal survival. . . . There may be no male thalidomide, but in fact isn't death more tragic? In this case, the effect is just more difficult to see."[183] Here, it's

not just the weakness of the evidence but the gendered lens through which this evidence is screened that makes the evidence more difficult to see.

This lack of visible human evidence has produced a vicious cycle for researchers. The funding is not there because the human evidence is absent or weak, and the human evidence is absent or weak largely because of difficulties with funding. As a result, the most promising areas of research seem to be in narrowly tailored animal studies that try to identify a "plausible biological mechanism" through which harm is transmitted from father to fetus. Animal studies have already long provided evidence of male-mediated effects. As Robaire, now working on animal studies in this area for more than fifteen years, has put it, "Without any doubt it is the animal data that makes me know that it happens. Animal data is repeated in different species, for different drugs and you get the same effects." Or as Barbara Hales observes, "It's reproducible. If you go to studies in Japan . . . they show the same defects. It's not random, they're the same thing. And they're different exposures, they're mice instead of rats. There are too many people across the world in the last few decades that have gotten the same thing. . . . You know it's not random. It's real." But researchers have not yet been able to pinpoint the biological mechanisms by which such effects are produced. Once the genetic and epigenetic processes are made clear in animals, it will be more difficult to deny their existence in human beings.[184]

As a result, these narrowly tailored animal studies demonstrating the effects of toxins on the male germ cell or on epigenetic processes—how genes work—are more likely to get funded. As Barbara Hales put it:

> If you ask specific focused questions and you're asking how these work, then there's funding. The basic science is fundable. What they're objecting to . . . [are] the human questions. So we can ask questions in animal models about specific little things of how it can happen—whether it's epigenetic or not—but we still can't do the human interface. Those studies are going to meet the same objections we

experienced the first time around—people still think it's implausible.[185]

Making the link to human effects raises questions of male vulnerability and culpability we seem to be unwilling to consider. It's an area of research, both Hales and Robaire believe, that is "threatening to a lot of males."[186]

Like the early critics of Friedler, some argue that biology itself justifies our near-exclusive focus on mothers because there is no equivalent link between fathers and fetuses. Unlike the direct and visible relation between mothers and fetuses, there seems to be no clear and simple connection between men and their children. The lack of attention to male-mediated fetal harm is the result, critics argue, not of some "imagined difference," but of the real biological differences between men and women in reproduction. Such skepticism was articulated in one 1993 editorial in a leading scientific journal:

> The people who make these accusations appear to believe that paternally mediated effects *must* occur in humans, for the sake of fairness. . . . It is argued that because father and mother make equal genetic contributions to the *conceptus,* they must have equal opportunity to transmit toxic effects. Students of developmental biology understand that there is nothing equal about male and female contributions to development. . . . There are several million unequivocal examples of children damaged by intrauterine exposure to toxicants encountered by the mother during gestation. There are no unequivocal examples for paternal exposures.[187]

Yet except for those rare and tragic cases where women are exposed to substances such as thalidomide that cause severe, visible deformities, the question of causality remains profoundly complicated for both women and men. Science has shown for more than thirty years that the levels of lead exposure permitted by OSHA in many industrial workplaces can cause abnormalities in sperm that may lead to birth defects in children.

It appears that it is not so much the nature of the risk but the nature of the population affected by risk that often determines the public response to potential harm.

This is not the same as arguing that men and women are entirely alike in their susceptibility to reproductive harm, nor is it to argue that gender equality requires that men be seen as just as vulnerable to reproductive risks as women or "equally" able to transmit harm to the fetus. But it is to argue that certain myths of masculinity have skewed the questions that have been asked, the research that has been done, and the answers we find acceptable in research on men. We will not and cannot know what men's reproductive vulnerabilities or culpabilities are until such myths are both revealed and challenged.

In the science of reproductive medicine, assumptions about masculinity affect not only the questions asked by scientific researchers but also what counts as an acceptable answer.[188] Knowledge of male-mediated harm posed certain risks to assumptions that men have the unassailable capacity to produce, provide for, and protect their children. That risk made certain answers simply unbelievable.

The Paradoxes of Reproductive Masculinity

Evidence that conflicts with norms of reproductive masculinity—evidence of men's vulnerabilities to harms, men's lack of virility, and men's central and critical connection to the health of their children—has been systematically met with skepticism at best and derision at worst from many scientists, policy makers, and even men themselves. Men do not want to be seen, nor do they want to see themselves, as the subjects of pain and suffering or, in this case, as those who are responsible for transmitting pain and suffering to their children.

By the turn of the twenty-first century, evidence of male-mediated fetal harm entered a public scene with masculinity already deep in crisis. Changing gender roles, the economic decline of traditionally male-dominated industries, and advances in reproductive technologies had all created a sense, whether real or imagined, that men's grip on reproductive power

was slipping. Evidence that men were being rendered sterile by toxins at work or at war or, worse, were transmitting harm to their children added insult to the injury already done to American masculinity. In this sense, the skepticism with which such evidence was met—by scientists and policy makers alike—was not surprising.

Ideals of masculinity rest on presumptions of men's ability to *produce, sustain, and protect* their children. Evidence of male reproductive harm threatened to undermine each of these presumptions. Men damaged by environmental or workplace toxins might not be able to produce children at all. A workplace that threatened to undermine male reproductive health might also undermine the family work ethic that drove men into the workplace in the first place. And wartime toxins could throw into question the ability—and the willingness—of men to go to war to protect nation, hearth, and home.

In science, as in all areas of human inquiry, the pursuit of knowledge is linked and often constrained by the implications of that knowledge. As ethicists have long observed, the question is never just "What can I know?" but always also "With that knowledge, what ought I do?"[189] If we were to know that certain toxins—workplace, wartime, lifestyle, or medical—produced fetal harm through men, what would we do with that knowledge? The politics of reproductive risks has focused primarily on the health risks and often "bad behavior" of women. If industrial workplaces were "too dangerous" for women, women could simply be removed from the job. If wartime exposures posed a risk to fertile or pregnant women's health, then women could be banned from service. If women's drug, alcohol, or nicotine addiction proved a threat to their "unborn children," then the state could post public warnings in bars and restaurants, print warnings on alcohol or cigarette packs, launch public education campaigns against drinking or drug use in pregnancy, and criminally prosecute pregnant women who chose to ignore such warnings. Would we really be prepared to do the same to men?

At what cost would we mandate a workplace safe for the reproductive health of both men and women? If workplace toxins posed a reproductive threat to men, would we be prepared to allow only sterile men

to work or shut down industry to make the workplace safe for men? Evidence that work harmed not only men but also men's ability to father healthy children might undermine the very incentives that drove men into toxic workplaces in the first place—the support of their wives and children. Indeed, the DBCP scandal galvanized workers, unions, researchers, and regulatory agencies in a way never before witnessed not because it threatened the health of men but because it suggested that work and manliness might be antithetical—that work might in fact undo manliness. The cultural prescription that had led to a profound neglect of men's health—the unwillingness to see male reproductive vulnerability—was the same cultural prescription that called for dramatic action once the damaging effects of DBCP became undeniable. The only way to reinstate the work ethic at the heart of masculinity was to virtually ban the chemical from production.

If wartime toxins proved a threat to the health of the future children of soldiers, would we ban such weapons of war or refuse to send men to the front lines? Evidence of male-mediated reproductive harm at war threatened the prescription that men rule and protect the nation. A state that had poisoned men on the battlefield and then masked its own complicity in the poisoning neither reflected the interests of its citizen-soldiers nor deserved their loyalty. Recognition of the reproductive vulnerability of men at war might throw into question not only the state's legitimacy in the eyes of soldiers but also the very willingness of soldiers to go to war. It was a recognition that also involved significant economic costs to both private producers of toxins and the public agencies that would be held responsible for the care of sick soldiers and their children. Only the political organizing of millions of Vietnam vets and the threatened loss of the state's legitimacy in the eyes of its citizen-soldiers generated action by the state. Recognition of male-mediated toxicity at work and at war posed the threat of structural change never posed in the same way by risks thought to be "contained" to pregnancy.

Evidence of male-mediated fetal harm from men's private behaviors threatened to throw into question men's reproductive self-sovereignty— their right to do whatever they pleased with their own bodies. If studies

showed, as they already have, that older men had higher risks of fathering children with birth defects, would we be prepared to recommend that men over the age of fifty not father children? Evidence of the damage wrought by men's drinking, drug use, or smoking might require interventions that the state has typically been unwilling to make, at least for men. If and when such interventions do come, they will most likely target (as the state has done in the case of women) those men most marginal in the hierarchy of masculinity—low-income men who use or abuse illegal drugs, "crack dads." In the meantime, ideals of reproductive masculinity make it all the more difficult to believe that such signs of manhood as beer drinking or cigarette smoking could potentially threaten both male seed and the health of the children such men father.

More equitable approaches to questions of male-mediated harm would subject male and female research to equal levels of scientific scrutiny. It would involve better protecting men from the harms of work, war, and environmental toxins. It would require educating both men and women about the risks of drug, alcohol, and cigarette use both before conception and throughout pregnancy. Where the evidence suggested equivalent levels of susceptibility, it would mean instituting public policies that recognize men's and women's common human vulnerabilities. And where the evidence suggested harms particular to one sex or the other, it would require differential treatment of men and women, as appropriate. But it would not assume, as much of the science and public policy has so far, that men are less susceptible to the harms of the outside world or more distant from the problems of human reproduction, including the children they father.

Research on male-mediated harm has been met with deep political, cultural, and scientific skepticism not only because it threatens to undermine assumptions of masculine invulnerability but also because it threatens to disrupt the fourth presumption of reproductive masculinity —the assumption of men's distance from the children they father. This distance is predicated on the assumption of a biological and social reproductive division of labor that presumably distances men from both physical production of and social responsibility for children. Assumptions

about the distance of men from fetal harm and the ultimate responsibility of women for the health of their children make the science of male-mediated toxicity simply more difficult to believe.

The fourth element of reproductive masculinity—the assumption that men are more distant from the children they father—has led to a profound skepticism of male-mediated harm. Yet the distance of men from the children they father appears to be produced as much by cultural belief as by the biology of reproduction. Despite the limitations of current research, studies of the father-fetal relationship have revealed deeper connections between men and their children. It has slowly extended the bridge from men to their babies from the moment of conception, across pregnancy, and now beyond birth. Such research first established men's contribution to couple infertility once thought to be primarily a "female" problem.[190] Research then demonstrated that problems in pregnancy—miscarriage, retarded fetal growth, developmental defects, and stillbirth loss—might also be attributable to men. And now research suggests connections between men and birth defects and childhood diseases. Men's contribution to procreation was no longer fleeting, no longer concluded by the fertilization of an egg.

Each extension of the bridge between men and their children has been met with increasing levels of resistance, not just because effects further from the point at which a sperm disappears into an egg are more difficult to prove but because such evidence places men closer and closer to culpability for the health problems of their children. As the avenues for male-mediated harm have multiplied, so, too, have men's responsibilities for fetal harm. Women would no longer bear the blame alone for the failure to conceive or for miscarriage, stillbirth, low birth weight, birth defects, or childhood diseases.

In the end, the failure to see the damage done to men and their children from reproductive toxins has more to do with what Friedler termed a "reluctance to look" than with what the evidence gives us to see. This reluctance has both privileged and damaged men. It has privileged men by perpetuating assumptions of the superior strength and invulnerability of the male body. It has also protected men from culpability for the

potential harm caused by their toxic exposures. But it is a privilege that has also come not just at men's expense—a price paid in the form of a profound neglect of the reproductive health of men—but at the expense of the men, women, and children whose health is increasingly placed at risk not just by the toxic work, wars, and drugs of the twenty-first century but by continuing myths of reproductive masculinity.

REPRODUCING MEN   **6**

We live in an age full of paradoxes and contradictions for men. While we expect men to be more sensitive to human needs, we champion the ideal of men as invincible soldiers. While we expect men to be the protectors of both nation and home, we subject them to toxic threats at work and war and fail to address their health needs when they suffer as a result. We expect men to be more involved in the care of children, while we belittle their biological contribution to human reproduction with arguments that testosterone makes men more aggressive and less sensitive to the needs of children. Male privilege persists in economic, political, and social structures, and men earn more and occupy more positions of power than women, yet the contradictory demands of manhood leave many men suffering the bitterness of masculine shame when they fail—physically, economically, or emotionally—to live up to ideals of masculinity.

The way out requires transforming—at a most fundamental level—the ideals of masculinity that both reward and burden men. This necessitates not just greater public attention to the reproductive health needs of men. It requires, more fundamentally, a transformation of the social system that makes, particularly for men, neediness, vulnerability, dependence on others, and deep connections to children a source of denigration and

shame. At this historical moment, there are both a profound need for and resistance to this transformation.

Ideals of masculinity have undergone significant challenge in the past fifty years. However disproportionately, men and women may now wage war together, they may be integrated into factories and corporate workplaces, and they may share the halls of political power. Yet despite, or perhaps because of, these challenges in all other spheres of life, myths of reproductive masculinity persist.

Men are more often present at the birth of children and provide more care for children than they have in the past. Yet still they are cast as less important to and less competent in the world of reproduction. It takes only a brief look at popular culture to see images of men blundering their way through child care, through household work, through tasks still depicted as fundamentally alien to men's character and as universally natural to women. In this era of wartime, it takes only the briefest look at news stories or popular films to see the icon of the invincible man, the machinelike soldier, the protector of women, children, and nation, as the ultimate expression of manhood. Although alternative images of men as sensitive caregivers and women as powerful warriors increasingly appear in social life, they still do so as exceptions to nature's rule that men play a secondary, less critical, and more distant role in human reproduction than women.

The human traits we see as essentially connected to procreation and human caregiving, to the needs and weaknesses of the human body, are seen as alien to the nature of men. Men may increasingly be caregivers, but they do not themselves need care. Men may serve the needs of others, but men are not themselves needy. We need only suggest the converse of current ideals of manhood to see the power such ideals still hold in our cultural imagination: men are weak, men are vulnerable, men are impotent, needy, and dependent. This is the image not of a man but of an "effeminate." It is an image of the end of manhood, the antithesis of masculinity.

As the reproductive needs of men increasingly come into public focus, they are met with equally powerful counterforces that seek to reinstate

ideals of manhood. We see Lance Armstrong suffering from testicular cancer and championed as the master of the Tour de France. We see Arnold Schwarzenegger starring in popular "Mr. Mom" films and elected as governor of one of the largest and most powerful states in the nation. We see commercials promoting chemical cures for male impotence, but they are invariably represented by powerful politicians, football coaches, and racecar drivers—icons of manhood. Each potential challenge to masculinity is met with an equally powerful reassertion of masculinity.

Yet such countervailing forces cannot fully reinstate masculinity because by their very nature they reveal that masculinity is not rooted in an ancient and unchangeable biology; rather, it is a social construction. The disjuncture between the veneer and the actuality of manhood reveals the distance between the ideal and the real lives of men. This is masculinity in crisis.

The transformation of masculinity would hold implications not just for men's relationship to human reproduction but also for assumptions about the presumed *differences* between men and women. Our understandings of human reproduction, like so many other realms of life, have been dominated by a polarized notion of masculinity and femininity. Men are *not like women*, and they are nowhere more not like women than in the realm of human reproduction. The extent to which we see the commonalities of the male and female bodies and of men and women's relationship to human reproduction is the extent to which we most undermine assumptions of gender difference.

This is not to deny all reproductive difference between the sexes. Although male and female anatomy may be transformed through surgery and hormonal treatments, and reproductive technologies make it possible to have more complex and multiple parenting relationships, reproductive biology is not infinitely malleable. The male body does not gestate or give birth to children. The female body produces ova and not sperm. Reproductive anatomy is, at this level (and at this time), beyond social construction. Perhaps in some distant future even this biology may be transformed. But for now we can question, at least, the social meanings we continue to project onto the most fundamental of human reproductive processes.

Cultural norms of masculinity and femininity continue to provide the lens through which we understand the most basic of biological reproductive functions: the nature of reproductive cells (sperm active, egg passive), reproductive fluids (sperm transitory, egg precious), reproductive drives (men polygamous, women monogamous), reproductive bodies (men invulnerable and "hard," women vulnerable and "soft"), and reproductive parenting (men father, women mother). These constructions continue to inform how we see men and how men perceive themselves. The solution does not lie in seeing all of reproductive biology as a mere construction of the cultural imagination but in seeing how reproductive difference has taken on meanings far beyond biology.

The form of reproductive masculinity that now holds sway is neither universal nor timeless. The purpose of this work has been to explore its history, its social production, and the social forces that have led to its transformation. The current challenge to masculinity has its roots in a range of social, political, economic, and technological forces. Social movements for gender equality have challenged assumptions of sexual difference. Technological developments have allowed us to better see and understand processes of human reproduction and to appreciate the equivalency of men's and women's genetic contributions to the creation of human life. Economics has made it profitable to reveal, and then to market and sell, treatments for male infertility. And men themselves, motivated by concern for the health of their own children, as well as by a sense of injustice and betrayal at the cavalier ways in which men's health is placed at risk in war and at work, have come forward, bound together through powerful men's organizations, to demand greater attention to these issues. These forces have greatly unsettled assumptions of reproductive masculinity.

Yet highly questionable assumptions still persist in our understanding of men's relationship to human reproduction. It is still assumed that men play a secondary role in biological reproduction. It is still assumed that the male body is relatively invulnerable to the harms of the outside world. Men are the protectors of women, children, and nation and not, therefore, in need of protection from the state or others. It is still assumed

that the male body is inherently virile. The ability to biologically father one's children remains a hallmark of one's manhood, and infertility remains a source of masculine shame. Male virility is also symbolic of the strength of the nation. It is still assumed that men are more distant from the health and well-being of children. The challenge lies in sorting out the distinctions between myth and reality in the politics of reproductive masculinity.

Men as Secondary to Biological Reproduction

Previous historical eras cast men as the carriers of the essence of human life. Current constructions cast men as secondary to the biology of reproduction. This presumed asymmetry of reproduction has been applied throughout all stages of the reproductive process—in fertilization, in gestation, and in parenthood. In fertilization, reproductive difference is projected onto the "character traits" of male and female gametes, with sperm the more dominant and aggressive partner and ova the more receptive and sedentary. These characterizations can be found in the history of the reproductive sciences and continue now through the use of military and war metaphors in both scientific and cultural descriptions of the processes of human fertilization. Sperm compete to conquer the waiting egg, penetrate the egg's outer shell, and deliver their payload to the egg's core. Militarized characterizations of sperm can also be found in debates over dropping sperm counts and hazards to the male reproductive system. Sperm are "under siege" from environmental toxins or remain "strong and hardy" in the face of such threats. They are men's "tiniest soldiers," fighting off the threat of estrogenated chemicals. Such character traits, writ back into gametes, in turn reinforce the idea of the immutable temperamental differences between the sexes, each suited to its "appropriate" future role in the reproductive process—one as warrior, the other as caregiver.

Assumptions of gender asymmetry even more deeply inform how we understand men's relationship to gestation. Indeed, it might seem odd to even suggest that men have a *biological* relationship to gestation beyond

their supporting social role as partners to pregnant women. Women gestate fetuses, and men do not. To many, this is the bottom line of reproductive gender difference. Yet evidence suggests otherwise. Research has demonstrated that problems in pregnancy—miscarriage and stillbirth—can often be attributed to men. Sperm damaged by "recreational" drugs and alcohol, by workplace hazards or environmental toxins, can contribute to fetal loss. And what is more essential to a pregnancy than whether gestation continues at all? Evidence suggests that men have an intimate biological relationship to gestation—a vital relation not only to conception but also to the quality of life so produced. Ideals of reproductive masculinity have rendered this connection nearly invisible in science, politics, and popular culture.

In parenthood, asymmetries of reproduction also presume that the male and female bodies are discrete and that related roles as mothers and fathers are rooted in that biological difference. Medical sciences, which once cast the male and female bodies as of one kind, now exaggerate the differences between male and female sexual and reproductive organs and characterize them as different in both quality and function, as if they were of different reproductive universes. But evidence suggests that such differences are not nearly so discrete. The smallest exposure to estrogenated toxins can "bend" gender categories altogether, producing the "intersexed" and blurring the line between male and female. The male body itself could be "feminized." Asymmetries of reproduction are challenged by this evidence—evidence that demonstrates the commonalities of male and female reproductive systems.

Male Invulnerability

Ideals of reproductive masculinity also codify the male body as relatively invulnerable to external harm and produce, as a result, a general denial of men's illnesses and injuries, particularly when they involve disorders of the reproductive system. Disorders of the male reproductive system—diseases and deformities—remain understudied and underdiagnosed by a social system that marks these as "unmanly." Illness and

disability have been feminized, and the manhood of men suffering from reproductive disorders thus compromised. The fact that we have no clear assessments of the health of the male reproductive system is evidence of our reluctance to see the weaknesses and vulnerabilities of the male reproductive body.

Evidence of men suffering the "assaults" of environmental chemicals throws presumptions of male invulnerability into question. Associations of vulnerability with femininity have made evidence of male harm less plausible and greatly increased the weight of evidence necessary to see such harm.

Indeed, evidence suggests that men are even more at risk than women. Male fetuses might be at greater risk than females: more likely to be lost during pregnancy, to be born with significant birth defects, or to pass along defects to their children once they were grown. The harm that men suffer in utero or as adults might be more severe and longer lasting than that suffered by women. Such evidence suggests that perhaps men more than women are in need of the protection and surveillance of the state. Nevertheless, the evidence that men might be more vulnerable to reproductive risks than women has been met with profound disbelief.

Politically, the need to reinforce the myth of male invulnerability has resulted in a lack of attention to questions of male reproductive health. Few occupational health and safety regulations take questions of male reproductive vulnerability seriously, even when such risks (like exposure to lead) have clearly damaging reproductive consequences for men. Only when toxins dramatically expose male vulnerability to harm, as in the case of DBCP and the sterility of male workers, does the state act to protect men from harm. With questions of male vulnerability so symbolic of their manhood, men would hardly stand up to demand greater attention to these issues. Such lack of attention has produced a self-fulfilling prophecy. As long as invulnerability to risk is symbolic of manhood, few men are willing to demand public attention to the issue. That lack of recognition then continues the illusion of male invulnerability to risk, while it perpetuates social practices that place the health of real men in danger.

Public recognition of the reproductive ailments of men continues to be a source of embarrassment and shame, not only to men suffering from such disorders but also for those politicians who seek to uphold the ideal of men as invulnerable fathers, soldiers, workers, and protectors of the nation. Writ large, the health of the male body remains symbolic of the health of the nation, with sperm counts a measure of national virility. The nation is weakened by the image of weakened men. Men who are weak, needy, or dependent on others can hardly symbolize national strength and honor. A nation of men under assault from environmental chemicals or a nation with falling sperm counts is a nation *emasculated*.

Male Virility

Norms of reproductive masculinity perpetuate the idea that the ability to father biological children is essential to one's standing as a man. This ideal has led historically to a neglect of attention to male infertility and the denigration of men who fail to live up to this ideal. The historical reluctance to examine sperm and to recognize the malformations that lead to male infertility perpetuates the assumption of the virility of all men and the assumption that women, not men, are the source of reproductive dysfunction.

The need to perpetuate the appearance of virility in men has also contributed to certain practices in the sperm banking industry. Male shame of infertility has led to the practice of "matching" sperm donors to the traits of nonbiological fathers to mask the infertility of those men procuring donor sperm. The need to keep the infertility of those men hidden has helped to produce the commodification of both sperm and sperm donors, whose traits are compartmentalized, categorized, and sold like other market commodities. Although the state has prohibited or heavily regulated the commodification of other body products, it allows such practices regarding sperm banking to flourish unfettered by social regulation. The industry remains unregulated precisely because such practices allow men to fulfill their function as fathers while disguising those male reproductive "failings" that make donor insemination necessary in the first place.

Assumptions of male virility also make research into dropping sperm counts socially and politically charged. Despite the fact that sperm counts alone do not predict the health of the male body or men's ability to father children, evidence of declining sperm counts threatens the presumption that men are capable of producing unlimited quantities of "vigorous" sperm. With sperm counts cast as the symbolic measure of manhood, a man faced with "low" sperm counts is "no longer a man."

Assumptions of male virility have also skewed research on the effects of toxins on sperm. Despite studies that have shown that sperm production is delicate in its sensitivities to heat, diet, weight gain, drugs, alcohol, and environmental toxins, both sperm and the male body are characterized as toughened to such assaults, and men so exposed are asserted to remain capable of producing healthy sperm. Until the association of men with virility is challenged, this research and the political responses to it will be skewed.

Men's Distance from Children

Ideals of reproductive masculinity also perpetuate the myth that men are more distant from the children they father. The presumed distance of men from children can be seen, in microcosm, in the premise that men have less attachment to their sperm than women have to their eggs. While eggs remain relatively protected from market exchange—more cherished by women and the social order—sperm are marketed as a "product" that men manufacture, and sperm "donation" just another form of "work" men do. Sperm "donation" becomes sperm "banking," with men presumed to have little more emotional attachment to their reproductive "assets" than they do to the dollar bills they deposit in a bank (or perhaps even less in that they are willing to trade their sperm for dollars). This presumed detachment contributes to the willingness to subject sperm donors to processes of commercialization, with their sperm bought and sold and packaged like other market commodities. The practices of the sperm banking industry thus rely on and perpetuate notions that men are more distant from the children they father.

Even those scientists of earlier centuries who assumed that sperm contained the entire preformed being presumed that it was women, through their bad actions (or even bad thoughts), who were responsible for producing malformations in children. In contemporary times, research on male-mediated harm has reflected, as well, the assumption of men's distance from the health and well-being of their children. Such research has been met with deep political, cultural, and scientific skepticism not only because the evidence is questionable but also because the evidence challenges assumptions of men's distance from reproductive responsibilities. From conception through infancy, it is women who are responsible for the health of children, and women who are assumed to be responsible when things go wrong.

But just as it was for women, the evidence suggests that toxins can pass through the male body to damage fetal and child health, casting more of the blame for these harms onto men. As a result, studies of male-mediated effects have been subject to a more critical level of scrutiny than have studies on female-mediated effects, for they potentially disrupt not just assumptions of male invulnerability but deeper assumptions of the reproductive division of labor between men and women.

The political implications of evidence of male-mediated harm have also surely been skewed by the potential ideas of reproductive responsibility for children. Presumptions of men's distance from the health of children have shielded men from the political culpability that comes with reproductive responsibilities for children. But the reluctance to see the intimate connections between men and their children has also come at a cost to their own health and the health of the children they father.

The State and Masculinity

Men have been too long absent in the politics of reproduction. This is reflected in the state's relative silence on questions of male reproduction, which can be seen in the lack of resources given to scientists engaged in primary research on male reproduction, from those exploring sperm count drops and increases in reproductive disorders in men to those

whose work examines male-mediated fetal harm. This silence can also be seen in the lack of regulation of the sperm banking industry, whose practices perpetuate forms of human commodification not tolerated in other realms. This silence speaks in the failure of the state to protect the health of men at work and at war when evidence clearly suggests that both damage the health of men and, potentially, the children men father.

When the state does act, it does so both reluctantly and selectively. The actions of the state seek not to protect the health of men but to reinstate presumptions of male reproduction and to empower men (or at least some men) to fulfill their traditional roles as fathers, workers, and soldiers. These responses appear to be more dedicated to reinstating presumptions of male virility and invulnerability, more focused on reinforcing assumptions of the traditional sexual division of labor in reproduction, than to actually protecting men.

The political response also reveals how reproductive masculinity is stratified—with the interests and concerns of some men given more weight and value than others. When the state acts to regulate the sperm banking industry, for instance, it does so by excluding gay men (or other marginalized men, like men in prison who are disproportionately poor men of color) from its practices. This is motivated less by articulated concerns about the transmission of disease than by unarticulated interests in reinforcing norms of reproductive masculinity for heterosexual men. Reproductive privilege—the power to become fathers—is not given to all men, only to those men who most closely resemble the traits of the "worthy."

State action has come most often in response to the demands of powerful male-dominated organizations: unions and veterans' associations. Only when these men, once recognizing not just the harm to themselves but to the children they father, are harmed do they demand action on the part of the state. Organized as workers and soldiers, these men have largely fulfilled the requirements of masculine ideals and are fairly assured of their masculine privilege. Those men at the bottom of the masculine order—working-class men and men of color—rarely have their concerns met by the state and as such pay the biggest price for the

perpetuation of assumptions of reproductive masculinity. Only "a few good men" are thus privileged through state policies of reproductive masculinity.

Transforming Reproductive Masculinity

What might be the alternatives that would more justly represent men's true relationship to human reproduction? A more just politics of reproduction would recognize the specific biological differences between the sexes while affirming men's and women's common humanity. It would affirm research on male as well as female reproduction. It would more strenuously regulate the forms of reproductive commodification visited most heavily on men. It would address the vulnerabilities of the male reproductive system through support of research on male reproductive illnesses and disorders. It would more heavily regulate the sources of those harms in environmental and "recreational" toxins. A more just politics of reproduction would recognize that men and women share an interest in the health and well-being of children. It would respect the self-sovereignty of its reproductive citizens while holding men as well as women accountable for the reproductive consequences of their actions.

When we see the price men pay for gender privilege, we must question how we think about power and privilege itself. Would we live in a more just world if we gave to women what men have—in toxic workplaces, in the neglect of their reproductive health needs, in the exploitation of their reproductive capacities, in the front lines of war? A more just social system requires that we rethink the polarization of human traits that we have so long projected onto male and female bodies.

The point is not just to recognize men's vulnerabilities but to challenge the denigration of those traits traditionally associated with the "feminine"—human needs, weaknesses, and vulnerabilities. These very same associations are the ones women have been fighting to leave behind for decades, so can we legitimately question when men do not want these very same tags applied to them?

Yet if we did not devalue the needs of the human body, would it be so necessary for men to hide their bodily needs? If we did not devalue and denigrate the dependency of one human being on another, would it be so necessary for men to hide their dependencies on others? If we did not undervalue the caregiving functions that have rested so heavily on the shoulders of women, would it be so necessary for men to diminish their connection to children? If we did not devalue human frailty, would it be so necessary to hide the weaknesses of men? A social system that denigrates these human traits is one that distorts human reproduction and perpetuates gender injustice for both men and women.

Transforming this system is the job not just of theorists and academics but of those who study the science of reproduction, of those medical practitioners who see and treat reproductive health problems, of those who make public policies that guide human behavior, of those social and political activists who strive to transform social, political, and economic injustices for men and women.

In the end, when men are valued for their comparable role in reproduction, then reproduction will surely come to be more highly valued by society as a whole. When men are recognized as vulnerable, then the vulnerability of all human beings may be more easily recognized and addressed. When the "invincible warrior" comes to be seen as not only vulnerable to the harms of war but also more likely to transmit those harms to coming generations, then we may be slower to engage in the risks of war and quicker to recognize the presumed interest of all of humanity in the preservation of human life.

Transforming reproductive masculinity means seeing men and women as equally essential to human reproduction, equally vulnerable to the hazards and threats of the world, equally moved by human tragedy and sorrow, and equally capable of being the protectors of the nation and the species. This would truly mark a most welcome "end of masculinity." But this will not come until all of these are seen not just as traits attributable to a particular sex but to the common humanity of both men and women.

NOTES

CHAPTER 2

1. See John Farley, *Gametes and Spores: Ideas about Sexual Reproduction, 1750–1914* (Baltimore: Johns Hopkins University Press, 1982), 18–19, and F. J. Cole, *Early Theories of Sexual Generation* (London: Oxford University Press, 1930), 195.

2. See reference to Aristotle in Thomas Laqueur, *Making Sex* (Cambridge, MA: Harvard University Press, 1990), 31.

3. As quoted by Laqueur, *Making Sex,* 25.

4. Laqueur, *Making Sex,* 25; see also Londa Schiebinger, *The Mind Has No Sex?* (Cambridge, MA: Harvard University Press, 1986), for a more general discussion of the history of scientific analyses of sexual difference.

5. As quoted by Angus McLaren, *Reproductive Rituals: The Perception of Fertility in England from the Sixteenth to the Nineteenth Century* (London: Methuen, 1984), 16.

6. The Aristotelian view, McLaren argues, was a minority view, against theories that recognized some more active, though not equivalent, role for the female (McLaren, *Reproductive Rituals,* 16, 20).

7. Angus McLaren, *A History of Contraception from Antiquity to the Present Day* (Oxford: Basil Blackwell, 1990), 19.

8. As quoted by McLaren, "Greece," in *Reproductive Rituals,* 19.

9. As quoted by McLaren, "Greece," in *Reproductive Rituals,* 19.

10. See McLaren, "Greece," in *Reproductive Rituals*, 24: The Hippocratic texts state, "The man must not be drunk, nor should he drink white wine, but strong unmixed wine, eat very strong food, not take a hot bath, be strong, in good health, abstain from unhealthful foods" (quoting from Aristotle, *Generation of Animals*, and article on the fourth century; see his note 51).

11. See McLaren on this point ("Greece," in *Reproductive Rituals*, 23).

12. McLaren, "Greece," in *Reproductive Rituals*, 29, note 78.

13. McLaren, "Greece," in *Reproductive Rituals*, 34. Exposure was a process by which newborn infants were abandoned, usually at a set place, where they could be adopted by another or left to die.

14. McLaren, *Reproductive Rituals*, 17

15. McLaren, *A History of Contraception*, 48.

16. McLaren notes that Roman fathers "were believed even to have the right to put their offspring to death" but that such rights were contingent upon their wealth. Among the lower classes, family structure was matrifocal" (*History of Contraception*, 43).

17. Clara Pinto-Correia, *The Ovary of Eve: Egg and Sperm and Preformation* (Chicago: University of Chicago Press, 1997), 221, referring to the work of Paracelsus in *De Natura Rerum* in 1572.

18. See Mary Fissel, "Gender and Generation: Representing Reproduction in Early Modern England," in *Sexualities in History: A Reader,* ed. Kim M. Phillips and Barry Reay (New York: Routledge, 2002), 107. Fissel argues that Laqueur overstates the predominance of the one-sex model due to his reliance on texts produced by and for a "social elite."

19. Historian Estelle Cohen argues that an alternative scientific tradition existed among "learned women" in which the "female was not defined by absence and passivity in important scientific texts, when male and female were construed as neither homologous nor mutually exclusive, neither different versions of the same model nor oppositional yet complementary"; see Estelle Cohen, "'What the Women at All Times Would Laugh At': Redefining Equality and Difference, circa 1660–1760," in *Women, Gender and Science: New Directions*, ed. Sally Gregory Kohlstedt and Helen Longino (*Osiris*, vol. 12, 1997), 127.

20. Angus McLaren, "The Pleasures of Procreation: Traditional and Biomedical Theories of Conception," in *Reproductive Rituals*, 20.

21. McLaren, "The Expert Midwife 1694," in *Reproductive Rituals*, 20.

22. McLaren, "The Practice of Physick, 1658," in *Reproductive Rituals*, 20.

23. As quoted by Pinto-Correia, *The Ovary of Eve*, 19.

24. McLaren, "The Pleasures of Procreation," in *Reproductive Rituals*, 24.

25. George Garden, as quoted by Pinto-Correia, *The Ovary of Eve*, 72.

26. As quoted in McLaren, "The Pleasures of Procreation," in *Reproductive Rituals*, 23.

27. McLaren, "The Pleasures of Procreation," in *Reproductive Rituals*, 23.

28. As quoted by Pinto-Correia, *The Ovary of Eve*, 64.

29. As quoted by Farley, *Gametes and Spores*, 26.

30. McLaren, "The Pleasures of Procreation," in *Reproductive Rituals*, 23.

31. McLaren, "The Pleasures of Procreation," in *Reproductive Rituals*, 24–25.

32. See Pinto-Correia, *The Ovary of Eve*, 71.

33. As quoted by Cohen, "'What the Women at All Times Would Laugh At,'" 128. Cohen was quoting a critic of this position, James Drake, anatomist of the early 1700s. Cohen argues that it is likely that Drake's sister, Judith Drake, may have written the chapter in his influential medical text on human generation, *Anthropologia Nova; or, A New System of Anatomy*. On the theory of maternal impression, see Pinto-Correia, *The Ovary of Eve*, 128.

34. M. Vandermonde, 1751 (as quoted by Pinto-Correia, *The Ovary of Eve*, 130).

35. This idea of children born monstrous from the maternal imagination can be traced to ancient times. See Pinto-Correia, *The Ovary of Eve*, 129, for her discussion of an account given by Hippocrates of a white woman giving birth to a dark-skinned child, presumably because she was looking at a portrait of a Moor at the foot of her bed during intercourse.

36. James Blondel, as quoted by Estelle Cohen, "'What the Women at All Times Would Laugh At,'" 128; italics in original.

37. Edward Ruestow, *The Microscope in the Dutch Republic: The Shaping of Discovery* (Cambridge: Cambridge University Press, 1996), 154

38. Ruestow, *The Microscope in the Dutch Republic*, 155.

39. Pinto-Correia, *The Ovary of Eve*, 65–66.

40. See Edward Ruestow, "Images and Ideas: Leeuwenhoek's Perception of the Spermatozoa," *Journal of the History of Biology* 16 (Summer 1983): 185–224; and Ruestow, *The Microscope in the Dutch Republic*. Nicolaas Hartsoeker is credited with the first drawing of a tiny man inside the head of the sperm in 1694. See Pinto-Correia, *The Ovary of Eve*, 211, for this image.

41. Pinto-Correia, *The Ovary of Eve*, 69.

42. Farley, *Gametes and Spores*, 29.

43. Farley, *Gametes and Spores*, 3.

44. Farley, *Gametes and Spores*, 112.

45. See McLaren, "The Pleasures of Procreation," in *Reproductive Rituals*, 20–21.

46. McLaren, "The Pleasures of Procreation," in *Reproductive Rituals*, 27.

47. McLaren, "The Pleasures of Procreation," in *Reproductive Rituals*, 26.

48. See McLaren, "The Pleasures of Procreation," in *Reproductive Rituals*, 27, and Laqueur, *Making Sex*, 188 (for an account of the discovery of virginal ovulation). Laqueur describes the autopsy of a young virginal woman in 1835 whose ovary showed evidence, in scar tissue, of ovulation.

49. As historian Thomas Laqueur, *Making Sex*, 57, has argued, "Much of the debate about the nature of the seed and of the bodies that produce it . . . are in fact not about bodies at all. They are about power, legitimacy, and fatherhood."

50. Karl Ernst von Baer in 1827 viewed with a simple microscope the ovum in the follicle, so clearly "that a blind man would hardly deny it" (as quoted by Ruestow, *The Microscope in the Dutch Republic*, 285). See Laqueur, *Making Sex*, 181, and also Farley, *Gametes and Spores*, 63. In 1853, scientists had viewed the sperm of a frog entering into the membrane surrounding the frog egg.

51. Farley, *Gametes and Spores*, 108.

52. As John Farley, *Gametes and Spores*, 30, has put it, "Epigenesis teaches that development is not the mere mechanical unfolding of preformed parts, but is a process of simultaneous growth and differentiation from a completely homogeneous beginning."

53. The development of the medical sciences, establishment of European teaching hospitals and availability of the corpses of the poor who availed themselves of these and because of the growth in the science of epidemiology which strove to find the sources of illness and disease within the human body, the interest of the state in discovering and preventing the spread of disease. All of these provided the conditions under which dissection of the human body became widespread. Development of these technologies led then to transformations in thinking about the structure of the reproductive organs and nature of human procreation. See Laqueur, *Making Sex*, 188.

54. See Cole, *Early Theories of Sexual Generation*.

55. Farley, *Gametes and Spores*, 41 and also 126.

56. Farley, *Gametes and Spores*, 55.

57. Farley, *Gametes and Spores*, 128.

58. See Farley on this point, *Gametes and Spores*, 126.

59. See Ornella Moscucci, *The Science of Woman: Gynaecology and Gender in England, 1800–1929* (Cambridge: Cambridge University Press, 1990), 2.

60. See Schiebinger, *The Mind Has No Sex?* 189. See also Nelly Oudshoorn, *Beyond the Natural Body: An Archeology of Sex Hormones* (New York: Routledge, 1994), 7.

61. See Schiebinger, *The Mind Has No Sex?* chapter 6.

62. Quote from Dr. Virchow in 1848, as quoted by Oudshoorn, *Beyond the Natural Body*, 8. As Oudshoorn has argued, "Physiological 'facts' were used to explain the passive nature of women." She argues that such differences were used to justify social and political inequalities between the sexes.

63. See Farley, *Gametes and Spores*, 259.

64. Oudshoorn, *Beyond the Natural Body*, 8.

65. Oudshoorn, *Beyond the Natural Body*, 60.

66. Emily Martin, "The Egg and the Sperm: How Science Has Constructed a Romance Based on Stereotypical Male-Female Roles," *Signs: Journal of Women in Culture and Society* 16 (1991): 485–501.

67. Jeremy Cherfas, *The Redundant Male: Is Sex Irrelevant in the Modern World?* (London: Bodley Head, 1984), 132. On the question of sociobiological interpretations of gamete size, also see Ruth Hubbard, "Have Only Men Evolved?" in *Discovering Reality: Feminist Perspectives on Epistemology, Metaphysics, Methodology and the Philosophy of Science*, ed. Sandra Harding and Merrill B. Hintikka (Dordrecht: Reidel, 1983), and Donna Haraway, "Investment Strategies for the Evolving Portfolio of Primate Females," in *Body/Politics*, ed. Mary Jacobus, Evelyn Fox Keller, and Sally Shuttleworth (New York: Routledge, 1990), 155–156.

68. Sociologist Donald Symons, as quoted by Michael Kimmel, ed., *The Gendered Society Reader*, 2nd ed. (New York: Oxford University Press, 2004), 25–26.

69. Although some claim that men who are violent have higher levels of testosterone, others argue that violent behavior produces higher testosterone in both men and women. The causal relation is very unclear. For a summary and criticism of hormonal studies, see Robert M. Sapolsky, "Testosterone Rules," in *The Gendered Society Reader*, 2nd ed., ed. Michael Kimmel (New York: Oxford University Press, 2004).

70. William. Marsiglio, *Procreative Man* (New York: New York University Press, 1998), 50–51.

CHAPTER 3

1. Editorial, "Andrology as a Specialty," *Journal of the American Medical Association* 17 (1891): 691.
2. Editorial, "Andrology as a Specialty," 691.
3. See Eugenia Rosemberg, "American Society of Andrology: Its Beginnings," *Journal of Andrology* 7 (1986): 72–75.
4. Nelly Oudshoorn, *The Male Pill: A Biography of a Technology in the Making* (Durham, NC: Duke University Press, 2003), 6.
5. Figures are from the International Society of Andrology Web site: http://andrology.org/.
6. As quoted by Thaddeus Mann, "Advances in Male Reproductive Physiology," *Fertility and Sterility* 23 (October 1972): 699.
7. As reported by Phillip Troen, "Andrology: Origins and Scope," in *Encyclopedia of Reproduction*, vol. 1 (New York: Academic Press, 1999), 214.
8. This was Edward Martin, considered to be the "founding father of modern clinical andrology," as reported by Troen, "Andrology," 215.
9. Steve Connor, "Science: Mystery of the Vanishing Sperm," *The Independent* (8 March 1992): 43.
10. Quote from Dolores Lamb, as quoted by Rita Rubin, "Shapely Swimmers Win Fertility Race," *Herald Sun* (10 November 2001): 32; accessed at Lexis Nexus Academic Universe [hereafter LNAU], 3/27/02. The same story ran in *USA Today* as "Sperm Shape, Swimming Ability Prove to Be Better Indicator of Fertility" (8 November 2001): 1, accessed LNAU, 3/27/02. These reported on the original article that appeared in *New England Journal of Medicine*, by David S. Guzick, James W. Overstreet, Pam Factor-Litvak, Charlene K. Brazil, Steven T. Nakajima, Christos Coutifaris, Sandra Ann Carson, Pauline Cisneros, Michael P. Steinkampf, Joseph A. Hill, Dong Xu, and Donna L. Vogel, for the National Cooperative Reproductive Medicine Network, "Sperm Morphology, Motility, and Concentration in Fertile and Infertile Men," *New England Journal of Medicine* 345 (8 November 2001): 1388–1393.
11. These techniques were developed both in reproductive health facilities, to assess male infertility problems, and through field research on male work-

ers exposed to toxic substances. Semen can be used as one quick measure of exposure rates. Because sperm are produced in the male body continuously and take about 72 days to reach full development in the male body, changes in seminal fluid may be evidence of recent toxic exposures. Sperm production may be decreased or stopped entirely. Sperm may be deformed or disabled. Regular monitoring of workers' semen in hazardous environments may be one way of tracking the impact of workplace exposures not just on reproductive health but on health more generally. As one researcher has put it, "What a man produces in his ejaculate is a read-out of what's happened in the past 10 weeks, because each sperm cell has taken about 10 weeks to manufacture" (Richard Sharpe, as quoted by Connor, "Science," 3).

12. Steven M. Schrader, R. E. Chapin, E. D. Clegg, R.O. Davis, J. L. Fourcroy, D. F. Katz, S. A. Rothmann, G. Toth, T. W. Turner, and M. Zinaman, "Laboratory Methods for Assessing Human Semen in Epidemiological Studies: A Consensus Report," *Reproductive Toxicology* 6 (1992): 275–279.

13. Sheldon Krimsky, *Hormonal Chaos: The Scientific and Social Origins of the Environmental Endocrine Hypothesis* (Baltimore: Johns Hopkins University Press, 1999), 31.

14. Lawrence Wright, "Silent Sperm," *The New Yorker* (15 January 1996): 42–55.

15. This was a study of 141 workers that the research team had access to through personal contacts. See Krimsky, *Hormonal Chaos*, 31.

16. Sperm counts dropped from 113 to 66 million per milliliter of semen. Although this was far from the 20 million generally assumed to be the minimum for male fertility, it raised concern that the downward trend could continue. See Elisabeth Carlsen, Aleksander Giwercman, Niels Keiding, and Niels E. Skakkebæk, "Evidence for Decreasing Quality of Semen during the Past Fifty Years," *British Medical Journal* 305 (1992): 609–612.

17. Carlsen et al., "Evidence," 611.

18. Carlsen et al., "Evidence," 612.

19. D. Marmor, V. Izard, D. Schahmaneche, G. Genoit, and A. Jardin, "Is Today's Man Really Less Fertile?" *Presse Med* 27 (October 1998): 1484–1490.

20. R. J. Sherins, "Are Semen Quality and Male Fertility Changing?" *New England Journal of Medicine* 332 (2 February 1995): 327.

21. In California, researcher Shanna Swan and her associates reevaluated the original 61 studies plus 40 other studies conducted between 1934 and 1996. See Shanna Swan, Eric P. Elkin, and Laura Fenster, "Have Sperm Densities

Declined? A Reanalysis of Global Trend Data," *Environmental Health Perspectives* 105 (1997): 128–132. See also Shanna H. Swan, Eric P. Elkin, and Laura Fenster, "The Question of Declining Sperm Density Revisited: An Analysis of 101 Studies Published 1934–1996," *Environmental Health Perspectives* 108 (October 2000): 961–966.

22. Jorma Toppari, John Chr. Larsen, Peter Christiansen, Aleksander Giwercman, Philippe Grandjean, Louis J. Guillette Jr., Bernard Jégou, Tina K. Jensen, Pierre Jouannet, Niels Keiding, Henrik Leffers, John A. McLachlan, Otto Meyer, Jørn Müller, Ewa Rajpert-De Meyts, Thomas Scheike, Richard Sharpe, John Sumpter, and Niels E. Skakkebæk, "Male Reproductive Health and Environmental Xenoestrogens," *Environmental Health Perspectives* 104 (Supplement 4, 1996): 768.

23. H. Fisch and E. T. Goluboff, "Geographic Variations in Sperm Counts: A Potential Cause of Bias in Studies of Semen Quality," *Fertility and Sterility* 65 (May 1996): 1044–1046.

24. This is reported by Gina Kolata, "Measuring Men Up," *New York Times* (5 May 1996): 4–4. As she reports: "Dr. Swerdloff and Dr. Larry Johnson of Texas A&M University collected the testicles of young men of Chinese, white and Hispanic ancestry who died suddenly. The investigators dissected the testicles to determine how many sperm they contained. The Chinese men, they discovered, had smaller testicles and fewer sperm."

25. As quoted by Thomas Barlow, "Body and Mind," *Financial Times* (London) (17 February 2001): 2; accessed LNAU, 3/28/03. The word *impotent* implies a compromised masculinity, not just a threat to the human environment.

26. Wright, "Silent Sperm," 45.

27. Niels Jørgensen, Anne-Grethe Andersen, Florence Eustache, D. Stewart Irvine, Jyrki Suominen, Jørgen Holm Petersen, Anders Nyboe Andersen, Jacques Auger, Elizabeth H. H. Cawood, Antero Horte, Tina Kold Jensen, Pierre Jouannet, Niels Keiding, Matti Vierula, Jorma Toppari, and Niels E. Skakkebæk, "Regional Differences in Semen Quality in Europe," *Human Reproduction* 16 (2001): 1012–1019.

28. This group of scholars was originally critical of the Danish study. The Paris study controlled for age, sexual activity, and techniques for assessing sperm quality. See J. Auger, J. M. Kunstmann, J. Czyglik, and P. Jouannet, "Decline in Semen Quality among Fertile Men in Paris during the Past 20 Years," *New England Journal of Medicine* 332 (2 February 1995): 281–285.

29. E. V. Younglai, J. A. Collins, and W. G. Foster, "Canadian Semen Quality: An Analysis of Sperm Density among Eleven Academic Fertility Centers," *Fertility and Sterility* 70 (July 1998): 76–80.

30. Rory Watson, "Chemicals Concern over Falling Sperm Counts," *The Herald* (Glasgow) (5 May 2000): 11.

31. J. Berlau, "Case of the Falling Sperm Counts," *National Review* (26 June 1995): 45–48.

32. Brian D. Acacio, Tamar Gottfried, Robert Israel, and Rebecca Z. Sokol, "Evaluation of a Large Cohort of Men Presenting for a Screening Semen Analysis," *Fertility and Sterility* 73 (March 2000): 595–597.

33. C. A. Paulsen, N. C. Berman, and C. Wang, "Data from Men in Greater Seattle Area Reveals No Downward Trend in Semen Quality: Further Evidence That Deterioration of Semen Quality Is Not Geographically Uniform," *Fertility and Sterility* 65 (1996): 1015–1020.

34. The researchers found a slight increase in sperm production, with donors producing on average a hardy 180 million sperm per ejaculation. See Julie Robotham, "Speedy Sperm, and Plenty of It," *Sydney Morning Herald* (20 February 2002): 3; accessed LNAU, 3/27/02.

35. Researchers reported that "time to pregnancy" success rates had improved from 65% to 80% in the first 3–4 months of trying over the past few decades. This was measured as attempts to conceive within the first four to six months of regular intercourse. The same study also noted that taxicab drivers still apparently have more trouble achieving conception than other men. Researcher Michael Joffe, an epidemiologist at Imperial College School of Medicine in London, interviewed 646 men and 894 women aged 16–59, asking them how long it took them to conceive and found time to conception was four to six months for 65% of the couples between 1961 and 1965, while between 1991 and 1993 it had increased to 80% of couples. See Steve Connor, "Fertility Rises Despite Falling Sperm Counts," *The Independent* (London) (2 June 2000): 15.

36. As quoted by Connor, "Fertility," 15.

37. See James Le Fanu "The Cure for Which There Is No Disease," *Daily Telegraph* (London) (3 October 2000): 22; accessed LNAU, 3/28/02.

38. Marilynne Marchione, "Potent News," *Milwaukee Journal Sentinel* (27 March 2000): 15.

39. Connor, "Mystery of the Vanishing Sperm," 3.

40. Jacqueline M. Moline, Anne L. Golden, Natan Bar-Chama, Ernest Smith, Molly E. Rauch, Robert E. Chapin, Sally D. Perreault, Steven M. Schrader, William A. Suk, and Phillip Landrigan, "Exposure to Hazardous Substances and Male Reproductive Health: A Research Framework," *Environmental Health Perspectives* 108 (September 2000): 803–813.

41. A. Ekbom and O. Akre, "Increasing Incidence of Testicular Cancer Birth Cohort Effects," *APMIS* 106 (January 1998): 225–231, as referenced in Moline et al., "Exposure to Hazardous Substances," 812.

42. Researchers suggest this is not due to better surveillance or detection because detection is still reliant on physical examination methods that have not changed significantly. Moline et al., "Exposure to Hazardous Substances," 805.

43. Moline et al., "Exposure to Hazardous Substances," 805; reference in "Stat Bite: U.S. Incidence of Testicular Cancer" [News], *Journal of the National Cancer Institute* 91 (1999): 1803.

44. Stephen H. Safe, "Endocrine Disruptors and Human Health—Is There a Problem? An Update," *Environmental Health Perspectives* 108 (June 2000): 1, accessed online at http://ehpnet1.niehs.nih.gov, April 11, 2000.

45. For early confirmation of this increase, see D. Schottenfeld and M. E. Warshauer, "Testis," in *Cancer Epidemiology and Prevention,* ed. D. Schottenfeld and J. F. Fraumeni Jr. (Philadelphia: Saunders, 1982), 947–957; and M. P. Coleman, J. Esteve, P. Damiecki, A. Arslan, and H. Renard, "Trends in Cancer Incidence and Mortality," *IARC Scientific Publications* 121 (1993): 521–542. See also R. Bergstrom, H. O. Adami, M. Mohner, W. Zatonski, H. Storm, A. Ekbom, S. Tretli, L. Teppo, O. Akre, and T. Hakulinen, "Increase in Testicular Cancer Incidence in Six European Countries: A Birth Cohort Phenomenon," *Journal of the National Cancer Institute* 88 (5 June 1996): 727–733. Also see Safe, "Endocrine Disruptors," 1.

46. Title of this section taken from "Bye Bye, Baby Boys," *Earth Island Journal* 13 (Spring 1998): 12, in reporting the results of the Canadian sex ratio study.

47. The 74 total births in Seveso from 1977 to 1984 produced 26 males and 48 females. Paolo Mocarelli, Paolo Brambilla, Pier Mario Gerthoux, Donald G. Patterson Jr., and Larry L. Needham, "Change in Sex Ratio with Exposure to Dioxin," *Lancet* 348 (10 August 1996): 409; on the human sex ratio, see W. H. James, "What Stabilizes the Sex Ratio?" *Annals of Human Genetics* 59 (1995): 243–249.

48. Paolo Mocarelli, Paolo Brambilla, Pier Mario Gerthoux, Donald G. Patterson Jr., and Larry L. Needham, "Paternal Concentrations of Dioxin and Sex Ratio of Offspring," *Lancet* 355 (27 May 2000): 1858–1863.

49. Devra Lee Davis, Michelle B. Gottlieb, and Julie R. Stampnitzky, "Reduced Ratio of Male to Female Births in Several Industrial Countries: A Sentinel Health Indicator?" *Journal of the American Medical Association* 279 (1998): 1018–1023.

50. Davis et al., "Reduced Ratio," 1020.

51. Researchers argued that while some of this decline can be attributed to hormonally induced ovulation, which was introduced to Denmark in 1985 and which typically produces more female births, it cannot explain the decrease in male births before 1985. Henrik Moller, "Change in Male:Female Ratio among Newborn Infants in Denmark," *Lancet* 348 (21 September 1996): 828–829. Also see W. H. James, "Male Reproductive Hazards and Occupation," *Lancet* 347 (1996): 773; and W. H. James, "The Human Sex Ratio, Part 1: A Review of the Literature," *Human Biology* 59 (1987): 721–752.

52. Bruce B. Allan and Rollin Brant, "Declining Sex Ratios in Canada," *Canadian Medical Association Journal* 156 (1 January 1997): 37.

53. Davis et al., "Reduced Ratio," 1019.

54. See H. Dimid-Ward, C. Hertzman, K. Teschke, R. Hershler, S. A. Marion, and A. Ostry, "Reproductive Effects of Paternal Exposure to Cholorophenate Wood Preservatives in the Sawmill Industry," *Scandinavian Journal of World Environmental Health* 22 (1996): 267–273; and W. H. James, "The Sex Ratio of Offspring Sired by Men Exposed to Wood Preservatives Contaminated by Dioxin," *Scandinavian Journal of World Environmental Health* 23 (1997): 69.

55. G. Potashnik, J. Goldsmith, and V. Insler, "Dibromochloropropane-Induced Reduction of the Sex-Ratio in Man," *Andrologia* 39 (1984): 85–89. Also see J. Goldsmith, G. Potashnik, and R. Israeli, "Reproductive Outcomes in Families of DBCP-Exposed Men," *Archives of Environmental Health* 16 (1984): 213–218.

56. Davis et al., "Reduced Ratio," 1021 (quote) and 1022.

57. Allan and Brant, "Declining Sex Ratios," 37.

58. For instance, high exposures to PCBs in an accident in Taiwan did not appear to produce a lower male birth rate. See W. J. Rogan, G. C. Gladen, Y.-L. Guo, and C. C. Hsu, "Sex Ratio after Exposure to Dioxin-Like Chemicals in Taiwan," *Lancet* 353 (1999): 206.

59. See Davis et al., "Reduced Ratio."

60. Theo Colborn and Richard Liroff, "Toxins in the Great Lakes," *EPA Journal* 16 (November/December 1990): 5.

61. Wright, "Silent Sperm," 55.

62. See Krimsky, *Hormonal Chaos*, 65.

63. Geoffrey Lean and Richard Sadler, "Chemicals in Water 'Lower Sperm Counts,'" *Independent* (London) (17 March 2002): 10; accessed LNAU, 3/27/02.

64. Lean and Sadler, "Chemicals in Water," 10.

65. See Jocelyn Kaiser, "Endocrine Disrupters: Scientists Angle for Answers," *Science* 274 (13 December 1996): 1837–1838. Also see Krimsky, *Hormonal Chaos*, 66.

66. Chris Gray, "Scientist Hot on Trail of Hormones; Chemical Clues Seen in Animals," *Times-Picayune* (New Orleans, LA) (23 December 1996): A1.

67. Louis J. Guillette Jr., Timothy S. Gross, Greg R. Masson, John M. Matter, H. Franklin Percival, and Allan R. Woodward, "Developmental Abnormalities of the Gonad and Abnormal Sex Hormone Concentrations in Juvenile Alligators from Contaminated and Control Lakes in Florida," *Environmental Health Perspectives* 102 (August 1994): 680–688. See also Kyla Dunn, "'Teeny Weenies,' Alligators in Florida's Lake Apopka Have Smaller Penises." PBS transcript (2 June 1998).

68. Dunn, "Teeny Weenies."

69. Doug Hamilton, "Interview with Fredrick vom Saal," *Frontline* (PBS, 2 June 1998).

70. Charles F. Facemire, Timothy S. Gross, and Louis J. Guillette Jr., "Reproductive Impairment in the Florida Panther: Nature or Nurture?" *Environmental Health Perspectives* (Suppl. 4, 1995): 79–86.

71. Facemire et al., "Reproductive Impairment in the Florida Panther."

72. "Testicular Dysgenesis Syndrome: Newly Coined TDS Encompasses Symptoms of Deteriorating Male Reproductive Function," *Health and Medicine Week* (6 August 2001): 49.

73. Carlsen et al., "Evidence."

74. Peter Pallot, "Tight Pants and Too Much Drinking Hit Sperm Count," *Daily Telegraph* (London) (9 March 1992): 3.

75. Claudia Fitzherbert, "Commentary: Terror on the Trouser Front," *Daily Telegraph* (London) (12 March 1992): 17.

76. As reported by Becky Wang-Cheng, "Dispelling a Myth about Boxer Shorts and Fertility," *Milwaukee Journal Sentinel* (2 October 2000), 1G, on the research of Robert Munkelwitz and Bruce Gilbert in the journal article "Are Boxer Shorts Really Better? A Critical Analysis of the Role of Underwear Type in Male Subfertility," *Journal of Urology* 160 (October 1998): 1329–1333.

77. German researchers (Wolfgang Sippell and his colleagues at the University of Kiel) reported in the journal *Archives of Disease in Childhood*, as reported by Sarah Boseley, "Nappies Cause Infertility Claim Stirs Controversy," *Guardian* (London) (26 September 2000): 6, and Express Staff, "Plastic Diapers Tied to Infertility," *Daily News* (New York) (26 September 2000): 2. C.-J. Partsch, M. Aukamp, and W. G. Sippell, "Scrotal Temperature Is Increased in Disposable Plastic Lined Nappies," *Archives of Disease in Childhood* 83 (October 2000): 364–368.

78. As quoted by Boseley, "Nappies," 6.

79. "Disposable Nappies Catch a Spray from Researchers," *The Age* (Melbourne) (27 September 2000): 3.

80. Reported at the World Life Sciences Forum in Lyons by Roger Highfield, "Folic Acid 'Is the Key to Fertility in Males,'" *Daily Telegraph* (London) (10 February 2001): 12.

81. Theo Colborn, Dianne Dumanoski, and John Peterson Myers, *Our Stolen Future: Are We Threatening Our Fertility, Intelligence, and Survival? A Scientific Detective Story* (New York: Dutton, 1996).

82. One of the primary researchers in this field was John McLachlan, who studied the transfer of toxins across the placenta (teratogenicity) in pregnant animals and found that of nicotine, caffeine, salicylate, and the pesticide DDT, the pesticide had the most significant and lasting effect. See Krimsky, *Hormonal Chaos*, 11.

83. Alejandro Oliva, Alfred Spira, and Luc Multigner, "Contribution of Environmental Factors to the Risk of Male Infertility," *Human Reproduction* 16 (August 2001): 1768–1776; as reported by Reuters, "Male Infertility May Be Linked to Pesticides," *Toronto Star* (27 July 2001): D02, accessed LNAU, 3/27/03.

84. J. Auger, F. Eustache, A. G. Andersen, D. S. Irvine, N. Jørgensen, N. E. Skakkebæk, J. Suominen, J. Toppari, M. Vierula, and P. Jouannet, "Sperm Morphological Defects Related to Environment, Lifestyle and Medical History of 1001 Male Partners of Pregnant Women from Four European Cities," *Human Reproduction* 16 (December 2001): 2710–2717.

85. These were Carlos Sonnenschein and Ana Soto at the Tufts University School of Medicine, as reported by Krimsky, *Hormonal Chaos*, 66.

86. J. Raloff, "Common Pollutants Undermine Masculinity," *Science News Online* 155 (3 April 1999): 1–4; accessed at www.sciencenews.org, 3/20/02; and James Le Fanu, "Behind the Great Plastic Duck Panic," *New Statesman* (22 November 1999): 11.

87. As quoted by Marilynn Larkin, "Male Reproductive Health: A Hotbed of Research," *Lancet* 352 (15 August 1998): 552.

88. Stephen H. Safe, "Environmental and Dietary Estrogens and Human Health: Is There a Problem?" *Environmental Health Perspectives* 103 (April 1995): 346–351.

89. Safe, "Environmental and Dietary Estrogens."

90. As quoted by Wright, "Silent Sperm," 52.

91. Facemire et al., "Reproductive Impairment in the Florida Panther."

92. Berlau, "Case of the Falling Sperm Counts," 45, 48.

93. According to one *Men's Health* magazine story entitled "Don't Worry, Be Fertile," stressed-out men produced sperm that were "sluggish swimmers." See "Don't Worry, Be Fertile," *Men's Health* 13 (June 1998): 34.

94. Arthur Hoppe, "Dealing with Heir Loss," *San Francisco Chronicle* (16 September 1992): A17.

95. "U.S. Men Face Extinction," *Earth Island Journal* (Winter 1999–2000): 3.

96. Anne Merewood, "Sperm Under Siege," *Health* (April 1991): 53–76; Meredith Small, "Sperm Wars," *Discover* (July 1991): 48–53.

97. Wright, "Silent Sperm."

98. Michael Castleman, "Down for the Count," *Mother Jones* (January–February 1996): 20–21; Maggie Fox, "Sperm Counts Falling around the World," *Reuters* (24 November 1997).

99. Roger Highfield, "Goodbye Macho Man?" *Daily Telegraph* (30 November 1992): 16.

100. For use of "hunting" terminology, see Associated Press, "Sperm Counts Reported to Drop," *Boston Globe* (11 September 1992): 19.

101. Hoppe, "Dealing with Heir Loss," A17.

102. Stewart Irvine, "Is the Human Testis Still an Organ at Risk?" *British Medical Journal* 312 (22 June 1996): 1557–1558.

103. On feminism, see Stewart Trotter, "Letter," *Independent* (15 March 1992): 23. The author suggests no reason for this association and perhaps assumes that it would be obvious to any reader.

104. One might think the sperm count rates, along with testosterone levels, might rise with the presence of women. See "Grades Aren't All That Are Dropping," *Washington Monthly* 33 (December 2001): 22.

105. Janet Raloff, "That Feminine Touch," *Science News Online* (22 January 1994), accessed LNAU, 3/20/02.

106. Bob Hunter, "Plastics Ain't So Fantastic, Lovers," *Eye Weekly* (Toronto's arts newspaper) (15 February 1996), accessed at www.eye.net/eye/issues/, 3/19/02.

107. Berlau, "Case of the Falling Sperm Counts," 48.

108. On war, see A. J. Forsyth, "Letter," *Independent* (London) (15 March 1992): 23.

109. R. M. Sharpe and N. E. Skakkebaek, "Are Oestrogens Involved in Falling Sperm Counts and Disorders of the Male Reproductive Tract?" *Lancet* 341 (29 May 1993): 1392–1395.

110. Karen Peterson, "Decreasing Sperm Counts Blamed on Environment," *USA Today* (28 May 1993): 1A.

111. As cited by Wright, "Silent Sperm," 48.

112. Tina Kold Jensen, Jorma Toppari, Niels Keilding, and Niels Erik Skakkebaek, "Do Environmental Estrogens Contribute to the Decline in Male Reproductive Health?" *Clinical Chemistry* 41 (1995): 1897.

113. Marla Cone, "Study Supports Finding of Male Fertility Decline," *Los Angeles Times* (2 February 1995): A22.

114. Wright, "Silent Sperm," 47.

115. For the stories in 1993 on female mediated estrogens, see Chris Mihill, "Raised Levels of Oestrogen Linked to Male Sex Disorders," *Guardian* (28 May 1993): 7; Jeremy Laurance, "Hormone Linked to Falling Fertility," *Times* (London) (28 May 1993); Robbie Dinwoodie, "Warning over Fall in Male Fertility," *Herald* (Glasgow, Scotland) (28 May 1993): 10; Dolores Kong, "Study Says Fetal Estrogen Exposure May Explain Male Ills," *Boston Globe* (28 May 1993): 3.

116. Hoppe, "Dealing with Heir Loss," A17.

117. Daniel Pinchbeck, "Downward Motility," *Esquire* (January 1996): 79–84.

118. Dunn, "Teeny Weenies."

119. Lean and Sadler, "Chemicals in the Water."

120. BBC/Discovery Production, "Assault on the Male" (4 September 1994; aired in 1993 in Great Britain).

121. Raloff, "That Feminine Touch"; Janet Raloff, "The Gender Benders," *Science News Online* (22 January 1994), accessed 3/20/02.

122. Editorial, "Masculinity at Risk," *Nature* 375 (15 June 1995): 522.

123. Christopher Lambton, "Mamas Maketh Man," *Guardian* (11 February 1993): 12.

124. Even stories dismissing claims of a sperm count drop made reference to sperm as a measure of one's manhood, with men reassured, in stories with titles like "Potent News," that men "produce as much sperm as their grandfathers" despite research that "tight underwear, pollution or bicycle seats might threaten sperm counts" (*Milwaukee Journal Sentinel* [24 March 2000]: 2G).

125. Pallot, "Tight Pants," 3.

126. Murray Freedman, "Counting Sperm" (Letter), *Times* (24 April 1993).

127. On seasonal variation of sperm counts, see "Human Sperm Count Peaks in Winter, Studies Say," *Toronto Star* (22 May 1993): A3.

128. Michael Castleman, "Big Drop," *Sierra* 78 (March–April 1993): 38.

129. On parking attendants and tunnel work, see Sylvia Thompson, "The Vanishing Sperm," *Irish Times* (19 October 1992): 10; on tight pants and drinking, see Pallot, "Tight Pants," 3. On stress, Houston Chronicle News Service, "Environment Pollutants Linked to a Large Drop in Sperm Count," *Houston Chronicle* (11 September 1992): 24; or Associated Press, "Sperm Counts Reported to Drop," 19.

130. David Freed, "Male Infertility Is an Overlooked Hazard of Toxic Exposure," *Los Angeles Times* (6 September 1993): A24.

131. Thomas Barlow, "Is the Number Up for Sperm Counts?" *Financial Times* (London) (17 February 2001): 2.

132. "The Gelding of America: Is DDT to Blame?" *Civil Defense Perspectives* 12 (November 1995).

133. Brian Halwell, "Plummeting Sperm Counts Cause Concern," *Futurist* (November 1999): 14–15.

134. The report was countered by a letter by Shanna Swan, written to the *New York Times*, who argued that the *Times* misrepresented the conclusion of the study and suggested that men presenting at fertility clinics might not be appropriate as subjects of study for the general population. Eric Nagourney, "American Sperm, as Hardy as Ever," *New York Times* (28 March 2000): F8; and Shanna Swan, "Letter" (29 March 2000).

135. As one reporter in Scotland put it, "Whatever happened to the red-blooded males, the fertile women, those heroic symbols of a healthy country? Has

our national sperm count dropped so low that we can no longer even pro-create properly?" See Magnus Linklater, "Why We Should Welcome Strang-ers Bearing Gifts," *Scotland on Sunday* (23 July 2000). Accessed via LNAU, 3/28/2002.

136. References are, respectively, local and wire dispatches, "Counting Sperm," *Pittsburgh Post-Gazette* (28 June 1993): C4; Jack R. Payton, "It's the Weird, the Wild, and the Wacky from Around the World," *St. Petersburg Times* (21 July 1993): 2A; Adam Nicolson, "Sunday Matters," *Daily Telegraph* (12 December 1993): 16.

137. Watson, "Chemicals Concern," 11.

138. Hoppe, "Dealing with Heir Loss," A17. For references to sperm as an en-dangered species, see "Scholars Find Drop in Sperm Counts," *Houston Chronicle* (16 November 1992): 3; "Sperm Counts Declining," *Buffalo News* (1 December 1992): 3. For religious revelation, see Roger Highfield, "Goodbye Macho Man?" 16. For "homo sapiens" reference, see Phil Jenkins, "Mystery Master Probes a Bleak and Barren Future," *Ottawa Citizen*, B7.

139. P. D. James, *The Children of Men* (London: Faber, 1992); for reviews, see Jenkins, "Mystery Master," B7, or Penny Perrick, "Future Shock," *Sunday Times* (20 September 1992), where James reports, "The idea came to me after I read about the reduction in the human sperm count."

140. Fitzherbert, "Commentary," 17.

141. Interestingly, it was one of only a few stories to also report "a correspond-ing dramatic increase in male genito-urinary abnormalities and testicular cancer," which was reported in the same *British Medical Journal* article. David Landis, "Sperm Count Slide," *USA Today* (11 September 1992): 1D.

142. Pennie Taylor, *Scotland on Sunday* (31 October 1993).

143. *ToxCat*, Vol. 2–2, Spring 1996 (TC Publications).

144. And, the story noted, this may explain the West's interest in cloning. "U.S. Men Face Extinction," 3.

145. For use of "hunting" terminology, see Associated Press, "Sperm Counts Reported to Drop," 19.

146. "Western Man's Fertility Counts Are Falling Fast: 12 Ways to Beat Sperm Crisis," *Sunday Mail* (SA) (18 February 2001): 118. Accessed LNAU 3/28/03.

147. Krimsky, *Hormonal Chaos*, 60.

148. See Krimsky, *Hormonal Chaos*, 68–70.

149. Krimsky, *Hormonal Chaos*, 68–69; HR 3293.

150. Environmental Protection Agency, "Endocrine Disruptor Screening and Testing Advisory Committee, Final Report, Chapter Seven, Compilation of EDSTAC Recommendations" (1998), ES-1. Available online at http://www.epa.gov/scipoly/oscpendo/docs/edstac/chap7v14.pdf.

151. EPA, "Endocrine Disruptor, Final Report," 6.

152. Environmental Protection Agency, Endocrine Disruptor Screening Program, "Report to Congress" August 2000, 16. In 2001, the EPA initiated a review of evidence regarding the effects of endrocrine disrupters. Available online at http://www.epa.gov.oscpmont/oscpendo/docs/edmvs/edmvs statusreporttocongressfinal.pdf.

153. Robert J. Kavlock, George P. Daston, Chris DeRosa, Penny Fenner-Crisp, L. Earl Gray, Steve Kaattari, George Lucier, Michael Luster, Michael J. Mac, Carol Maczka, Ron Miller, Jack Moore, Rosalind Rolland, Geoffrey Scott, Daniel M. Sheehan, Thomas Sinks, and Hugh A. Tilson, "Research Needs for the Risk Assessment of Health and Environmental Effects of Endocrine Disruptors: A Report of the U.S. EPA-Sponsored Workshop," *Environmental Health Perspectives* 104 (Suppl. 4, August 1996): 715–740, quote from 33.

154. Committee on Hormonally Active Agents in the Environment, Board on Environmental Studies and Toxicology, Commission on Life Sciences, National Research Council, *Hormonally Active Agents in the Environment* (henceforth HAAE) (Washington, DC: National Academy Press, 1999), Executive Summary, 1.

155. Colin Macilwain, "U.S. Panel Split on Endocrine Disruptors," *Nature* 395 (1998): 828.

156. HAAE, 2.

157. HAAE, 4.

158. HAAE, 146.

159. HAAE, 5.

160. HAAE, 1.

161. HAAE, 266.

162. HAAE, 135.

163. HAAE, 170.

164. Michael Fumento, "Hormonally Challenged," *American Spectator* 32 (October 1999): 2.

165. HAAE, 2.

166. As noted in Kavlock et al., "Research Needs," 20.

167. Wright, "Silent Sperm," 47.

CHAPTER 4

1. For examples of racial identifications, see their donor list at http://www .cyrobank.com/catalog/indexb.cfm.

2. As Cryobank puts it, "To ensure that the man standing at the donor desk is really donor #500." Cryobank, *Donor Information*, 2000; see www .cryobank.com.

3. At most sperm banks, donors may be rejected if they fail any one of the monthly blood or urine tests administered to all donors for drug use, HIV, and a range of other infectious diseases. It is, indeed, no surprise that one observer noted that "being accepted as a sperm donor can be as difficult as entering Harvard." See Xytex Corporation, *Donor Screening Guide*.

4. As reported by Sonia Fader, "Sperm Banking: A Reproductive Resource" (California Cryobank, 1993), at http://www.cryobank.com/sbanking.cfm.

5. As quoted in K. J. Betteridge, "An Historical Look at Embryo Transfer," *Journal of Reproduction and Fertility* 62 (1981): 3.

6. J. Marion Sims described experiments in uterine insemination in the 1860s, including his repeated inseminations of six women. Only one case resulted in a pregnancy, which was later miscarried. The treatments were typically instituted because the women suffered from malformed cervixes that blocked the entry of the sperm into the uterus. Sims's efforts are described in Margaret Marsh and Wanda Ronner, *The Empty Cradle: Infertility in America from Colonial Times to the Present* (Baltimore: Johns Hopkins University Press, 1996): 64–68.

7. Elaine Tyler May, *Barren in the Promised Land* (New York: Basic Books, 1995). May believes Hard was the donor.

8. R. T. Seashore, "Artificial Impregnation," *Minnesota Medicine* 21 (1938): 641–644.

9. For example, see C. Travers Stepita, "Physiologic Artificial Insemination," *American Journal of Surgery* 21 (1933): 450–451; Walter R. Stokes, "Artificial Insemination," *Medical Annals of the District of Columbia* 7 (1938): 218–219, on the technique; and on the law Frances I. Seymour and Alfred Koerner, "Medicolegal Aspects of Artificial Insemination," *Journal of the American Medical Association* 107 (1936): 1531–1534.

10. Seashore, "Artificial Impregnation," 643.

11. "Eugenic Babies: Medical Science Finds a Way, Even with Sterile Husbands," *Literary Digest* (21 November 1936): 23–25. See also Frances Seymour,

"Eugenics in Practice: Cross Artificial Insemination," *Marriage Hygiene* 3 (1936): 46.

12. Abner I. Weisman, "The Selection of Donors for Use in Artificial Insemination," *Western Journal of Surgery, Obstetrics, and Gynecology* 50 (1942): 144.

13. On eugenics, see Daniel J. Kevles, *In the Name of Eugenics: Genetics and the Uses of Human Heredity* (Cambridge, MA: Harvard University Press, 1985), and Diane B. Paul, *Controlling Human Heredity, 1865 to the Present* (New York: Humanities Press, 1995).

14. In succeeding decades, critics demonstrated that there was no biological evidence to support the claims of eugenicists. They could find no genetic basis for behavior and demonstrated that IQ test scores changed in individuals according to their environment. The racial hygiene policies of the Nazis also dealt a blow to the claims of eugenicists. See Kevles, *In the Name of Eugenics*.

15. Alan Frank Guttmacher, "Practical Experience with Artificial Insemination," *Journal of Contraception* 3 (1938): 76.

16. Seymour, "Eugenics in Practice," 46.

17. Grant S. Beardsley, "Artificial Cross Insemination," *Western Journal of Surgery, Obstetrics and Gynecology* 48 (1940): 95.

18. Guttmacher, "Practical Experience," 76.

19. Alan F. Guttmacher, "A Physician's Credo for Artificial Insemination," *Western Journal of Surgery, Obstetrics and Gynecology* 50 (1942): 358–359.

20. "'Ghost' Fathers: Children Provided for the Childless," *Newsweek* 3 (12 May 1934): 16.

21. "Proxy Fathers," *Time* (26 September 1938): 28.

22. "Proxy Fathers," 28.

23. "Eugenic Babies," 23–25.

24. Anthony M. Turano, "Paternity by Proxy," *American Mercury* 43 (1938): 418–424. The terms "Nordic" and "Mediterranean" were the racial categorizations used by eugenicists and others who supported immigration restriction for the latter and who feared "mongrelization" of the races, resulting in a decline in good American stock.

25. Robert A. Ersek, "Frozen Sperm Banks" *Journal of the American Medical Association* 220 (5 June 1972): 1365.

26. Keith D. Smith and Emil Steinberger, "Survival of Spermatozoa in a Human Sperm Bank: Effects of Long-Term Storage," *Journal of the American Medical Association* 223 (12 February 1973): 774; R. G. Bunge and J. K.

Sherman, "Fertilizing Capacity of Frozen Human Spermatozoa," *Nature* 172 (1953): 767–768; W. C. Keettel, R. G. Bunge, J. T. Bradbury, and W. O. Nelson, "Report of Pregnancies in Infertile Couples," *Journal of the American Medical Association* 160 (January 1956): 102–105.

27. As quoted by S. J. Behrman and D. R. Ackerman, "Freeze Preservation of Human Sperm," *American Journal of Obstetrics and Gynecology* 103 (1969): 660–661.

28. Albert Rosenfeld, "The Futuristic Riddle of Reproduction," *Coronet* 54 (1959): 122.

29. "Frozen Fatherhood," *Time* (8 September 1961); Barbara J. Cullitan, "Sperm Banks Debated," *Science News* 92 (1967): 208–209. See also "Urge Human Sperm Banks," *Science News Letter* 80 (9 September 1961): 163. The radical potential of such a sperm bank did not escape one writer, who mused about a world with a few selected males to keep up the stocks of frozen sperm and a race of "Amazonian women, of whom only the fittest individuals would be allowed to reproduce." And in which only women were born, thanks to sperm separating techniques. A. J. Burton, "Are Men Really Necessary?" *Science Digest* 49 (April 1961): 6–7.

30. "Toward a 'Sperm Bank,'" *Newsweek* (18 April 1966): 101. Expert S. J. Behrman noted, "The day when we can preserve the sperm, the life cells, of an Einstein or a Beethoven for reproduction in future centuries is a long way off" in Hugh Wray-McCann, "Fatherhood in Deep Freeze," *Science Digest* 60 (14 July 1966): 14. Of course, Beethoven suffered from deafness and probably would not have qualified as a sperm donor!

31. Hannah Lees, "Born to Order," *Collier's* (April 1946): 20. For other descriptions of "superior" AID children see J. D. Ratcliff, "Are These the Most Loved Children?" *Women's Home Companion* 82 (March 1955): 46–47, 51, 54, 56.

32. See Behrman and Ackerman, "Freeze Preservation."

33. S. Leon Isreal, in "Discussion," following reprint of Behrman and Ackerman's lecture in "Freeze Preservation": 662.

34. Isreal, "Discussion," 662, and Behrman and Ackerman, "Freeze Preservation," 661.

35. During the 1970s, those who promoted cryopreservation continued to use language reminiscent of their eugenic predecessors', arguing that pregnancies—and children—produced by frozen semen were "healthier" than children produced the "usual" way, with lower rates of both miscarriage and genetic abnormalities. See Ersek, "Frozen Sperm Banks," 1365.

36. See, for example, "Domestic Relations: The Child of Artificial Insemination," *Time* 89 (14 April 1967): 79–80; "Test Tube Babies: The Controversy over Artificial Insemination," *Good Housekeeping* 166 (February 1968): 163–165; and Mark S. Frankel, "Human-Semen Banking: Implications for Medicine and Society," *Connecticut Medicine* 39 (May 1975): 313–317.

37. The number of 300 in 1972 was reported by Robert A. Ersek, "Frozen Sperm Banks," 1365. The number of 500 was reported by Mark S. Frankel, "Role of Semen Cryobanking in American Medicine," *British Medical Journal* (7 September 1974): 619–621. The number of 1,000 in 1977 was reported by Warren G. Sander and James D. Eisen, "Cryogenically Preserved Human Semen: Clinical Applications," *Nebraska Medical Journal* (December 1977): 422.

38. Rudi Ansbacher, "Artificial Insemination with Frozen Spermatozoa," *Fertility and Sterility* 29 (April 1978): 378.

39. Amnon David and Dalia Avidan, "Artificial Insemination Donor: Clinical and Psychological Aspects," *Fertility and Sterility* 27 (May 1976): 528–532; quotes from 531, 532.

40. David and Avidan, "Artificial Insemination Donor," 531, 532.

41. David and Avidan, "Artificial Insemination Donor," 532.

42. W. Leslie, G. Quinlivan, and Herlinda Sullivan, "The Immunologic Effects of Husband's Semen on Donor Spermatozoa during Mixed Insemination," *Fertility and Sterility* 28 (April 1977): 448–450.

43. Joseph Barkay and Henryk Zuckerman, "Further Developed Device for Human Sperm Freezing by the Twenty-Minute Method," *Fertility and Sterility* 29 (March 1978): 304–308. See image of instrument on 305.

44. Roy Witherington, John B. Black, and Armand M. Karow Jr., "Semen Cryopreservation: An Update," *Journal of Urology* 118 (1977): 510.

45. Witherington et al., "Semen Cryopreservation," 510.

46. As Mary Douglass points out in *Purity and Danger: An Analysis of the Concepts of Pollution and Taboo* (New York: Routledge and Kegan Paul, 1966).

47. The historical practice of human slavery, in the United States, was justified on the grounds that slaves were less than human and thus exempt from such prohibitions.

48. Lewis Hyde argues: "It is the cardinal difference between gift and commodity exchange that a gift establishes a feeling-bond between two people, while the sale of a commodity leaves no necessary connection"; *The Gift: Imagination and the Erotic Life of Property* (New York: Vintage, 1983): 56; or as Elizabeth Anderson has stated: The "gift exchange affirms and perpetuates the ties that

bind the donor and the recipient"; *Value in Ethics and Economics* (Cambridge, MA: Harvard University Press, 1993): 151. See also Margaret Jane Radin, *Contested Commodities* (Cambridge, MA: Harvard University Press, 1996).

49. Richard M. Titmuss, *The Gift Relationship: From Human Blood to Social Policy* (London: Pantheon, 1971); Viviana Zelizer, *Pricing the Priceless Child: The Changing Social Value of Children* (New York: Basic Books, 1985); and Janet Golden, "From Commodity to Gift: Gender, Class and the Meaning of Breast Milk in the Twentieth Century," *Historian* 59 (1996): 75–87. For a discussion of the international marketing of plasma, see Gilbert M. Gaul, "The Blood Brokers—America: The OPEC of the Global Plasma Industry," *Philadelphia Inquirer* (28 September 1989) at www.bloodbank.com/part-3 .html (accessed 2/17/02) and Douglas Starr, *Blood: An Epic History of Medicine and Commerce* (New York: Alfred A. Knopf, 1998), esp. 207–265.

50. See Golden, "From Commodity to Gift."

51. Radin, *Contested Commodities*, and A. Appadurai, ed., *The Social Life of Things: Commodities in Cultural Perspective* (Philadelphia: University of Pennsylvania Press, 1986).

52. The poem, titled "Seminal Gelation," is by L. Fred Ayvazian and first appeared in *New England Journal of Medicine* 279 (1968): 436. It is quoted by S. J. Behrman in an exchange over ethical objections to sperm banking in Behrman and Ackerman, "Freeze Preservation of Human Sperm," 664.

53. New England Cryogenics reports successful use of semen after 20 years of cryopreservation.

54. In 1996, the federal government issued guidelines for tissue banks to prevent the spread of HIV: "Guidelines for Preventing Transmission of Human Immunodeficiency Virus through Transplantation of Human Tissue and Organs," *Federal Register* (Health Care Financing Administration, Department of Health and Human Services, Appendix A to Subpart G of Part 486, effective 2 May 1996).

55. S. J. Berhman, "Artificial Insemination," in *Progress in Infertility*, 2nd ed., ed. S. J. Berhman and Robert W. Kistner (Boston: Little Brown, 1975): 785. For a popular discussion of this, see Wray-McCann, "Fatherhood in Deep Freeze." Both frozen and fresh donor semen were better than homologous or AIH in terms of pregnancy rates. See also Mark S. Frankel, "Human-Semen Banking," who suggested, "With an increase in commercial frozen-semen banks, the country may witness an increasing commercialization of semen-donor relationships" (p. 315).

56. The full name of the organization was the Herman J. Muller Repository for Germinal Choice. Muller was deceased, and his widow objected to the name, according to Kevles, *In the Name of Eugenics*, 262–263. It opened in 1971 but did not begin collecting donations until several years later. R. B. Brenner, "Sperm Repository, Marking 10th Year, Still Has Same Goal—Genius," *San Diego Union-Tribune* (22 July 1990) [LNAU]. By 1990, there were no longer any Nobelists among the twenty anonymous donors whose sperm was stored in the facility. The repository ultimately closed its doors.

57. The popular press reported such openings in feature news stories. For instance, see "Sperm Banks: Fatherhood on Ice," *Chicago Tribune* (18 November 1972) [LNAU], and "Bad Seed: How Sperm Bank Lost Its Deposits," *San Francisco Chronicle* (27 June 1971 and 18 July 1975) [LNAU]. By the end of 1973, there were reported to be sixteen U.S. sperm banks, including three major commercial banks with a combined total of seven branch offices. For instance, IDANT Corporation opened sperm banks in four cities: New York, Baltimore, Ann Arbor, and Minneapolis in 1973. See Frankel, "Role of Semen Cryobanking."

58. John K. Critser estimated that 135 semen banks were in operation in the United States in 1989 (defined as a facility providing anonymous donor samples). See John K. Critser, "Current Status of Semen Banking in the USA," *Human Reproduction* 13 (Suppl. 2, 1998): 55–66.

59. M. Curie-Cohen, L. Luttrell, and S. Shapiro, "Current Practice of Artificial Insemination by Donor in the United States," *New England Journal of Medicine* 300 (1979): 585–590; and Office of Technology Assessment (OTA), Congress of the United States, *Artificial Insemination Practice in the United States. Summary of a 1987 Survey. Background Paper* (Washington, D.C.: Office of Technology Assessment, Congressional Board of the 100th Congress, U.S. Congress, 1988). Also see G. M. Centola, "American Organization of Sperm Banks" in *Donor Insemination*, ed. C. L. R. Barratt and I. D. Cooke (Cambridge: Cambridge University Press, 1993), 143–151.

60. G. J. Stewart, J. P. Tyler, A. L. Cunningham, J. A. Barr, G. L. Driscoll, J. Gold, and B. J. Lamont, "Transmission of Human T-Cell Lymphotropic Virus Type III (STLV-III) by Artificial Insemination by Donor," *Lancet* 2 (14 September 1985): 581–585.

61. M. A. Chiasson, R. L. Stoneburner, and S. C. Joseph, "Human Immunodeficiency Virus Transmission through Artificial Insemination," *Journal of Acquired Immune Deficiency Syndrome* 3 (1990): 69–72; M. R. Araneta, L.

Mascola, A. Eller, L. O'Neil, M. M. Ginsberg, M. Bursaw, J. Marik, S. Friedman, C. A. Sims, M. L. Rekart, et al., "HIV Transmission through Donor Artificial Insemination," *Journal of the American Medical Association* 273 (March 1995): 854–858.

62. Critser, "Current Status of Semen Banking in the USA."

63. Interviews with BioGenetics director Albert Anouna (interview with C. Daniels, 3/27/01) and New England Cryobank director John R. Rizza (interview with C. Daniels, 10/24/01).

64. Seven were in California, three in New York and three in Minnesota. The remaining banks were scattered across the country, including the states of Washington, Ohio, New Jersey, Colorado, Massachusetts, Utah, Georgia, Illinois, Louisiana, Indiana, Virginia, Missouri, and Arizona.

65. The one sperm bank to decline provides donor information only after a potential client has filed a "matching" form, which the bank then uses to select an "appropriate" sperm donor.

66. These banks were California Cryobank (168), New England Cryogenic Center (120), Fairfax Cryo (119), Cryobiology-OH (96), and Cryogenic Labs (90).

67. Most sperm banks do not because the procedure cannot guarantee the sex of the child, only improve the odds of having one sex over the other.

68. See www.sperm1.com/biogenetics/faq.html (2001).

69. Park Avenue Fertility Center in New York City.

70. Fairfax Cryobank.

71. See, for instance, Swedish Medical in the state of Washington. Only two banks recognized that "hispanic" is not a racial category, listing a number of donors as Caucasian/hispanic.

72. Racial breakdown of donors and U.S. population:

Racial Categories	Numbers	Percentage	U.S. Population Percentage
White	1,038	80	71
Asian	106	8	4
Mixed	62	5	N/A
Black	62	5	12
Hispanic	30	2	12
All	1,298	100	99

The U.S. population percentages are estimates for November 2000, based on the *1990 U.S. Population Census*, available at http://factfinder.census.gov/

servlet/DatasetMainPageServlet?_program=DEC&_lang=en. These are rough estimates, as the categories used by sperm banks are not coterminous with those used by the U.S. Census. For instance, the U.S. Census estimates that 0.7 % of the U.S. population is "American Indian, Eskimo, or Aleut, not Hispanic," and donors in these categories may be listed by sperm banks as "others" or "mixed" race.

73. From the U.S. Census Bureau, *Population Estimates Program*, Population Division, 2002.

74. On donor insemination demands among African Americans, see Marsh and Ronner, *Empty Cradle*, which suggests at one point that many sought treatment.

75. Although the selection of donors by ethnicity may reflect the consumer's use of this categorization as a proxy for "looking like" the preferred type of partner, the use of religion is more puzzling. No one has ever claimed religion is a heritable characteristic. Bank directors report that religious affiliation is most important for Jewish recipients.

76. Cryobank (2001).

77. These are Fairfax Cryo in Virginia and Procreative Technologies in St. Louis.

78. On the complexity of heritability of simple human traits, see H. Eldon Sutton and Robert P. Wagner, *Genetics: A Human Concern* (New York: Macmillan, 1985).

79. Northwest Andrology and Cryobank.

80. To be accredited by the American Association of Tissue Banks (AATB), the only professional organization conducting inspections of sperm banks, a bank must reject gay donors. Although only seven banks are accredited, most others follow the standards set by AATB. The American Society for Reproductive Medicine (ASRM, formerly the American Fertility Society) also recommends against the use of semen from gay donors, as a "high risk" group for HIV transmission. The FDA is currently considering regulations that would impose a federal ban on the use of semen from gay donors. See "Suitability Determination for Donors of Human Cellular and Tissue-Based Products," *Federal Register* (Department of Health and Human Services, Food and Drug Administration, 9 January 2001).

81. Some banks provide consumers with reproductive questionnaires to determine their priority of desired traits. The consumer questionnaire provided by the Swedish Medical Center in Washington State puts it most

bluntly: "How important is race to you? Very important? Somewhat important? Not important?" "How important is hair color? Hair texture? Eye color? Complexion?"

82. According to the 2000 CDC Growth Charts, this is median height for a male at age twenty; National Center for Health Statistics, Centers for Disease Control at www.cdc.gov/nchs (2/10/02).

83. As reported in Beth Ann Krier, "King of the Anonymous Fathers," *Los Angeles Times* (21 April 1989): 10.

84. As indicated by Daniels's interviews with the directors of New England Cryobank, BioGenetics, and Cambridge/California Cryobank.

85. Anouna interview, 3/27/01.

86. The CDC also publishes growth charts for use by the medical profession in monitoring the growth of children and adolescents. These charts go only to age twenty, and it may not be appropriate to use these measures with respect to evaluating weight range. See CDC, *2 to 20 years: Boys Body Mass Index-for-Age Percentiles* (2000) at www.cdc.gov/growthcharts.

87. www.cdc.gov/nchs/data/hus/tables/2003/03hus068.pdf.

88. This study also found 51% of all young men (20–34 years) to be of healthy weight (compared with donors at 65%), 33% of all young men to be overweight (compared with donors at 29%), and 14% to be obese (compared with donors at 6%). These categories are defined by the CDC as: Underweight: BMI of <18.5; Healthy weight: BMI of 18.5 to <25; Overweight: BMI of 25 or over; Obese: BMI of 30 or over. See www.cdc.gov/nchs/data/hus/tables/2003/03hus068.pdf.

89. The CDC publishes percentile charts on stature for use by health professionals. The guidelines go through age twenty; although weight would continue to change with age, height at age twenty can reasonably be considered as a man's full adult height. See CDC, *2 to 20 years: Boys Stature-for-Age and Weight-for-age Percentiles* (2000) at www.cdc.gov/growthcharts.

90. In the sample of donors, twenty-one of twenty-seven sperm banks provided information on level of education achieved. The three banks that did not provide this information were IDANT Laboratories, Sperm Bank of California, and—surprisingly—Heredity Choice. This affected a total of seventy records in our database.

91. This included Egypt, Iran, the Gulf countries, Indonesia, Jordan, Lebanon, Morocco, Malaysia, Pakistan, and Turkey. Sperm donation is also

prohibited in Japan, Norway, and Taiwan. Although most Christian religions prohibit sperm donation, countries that are dominated by the Catholic Church, including Spain and Italy, still permit sperm donation. D. Meirow and J. G. Schenker, "The Current Status of Sperm Donation in Assisted Reproduction Technology: Ethical and Legal Considerations," *Journal of Assisted Reproduction and Genetics* 14 (March 1997): 134.

92. Some countries allow donors to restrict the categories of recipients who may receive their sperm, such as older women or lesbian women. See Meirow and Schenker, "The Current Status of Sperm Donation," 136.

93. Two professional associations in the United States currently provide voluntary health, safety, and (minimal) ethical guidelines for sperm banks to follow: The American Society for Reproductive Medicine (ASRM; formerly known as the American Fertility Society) and the American Association of Tissue Banks (AATB). The ASRM offers a set of voluntary guidelines that banks may follow, and the AATB offers formal accreditation of sperm banks for a fee.

94. In 1988, the Congressional Office of Technology Assessment (OTA) found that donor testing was severely deficient, particularly when physicians obtained their own donors rather than using sperm banks. By 1990, lawsuits had been successfully brought against sperm banks accused of transmitting infectious diseases to artificially inseminated women through "tainted" sperm. In 1990, a woman who claimed to have been infected with a herpes-like virus through artificial insemination in 1986 settled out of court with the accused sperm bank (the Fertility Center of California) for $450,000. See Associated Press, "Lawsuit over Infection Settled by Sperm Bank," *Los Angeles Times* (2 November 1990): 9B.

95. Sperm banks vary in their restrictions on tattooing and piercing for sperm donors, with many prohibiting donation by those who have had either done within the preceding twelve months, as they consider this to place the donor at higher risk of infection from HIV and other blood-borne infections. Most sperm banks follow the recommendations of the AATB regarding this ruling.

96. In addition, the ASRM guidelines recommend that donors be between the ages of 18 and 40 and that, because of potential ethical conflicts, no lab owner or physician performing the service provide donor semen. To minimize the risks of consanguinity—half-brothers and half-sisters unknowingly produc-

ing children together—the ASRM guidelines also recommend that donors be allowed to contribute to no more than twenty-five pregnancies in a total population area of 800,000. In the donor selection process, the ASRM also recommends: "The couple should be encouraged to list the characteristics that they desire in a prospective donor, including race, and/or ethnic group, height, body build, complexion, eye color, and hair color and texture." ASRM, "Guidelines for Gamete and Embryo Donation," at www.asrm.org.

97. ASRM, "Guidelines," 16 of 21.

98. In 1996, the American Association of Tissue Banks, the professional association representing those working in the field of tissue donation (including internal organs, cornea, etc.) initiated an inspection and accreditation program for tissue banks, including sperm banks. The AATB standards essentially mirror the ASRM's, requiring the use of only frozen semen and the health screening and testing of sperm donors. In addition to the health standards set out by ASRM, the AATB also requires banks to screen donors for educational and occupational background, personal drug and alcohol use, interests, talents, attitudes, and general reliability as potential donors. See Critser, "Current Status," 63.

99. AATB, "Ethical Guidelines for Commercial Activities and Advertising," at www.aatb.org.

100. AATB, "Statement of Ethical Principles," at www.aatb.org.

101. Despite the market advantages that one might think accreditation would bring to a sperm bank, by the year 2001 only seven U.S. sperm banks had undergone AATB accreditation. Accredited banks are Andrology Lab (Cleveland, OH), BioGenetics (NJ), California Cryobank (Los Angeles), Cryobiology, Inc. (Columbus, OH), Cryogenic Labs (MN), IDANT Corporation (New York), and New York Cryobank (Great Neck, NY). Source: American Association of Tissue Banks; E-mail correspondence with C. R. Daniels (March 22, 2000).

102. State of New York, *Public Health Law*, Section 4365, Part 52, "Tissue Banks and Nontransplant Anatomic Banks," Subpart 52–8, 26.

103. State of New York, *Public Health Law*, "Tissue Banks," 66.

104. In an interesting admission of the damage that could be transmitted to the fetus through paternal exposures to toxins, New York State (as well as both ASRM and AATB) also restricts donations from men who work with or have a history of working with radiation or chemical exposures or men with a

history of alcohol abuse. Because of increased risks of birth defects from older men, New York regulations also discourage the use of semen from donors over age forty-four. State of New York, *Public Health Law,* "Tissue Banks," 66.

105. Associated Press, "44% of Doctors Report Tests for AIDS on Donated Semen," *New York Times* (11 August 1988), [LNOS].

106. FDA, "Suitability Determination for Donors of Human Cellular and Tissue-Based Products," 21 CFR Parts 210, 211, 820, 1271, Docket #97N-484S.

107. Anouna interview, 3/27/01.

108. Some members of the AATB appear to welcome such standards. As an AATB news bulletin puts it, "Mandatory registration would also force any small irregular operations to acknowledge their participation in a regulated activity." See FDA, "Suitability Determination," 39/52711. See also AATB, "FDA Final Rule: Registration and Listing," AATB Information Alert XI (January 18, 2001) at www.aatb.org. For final FDA regulations, see "Eligibility Determination for Donors of Human Cells, Tissues, and Cellular and Tissue-Based Products," *Federal Register,* 21 CFR Parts 210, 211, 820, and 1271, May 25, 2004.

109. As this objection was put by the National Center for Lesbian Rights: "It remains our concern that the guidance will simply adopt, as to sperm donors, the 1994 CDC guidelines, which ban any men who have had sex with men (MSM) within the preceding five years from being blood or tissue donors. The designation of MSMs as unsuitable donors operates regardless of the results of any HIV test, the sexual behavior of the potential donor and with no accounting for the fact that the blood of the donor can be tested, and that semen, unlike other types of tissue, can be stored in quarantine for six months until the donor is retested. Simply put, we believe that the guidance should not designate MSMs as unsuitable sperm donors without adequate scientific support." See www.fda.gov/ohrms/dockets/dailys/00/jan00/010500/emc0019.rtf.

110. FDA, "Eligibility Determination," 29806.

111. If we widen the lens, we can see that the state only selectively maintains principles of reproductive liberty and that these are skewed by gender. Since the 1980s, the state has increasingly burdened women's right to abortion. The state has also restricted the development of new contraceptives for women, like RU 486, and has provided only limited support for male con-

traceptives that might free women from the primary responsibility for birth control. See Nelly Oudshoorn, *The Male Pill: A Biography of a Technology in the Making* (Durham, NC: Duke University Press, 2003).

112. David Blankenhorn, *Fatherless America* (New York: Basic Books, 1995), 171–172.

113. Perhaps this is compensation for the ancient male uncertainty of paternity—"mother's baby, father's maybe"—which, until the advent of artificial insemination, could never be certain.

114. This term was developed by famed British eugenicist Herbert Brewer in the 1930s. See Kevles, *In the Name of Eugenics*, and Daniel J. Kevles, "Brave New Biology: The Dreams of Eugenics," http://invisible.gq.nu/wake/texts/BRAVENEWBIOLOGY.html (accessed 5/21/03).

115. Kevles, "Brave New Biology," 5.

116. See Marilyn Strathern, "Displacing Knowledge: Technology and the Consequences for Kinship," in *Conceiving the New World Order*, ed. Faye D. Ginsburg and Rayna Rapp (Berkeley: University of California Press, 1995), 346–364.

CHAPTER 5

1. Gladys Friedler, telephone interview with C. Daniels (13 February 2001).

2. Gladys Friedler, telephone interview with C. Daniels (7 February 2001).

3. Friedler interview (13 February 2001).

4. Friedler interview (13 February 2001).

5. Friedler interview (7 February 2001).

6. Laws 6:775, quoted by Ernest L. Abel, "Paternal Exposure to Alcohol," in *Perinatal Substance Abuse*, ed. T. B. Sonderegger (Baltimore: Johns Hopkins University Press, 1992), 133.

7. Gladys Friedler, "Paternal Exposures: Impact on Reproductive and Developmental Outcome: An Overview," *Pharmacology Biochemistry and Behavior* 55 (1996): 691–700.

8. The "gin epidemic" refers to England between 1720 and 1751, when gin became very cheap and gin consumption increased from 2 million to 11 million gallons per year, spurring a series of social reforms aimed at limiting alcohol consumption, particularly by the poor and working classes. See T. G. Coffey, "Beer Street: Gin Lane; Some Views of 18th Century Drinking," *Quarterly Journal of Studies on Alcohol* 27 (1966): 669–692; Ernest L.

Abel, "Gin Lane: Did Hogarth Know about Fetal Alcohol Syndrome?" *Alcohol and Alcoholism* 36 (2001): 131–134.

9. Janet Golden and Cynthia R. Daniels, "The Politics of Paternity: Fetal Risks and Reproductive Responsibility," in *Current Issues in Law and Medicine 3*, ed. M. Freeman (London: Oxford University Press, 2000), 363–378.

10. Young male chimney sweeps were often lowered into chimneys to clean them, resulting in higher levels of scrotal skin cancer. The study resulted in one of the earliest health and safety reforms in requiring cleaning facilities for chimney sweeps. See Steven M. Schrader, R. E. Chapin, E. D. Clegg, R. O Davis, J. L. Fourcroy, D. F. Katz, S. A. Rothmann, G. Toth, T. W. Turner, and M. Zinaman, "Laboratory Methods for Assessing Human Semen in Epidemiological Studies: A Consensus Report," *Reproductive Toxicology* 6 (1992): 275–279.

11. Even though these reports suggested effects on both men and women, only women were banned from the lead trades. See Susan M. Barlow and Frank M. Sullivan, *Reproductive Hazards of Industrial Chemicals: An Evaluation of Animal and Human Data* (New York: Academic Press, 1982).

12. Barlow and Sullivan, *Reproductive Hazards*; Schrader et al., "Laboratory Methods."

13. This research, although muted, was never entirely absent. For instance, see references in Friedler, "Paternal Exposures," for a few studies continuing from the 1950s through the 1970s.

14. Hales and Robaire report that their early research proposals on male-mediated toxicity were rejected by funders because they believed that sperm were "forever young." Not recognized was the ways in which the aging of stem cells, which produce sperm, might produce more defects as men age. Barbara Hales and Bernard Robaire, interviews with C. Daniels (23 June 2001).

15. E. J. Burger, R. G. Tardiff, A. R. Scialli, and H. Zenick, ed., *Sperm Measures and Reproductive Success* (New York: Alan R. Liss, 1989).

16. See Emily Martin, "The Egg and the Sperm: How Science Has Constructed a Romance Based on Stereotypical Male-Female Roles," *Signs: Journal of Women in Culture and Society* 16 (1991): 485–501.

17. Robin Baker and Mark A. Bellis, "'Kamikaze' Sperm in Mammals?" *Animal Behaviour* 36 (1988): 936–939; Mark Bellis and Robin Baker, "Do Females Promote Sperm Competition? Data for Humans," *Animal Behaviour*

40 (1990): 997–999; and G. A. Parker, "Sperm Competition and Its Evolutionary Consequences in the Insects," *Biological Review* 45 (1970): 525–567.

18. As quoted by Meredith Small, "Sperm Wars," *Discover* (July 1991): 50. Publications as diverse as *Cell, Esquire,* and the *New York Times* share accounts that impart a consciousness to sperm. The "kamikaze" and "sperm competition" theories of Bellis and Baker suggest that sperm collaborate and compete as fraternity "brothers" or "enemies." One article in the *New York Times* reporting Bellis and Baker's research suggested that kamikaze sperm are "self-sacrificing" as they "commit suicide" for the good of the group. In part, this characterization was generated directly from reports in scientific journals. For instance, in an article in *Cell,* Bennett Shapiro suggests that sperm face three existential dilemmas in reproduction—whether to swim, whether to pursue an egg, and whether to fertilize an egg—all of which shorten the "life span" of the sperm. Popularized accounts of Shapiro's theory capitalized on his imagery, suggesting that human sperm were faced with the ultimate question, "Do I give up my autonomy and individuality for the chance to fertilize an egg, or do I spurn responsibility and lead an independent and happy-go-lucky—but meaningless—existence?" Bennett M. Shapiro, "The Existential Decision of a Sperm," *Cell* 49 (1987): 293–294.

19. Small, "Sperm Wars," 50.

20. Small, "Sperm Wars," 50.

21. George Mason, "Female Infidelity—May the Best Sperm Win," *New Scientist* (January 1991): 29; and Bellis and Baker, "Do Females Promote Sperm Competition?" 997. Multiple mating, Bellis and Baker argue, is most useful when a female is "unable to judge ejaculate quality from a male's appearance."

22. Small, "Sperm Wars," 51.

23. Carol Cohn has documented the extensive use of sexual metaphors in military planning for nuclear war. Apparently, the reverse is also true. Carol Cohn, "'Clean Bombs' and Clean Language," in *Women, Militarism and War,* ed. Jean Bethke Elshtain and Sheila Tobias (Savage, MD: Rowman and Littlefield, 1990), 35–56.

24. Small, "Sperm Wars," 53.

25. Small, "Sperm Wars," 49. In fact, when fertility researchers began to develop a method of piercing the outer layer or zona pellucida of a fertile egg to assist the sperm in penetration, some scientists feared this might increase the

chance of birth defects in offspring because "immobile or feeble sperm—which normally don't stand much chance of penetrating the egg's inner sanctum—might be more likely to harbor serious DNA mutations than their more vigorous counterparts" (Richard D. Amelar of New York University, quoted in Kathy A. Fackelmann, "Zona Blasters: There's More Than One Way to Crack an Egg," *Science News* 138 [15 December 1990]: 376–379).

26. Ernest L. Abel, interview with C. Daniels (24 January 2001).

27. Abel interview (24 January 2001).

28. Abel interview (24 January 2001).

29. Able interview (24 January 2001).

30. Bernard Robaire, interview with C. Daniels (23 June 2001).

31. Robaire interview (23 June 2001).

32. Ellen Silbergeld, interview with C. Daniels (22 June 2001).

33. Silbergeld interview (22 June 2001).

34. Shapiro, "The Existential Decision of a Sperm."

35. D. Ralt, M. Goldenberg, P. Fetterolf, D. Thompson, J. Dor, S. Mashiach, D. L. Garbers, and M. Eisenbach, "Sperm Attraction to a Follicular Factor(s) Correlates with Human Egg Fertilizability," *Proceedings of the National Academy of Sciences* 88 (1991): 2840–2844.

36. C. Ezzell, "Eggs Not Silent Partners in Conception," *Science News* 139 (1991): 214.

37. N. Angier, "Genetic Mutation Tied to Father in Most Cases," *New York Times* (17 May 1994): C12.

38. S. Blakeslee, "Research on Birth Defects Shifts to Flaws in Sperm," *New York Times* (January 1991): A1.

39. Martin, "The Egg and the Sperm."

40. Thomas H. Maugh II, "Protein's Discovery May Aid Birth Control," *Chicago Sun-Times* (19 March 1992): 3.

41. Emily Martin has noted that scientists confronted with this new evidence in the late 1980s vacillated between a model that emphasized the egg as seductress and the more mutual paradigm of sperm-egg fusion. See Martin, "The Egg and the Sperm."

42. Yet a mutual picture of procreation did not necessarily lessen women's culpability for fetal harm. In the "aggressive egg" model, women were once again at fault for seducing, if not "bad men," then at least "bad sperm." Although potentially drawing men into the circle of causality with women,

cultural constructions embedded in scientific magazines and newspaper stories continued to lay the blame at women's door.

43. As cited by Friedler, "Paternal Exposures," 691.

44. Rafael Moure, telephone interview with C. Daniels (25 January 2001).

45. James C. Robinson, *Toil and Toxics: Workplace Struggles and Political Strategies for Occupational Health* (Berkeley: University of California Press, 1991); Ted Schettler, Gina Solomon, Maria Valenti, and Annette Huddle, *Generations at Risk: Reproductive Health and the Environment* (Cambridge, MA: MIT Press, 1999), 122.

46. *Federal Register* 43(53)—Friday March 17, 1978. Title 29–Labor, Chapter XVII—Occupational Safety and Health Administration, Department of Labor, Part 1910—Occupational Safety and Health Standards, Occupational Exposure to 1,2–Dibromo-3–Chloropropane (DBCP), [4510–26] 11514–11520.

47. *Federal Register* 43(53) Title 29—Labor, Chapter XVII, 11514.

48. Moure Interview (25 January 2001).

49. *Federal Register* 43(53) Title 29—Labor, Chapter XVII, 11515.

50. *Federal Register* 43(53) Title 29—Labor, Chapter XVII, 11514.

51. Moure interview (25 January 2001).

52. Moure interview (25 January 2001).

53. *Federal Register* 43(53) Title 29–Labor, Chapter XVII, 11514.

54. M. Donald Whorton, "Male Occupational Reproductive Hazards," in *Occupational Medicine*, 3rd ed., ed. Carl Zenz, O. Bruce Dickerson, and Edward P. Hovarth (St. Louis, MO: Mosby-Year Book, 1994), 871.

55. M. Kharrazi, G. Patashnik, and J. R. Goldsmith, "Reproductive Effects of Dibromochloropropane," *Israel Journal of Medical Science* 6 (1980): 403–406; risk ratio of 3.0; 95% CI, 1.3–7.0 (as analyzed by David A. Savitz, Nancy L. Sonnenfeld, and Andrew F. Olshan, "Review of Epidemiologic Studies of Paternal Occupational Exposure and Spontaneous Abortion," *American Journal of Industrial Medicine* 25 [1994]: 361–383, Table V, p. 371).

56. Schettler et al., *Generations at Risk*, 123; Schettler et al. report positive associations but do not evaluate the strengths of these associations.

57. Laura Oren, "Protection, Patriarchy, and Capitalism: The Politics and Theory of Gender-Specific Regulation in the Workplace," *UCLA Women's Law Journal* 6 (Spring 1996): 349.

58. As quoted by Oren, "Protection, Patriarchy, and Capitalism," 351.

59. Jeanne Stellman, interview with C. Daniels (22 March 2001).

60. While achieving only limited political success, the coalition represented the first organized effort to defend the reproductive health of both men and women at work and generated new interest in research specifically on the reproductive effects on men. See Oren, "Protection, Patriarchy, and Capitalism," 351.

61. H. Lancranjan, I. Popescu, O. Gavanescu, I. Klepsch, and M. Serbanescu, "Reproductive Ability of Workmen Occupationally Exposed to Lead," *Archives of Environmental Health* 30 (1975): 396–401.

62. Jeanne Stellman, telephone interview with C. Daniels (21 March 2001).

63. 29 U.S.C. 654 (a)(1).

64. As quoted by Jane Terry, "Conflict of Interest: Protection of Women from Reproductive Hazards in the Workplace," *Industrial and Labor Relations Forum* 15 (1981): 48.

65. See Wendy Williams, "Firing the Woman to Protect the Fetus: The Reconciliation of Fetal Protection with Employment Opportunity Goals under Title VII," *Georgetown Law Journal* 69 (1981): 641–704; and Lisa J. Raines and Stephen P. Push, "Protecting Pregnant Workers," *Harvard Business Review* (May–June, 1986): 26–30.

66. In 1982, the Johnson Controls Company had instituted a policy nearly identical to American Cyanamid's in its battery production plant in Bennington, Vermont. See *UAW v. Johnson Controls*, 111 S.Ct. 1196 (1991), and Cynthia R. Daniels, *At Women's Expense: State Power and the Politics of Fetal Rights* (Cambridge, MA: Harvard University Press, 1993), chapter 3, for a more complete analysis of the Johnson Controls case.

67. In addition to the DBCP scandal, a number of other environmental disasters in the 1970s brought reproductive hazards to public attention. In Minamata and Niigata, Japan, the public waters were heavily contaminated with mercury from industrial pollution. Adults began to die from the poisoning, and the rate of severe birth defects skyrocketed. In Seveso, Italy, an explosion at a chemical plant released clouds of dioxin into the local town, producing illness and birth defects in those exposed (Barlow and Sullivan, *Reproductive Hazards*, 3).

68. D. L. Davis, G. Friedler, D. Mattison, and R. Morris, "Male-Mediated Teratogenesis and Other Reproductive Effects: Biological and Epidemiologic Findings and a Plea for Clinical Research," *Reproductive Toxicology* 6 (1992): 289–292; Friedler, "Paternal Exposures"; Schletter et al., *Generations at Risk*.

69. See Friedler, "Paternal Exposures"; Schettler et al., *Generations at Risk*.

70. W. J. Schull, M. Otake, and J. V. Neel, "Genetic Effects of the Atomic Bombs: A Reappraisal," *Science* 213 (1987): 1220–1227.

71. Y. Yoshimoto, "Cancer Risk among Children of Atomic Bomb Survivors: A Review of RERF Epidemiologic Studies," *Journal of the American Medical Association* 264 (1990): 596–600; A. F. Olshan and E. M. Faustman, "Male-Mediated Developmental Toxicity," *Reproductive Toxicology* 7 (1993): 191–202; Friedler, "Paternal Exposures," 696.

72. M. J. Gardner, M. P. Snee, A. J. Hall, C. A. Powell, S. Downes, and J. D. Terrell, "Results of Case-Control Study of Leukaemia and Lymphoma among Young People near Sellafield Nuclear Plant in West Cumbria," *British Medical Journal* 300 (17 February 1990): 423–429.

73. This study showed an odds ratio of 1.25 for stillbirth after 100 mSv lifetime exposure, and the odds ratio increased to 1.7 for stillbirth with a neural tube defect. See L. Parker, M. S. Pearce, H. O. Dickinson, M. Aitkin, and A. W. Craft, "Stillbirths among Offspring of Male Radiation Workers at Sellafield Nuclear Reprocessing Plant," *Lancet* 354 (23 October 1999): 1407–1414. Parker et al. tracked radiation exposures of workers from individual film badges and for annual exposure records for each worker, as well as for a control group.

74. H. Inskip, "Stillbirth and Paternal Preconceptional Radiation Exposure," *Lancet* 354 (23 October 1999): 1400–1401.

75. Schettler et al., *Generations at Risk*, 333–335. These include (solvents) epichlorohydrin, glycol ethers, percholoroethylene, styrene, toluene; (metals) cadmium; (pesticides) benomyl, dicofol dimethoate, dithiocarbamate, endosulfan, ethylene dibromide, ethylene oxide, lindane, methyl bromide, parathion; and (other) dioxin and phthalates.

76. Olshan and Faustman, "Male-Mediated Developmental Toxicity," 196.

77. Whorton, "Male Occupational Reproductive Hazards," 872. Levels of 40–70 ug/dl have produced this effect. This level is reportedly not uncommon in workplaces where lead is used in production. According to OSHA, "The best way to prevent all forms of lead-related impairments and diseases—both short term and long term—is to maintain your PbB below 40 ug/100g." See www.osha.gov/pls/oshaweb/owadisp.show_document?p_table=STANDARDS&p_id=10031.

78. Olshan and Faustman, "Male-Mediated Developmental Toxicity," 195; Schettler et al., *Generations at Risk*.

79. Whorton, "Male Occupational Reproductive Hazards," 872.

80. Schettler et al., *Generations at Risk*.

81. D. S. Rupa, P. P. Reddy, and O. S. Reddi, "Reproductive Performance in Population Exposed to Pesticides in Cotton Fields in India," *Environmental Research* 55 (1991): 123–128.

82. Schettler et al., *Generations at Risk*, 117, 119.

83. E. N. Cohen, B. W. Brown, M. L. Wu, C. D. Whitcher, J. B. Brodsky, H. C. Gift, W. Greenfield, T. W. Jones, and E. J. Driscoll, "Occupational Disease in Dentistry and Chronic Exposure to Trace Anesthetic Gases," *Journal of the American Dental Association* 101 (1980): 21–31; P. H. Rosenberg and H. Van Hinen, "Occupational Hazards to Reproduction and Health in Anaesthetists and Paediatricians," *Acta Anaesthesiology Scandinavia* 22 (1978): 202–207.

84. Olshan and Faustman, "Male-Mediated Developmental Toxicity," 196.

85. C. F. Colie, "Male Mediated Teratogenesis," *Reproductive Toxicology* 7 (1993): 7.

86. D. A. Savitz and J. Chen, "Parental Occupation and Childhood Cancer: Review of Epidemiological Studies," *Environmental Health Perspectives* 88 (1990): 325–337.

87. See Andrew Olshan and Edwin van Wijngaarden, "Paternal Occupation and Childhood Cancer," in *Advances in Male Mediated Developmental Toxicity*, ed. Bernard Robaire and Barbara F. Hales (New York: Kluwer Academic, 2003), 147–162.

88. Savitz and Chen, "Parental Occupation and Childhood Cancer"; L. M. O'Leary, A. M. Hicks, J. M. Peters, and S. London, "Parental Occupational Exposures and Risk of Childhood Cancer: A Review," *American Journal of Industrial Medicine* 20 (1991): 17–35.

89. Friedler, "Paternal Exposures," 696.

90. Quote from talk given by David Savitz at the second International Conference on Male-Mediated Developmental Toxicity, June 2001, Montreal, Canada. Also see David A. Savitz, "Paternal Exposure to Known Mutagens and Health of the Offspring: Ionizing Radiation and Tobacco Smoke" in *Advances in Male Mediated Developmental Toxicity*, ed. Bernard Robaire and Barbara F. Hales (New York: Kluwer Academic/Plenum, 2003), 49–58.

91. Quote from talk given at the second International Conference on Male-Mediated Developmental Toxicity, June 2001, Montreal, Canada. Also see Olshan and Wijngaarden, "Paternal Occupation and Childhood Cancer."

92. See J. P. Bonde, H. I. Hjollund, T. B. Henriksen, T. K. Jensen, M. Spano, H. Kolstad, A. Giwercman, L. Storgaard, E. Ernst, and J. Olsen, "Epidemiologic Evidence on Biological and Environmental Male Factors in Embryonic Loss," in *Advances in Male Mediated Developmental Toxicity*, ed. Bernard Robaire and Barbara F. Hales (New York: Kluwer Academic/Plenum, 2003), 25–36.

93. See Ellen K. Silbergeld, Betzabet Quintanilla-Vega, and Robin E. Gandley, "Mechanisms of Male Mediated Developmental Toxicity Induced by Lead," in *Advances in Male Mediated Developmental Toxicity*, ed. Bernard Robaire and Barbara F. Hales (New York: Kluwer Academic/Plenum, 2003), 37–48. See also V. M. Stowe and R. Goyer, "Reproductive Ability and Progeny of F1 Lead-Toxic Rats," *Fertility and Sterility* 22 (1971): 755–760; K. Brady, Y. Herrera, and H. Zenick, "Influence of Paternal Lead Exposure on Subsequent Learning Ability of Offspring," *Pharmacology, Biochemistry and Behavior* 3 (1975): 561–565.

94. The three substances are lead, DBCP, and ethylene oxide. The 1,000 substances identified as reproductive hazards were established in the 1994 Register of Toxic Effects of Chemical Substances. See OSHA, 2000, www.osha.gov/SLTC/reproductivehazards/standards.html.

95. Steven M. Schrader, "Towards a Safer Occupational Environment: The U.S. Approach, the Example of Glycol Ethers," *Middle East Fertility Society Journal* 3 (1998): 70.

96. State law may vary in specific negligence cases.

97. Daryl Alexander, interview with C. Daniels (16 January 2001).

98. Alexander interview (16 January 2001).

99. Theresa Schnorr, telephone interview with C. Daniels (18 January 2001).

100. Mazzocchi, as well as others in the labor movement, have worked to develop special programs to train physicians in occupational health, most notably through Yale University. Anthony Mazzocchi, interview with C. Daniels (19 January 2001).

101. As quoted by Gerald Nicosia, *Home to War* (New York: Crown, 2001), 590.

102. As quoted by Linda Kanamine, "Congress Considering Children-of-War Measure," *USA Today* (12 September 1996): 4A.

103. Earl Lane, "Study: Agent Orange Linked to Spina Bifida," *Houston Chronicle* (15 March 1996): 10.

104. Occupational health practitioners in the United States had also reported increased rates of a skin disease, chloracne, in the men who worked

producing the chemical in New Jersey in 1962. Lane, "Study: Agent Orange," 10.

105. Jan Barry, "Troubling Questions about Dioxin," *New York Times* (11 September 1983): 26.

106. Mary McGrory, "Justice for Vietnam Veterans," *Washington Post* (9 May 1989): A2.

107. S. Stellman and J. Stellman, "Health Problems among 535 Vietnam Veterans Potentially Exposed to Herbicides," *American Journal of Epidemiology* 112 (1980): 444.

108. Stellman interview (12 June 2001).

109. Clark Brooks, "Fatal Flaws: How the Military Misled Vietnam Veterans and Their Families about the Health Risks of Agent Orange," *San Diego Union-Tribune* (1 November 1998): A1.

110. McGrory, "Justice for Vietnam Veterans," A2.

111. Barry, "Troubling Questions about Dioxin," 26.

112. J. D. Erickson, J. Mulinare, P. W. McClain, T. G. Fitch, L. M. James, A. B. McClearn, and M. J. Adams Jr., "Vietnam Veterans' Risks for Fathering Babies with Birth Defects," *Journal of the American Medical Association* 252 (August 1984): 903–912. Also see, for analysis of this and other related studies, Lowell E. Sever, Tye E. Arbuckle, and Anne Sweeney, "Reproductive and Developmental Effects of Occupational Pesticide Exposure: The Epidemiologic Evidence," *Occupational Medicine: State of the Art Reviews* 12 (April–June 1997).

113. Pete Earley, "Second Federal Study; Agent Orange Risk Doubted," *Washington Post* (17 August 1984): A1.

114. Earley, "Second Federal Study," A1; McGrory, "Justice for Vietnam Veterans," A2.

115. McGrory, "Justice for Vietnam Veterans," A2.

116. Stellman interview (21 March 2001).

117. A 1999 GAO investigatory report confirmed that in "1984 and 1985, Air Force management and the White House at the time tried to direct certain aspects of the Air Force scientists' research." See U.S. General Accounting Office. "Agent Orange: Actions Needed to Improve Communications of Air Force Ranch Hand Study Data and Results," in *Report to the Ranking Minority Member Committee on Veterans Affairs*, House of Representatives (December 1999): GAO/NSIAD-00-31.

118. *Nehmer v. U.S. Veterans' Administration,* 712 F. Supp. 1404 (N.D. Cal.1989); also see USGAO, "Agent Orange."

119. For an interesting account of political manipulation of the Air Force study and the role of Zumwalt, see Brooks, "Fatal Flaws," A1.

120. Institute of Medicine, National Academy of Sciences, *Veterans and Agent Orange: Health Effects of Herbicides Used in Vietnam* (Washington, DC: National Academy Press, 1994).

121. Brooks, "Fatal Flaws," A1.

122. USGAO, "Agent Orange," 4.

123. These included non-Hodgkin's lymphoma, soft-tissue sarcoma, Hodgkin's disease, porphyria cutanea tarda (a liver disease known as PCT), multiple myeloma, and respiratory cancers of the lungs, bronchus, larynx, and trachea. Institute of Medicine, *Veterans and Agent Orange: Update 1996* (Washington, DC: National Academy Press, 1997).

124. USGAO, "Agent Orange," 5.

125. USGAO, "Agent Orange," 12.

126. Earl Lane, "Study: Agent Orange," 10.

127. See reports in Paul Richter, "Clinton Expands U.S. Benefits for Veterans Exposed to Agent Orange," *Los Angeles Times* (29 May 1996): 18; Ron Fournier, "Agent Orange Aid Expanded," *Chicago Sun-Times* (29 May 1996): 31; John F. Harris and Bill McAllister, "President Adds VA Benefits after AO Study; Prostate Cancer, Nervous Disorder Covered," *Washington Post* (29 May 1996): A01.

128. Spina bifida is a birth defect in which the backbone fails to close, allowing for possible herniation of the spinal cord.

129. As quoted by Kanamine, "Congress Considering Children-of-War Measure," 4A.

130. Philip Shenon, "Air Force Links Agent Orange to Diabetes," *New York Times* (29 March 2000): A23.

131. The specific form of leukemia is acute myelogenous leukemia (AML). David Brown, "Children's Leukemia Risk Tied to Agent Orange; Panel's Finding of Possible Causation Means Vietnam Vets' Offspring May Be Compensated," *Washington Post* (20 April 2001): A2.

132. Brown, "Children's Leukemia Risk," and Kathleen Sullivan, "Lawyers Badger VA to Help Vets Hurt by Dioxin," *San Francisco Chronicle* (11 March 2001): A17.

133. USGAO, "Agent Orange."

134. Stellman telephone interview (7 June 2001).

135. Stellman interview (21 March 2001).

136. Julie Schmit, "Countries Consider Joint Study of Agent Orange," *USA Today* (16 March 2000): 15A.

137. See J. R. Moehringer on Yorba: "Legacy of Worry," *Los Angeles Times* (22 October 1995): A3; Richard Serrano on Fayetteville: "Birth Defects in Gulf Vets' Babies Stir Fear, Debate," *Los Angeles Times* (14 November 1994): A1.1; Simon Tisdall on Mississippi: "Gulf Babies Maimed at Birth, *Guardian* (23 December 1993): Al.

138. For a more complete analysis of the science of paternally mediated fetal effects and social construction of paternal-fetal harm, see Cynthia R. Daniels, "Between Fathers and Fetuses: The Social Construction of Male Reproduction and the Politics of Fetal Harm," *Signs: Journal of Women in Culture and Society* 22 (1997): 579–616.

139. U.S. General Accounting Office, *Gulf War Illnesses*, 42, 43, and 46.

140. One study was conducted by the U.S. Department of Veteran Affairs, the Mississippi State Department of Health, and the Centers for Disease Control and Prevention. See Alan D. Penman, Russell S. Tarver, and Mary M. Currier, "No Evidence of Increase in Birth Defects and Health Problems among Children Born to Persian Gulf War Veterans in Mississippi," *Military Medicine* 161 (January 1996): 1–6. Also see David N. Cowan, Robert F. DeFraites, Gregory C. Gray, Mary B. Goldenbaum, and Samuel M. Wishik, "The Risk of Birth Defects among Children of Persian Gulf War Veterans," *New England Journal of Medicine* 336 (5 June 1997): 1650–1656.

141. U.S. General Accounting Office, *Depleted Uranium Health Effects*, U.S. GAO/ NSIAD (2000), 6.

142. USGAO, *Depleted Uranium*, 7.

143. USGAO, *Depleted Uranium*, 9; and see M. A. McDiarmid, J. P. Keogh, F. J. Hooper, K. McPhaul, K. Squibb, R. Kane, R. DiPino, M. Kabat, B. Kaup, L. Anderson, D. Hoover, L. Brown, M. Hamilton, D. Jacobson-Kram, B. Burrows, and M. Walsh, "Health Effects of Depleted Uranium on Exposed Gulf War Veterans," *Environmental Research* 82 (February 2000): 168–180.

144. Studies also continue on the 51,000 British soldiers deployed to the war, as well as the 4,500 Canadian soldiers sent to the Gulf. CBC News Online, "Pentagon Looking at Possible Cause of Gulf War Syndrome" (19 October

1999); Jim Bronskill, "Health Woes Plague Gulf War Babies," *Ottawa Citizen* (29 June 1998).

145. USGAO, *Gulf War Illnesses*, 42.

146. USGAO, *Depleted Uranium*, 13.

147. Howard M. Kipen and Nancy Fiedler, "Invited Commentary: Sensitivities to Chemicals—Context and Implications," *American Journal of Epidemiology* 150 (1999): 13–16. Quote from p. 16.

148. Stellman interview (21 March 2001).

149. As quoted by Brain S. Katcher, "The Post-Repeal Eclipse in Knowledge about the Harmful Effects of Alcohol," *Addiction* 88 (1993): 735.

150. Thomas Trotter, *An Essay, Medical, Philosophical, and Chemical, on Drunkenness, and its Effects on the Human Body* (Philadelphia: Anthony Finley, 1813), as cited in Abel, "Gin Lane," 134. As quoted by Rebecca H. Warner and Henry L. Rosett, "The Effects of Drinking on Offspring: An Historical Survey of the American and British Literature," *Journal of Studies on Alcohol* 36 (1975): 1395.

151. Ernest L. Abel, *Psychoactive Drugs and Sex* (New York: Plenum, 1985); T. B. Sonderegger, ed., *Perinatal Substance Abuse* (Baltimore: Johns Hopkins University Press, 1992); Davis et al., "Male-Mediated Teratogenesis"; Olshan and Faustman, "Male-Mediated Developmental Toxicity"; Gladys Friedler, "Developmental Toxicology: Male-Mediated Effects," in *Occupational and Environmental Reproductive Hazards*, ed. Maureen Paul (Baltimore: Williams and Wilkins, 1993), 52–59; Colie, "Male Mediated Teratogenesis"; A. F. Olshan and D. R. Mattison, *Male-Mediated Developmental Toxicity* (New York: Plenum, 1994).

152. Abel, *Psychoactive Drugs and Sex*.

153. Abel, "Paternal Exposure to Alcohol."

154. D. Savitz, P. J. Schwingle, and M. A. Keels. "Influence of Paternal Age, Smoking and Alcohol Consumption on Congenital Anomalies," *Teratology* 44 (1991): 429–440.

155. See Colie, "Male Mediated Teratogenesis"; T. J. Cicero, B. Nock, L. H. O'Connor, B. N. Sewing, M. L. Adams, and E. R. Meyer, "Acute Paternal Alcohol Exposure Impairs Fertility and Foetal Outcome in the Male Rat," *Life Sciences* 55 (1994): 901–910; Savitz et al., "Influence of Paternal Age."

156. Savitz et al., "Influence of Paternal Age."

157. Jun Zhang and Jennifer Ratcliffe, "Paternal Smoking and Birthweight in Shanghai," *American Journal of Public Health* 83 (1993): 207–210; Fernando

Martinez, Anne Wright, Lynn Taussig, and Group Health Medical Associates, "The Effect of Paternal Smoking on the Birthweight of Newborns Whose Mothers Did Not Smoke," *American Journal of Public Health* 84 (1994): 1489–1491.

158. D. Savitz and D. P. Sandler, "Prenatal Exposure to Parents' Smoking and Childhood Cancer," *American Journal of Epidemiology* 133 (1991): 123–132; D. L. Davis, "Paternal Smoking and Fetal Health," *Lancet* 337 (1991): 123.

159. Jun Zhang, David A. Savitz, Pamela J. Schwingle, and Wen-Wei Cai, "A Case-Control Study of Paternal Smoking and Birth Defects," *International Journal of Epidemiology* 21 (1992): 273–278.

160. Zhang et al., "A Case-Control Study," 273.

161. K. F. Schmidt, "The Dark Legacy of Fatherhood," *U.S. News and World Report* (14 December 1992): 92.

162. M. B. Bracken, B. Eskenazi, K. Sachse, J. E. McSharry, K. Hellenbrand, and L. Leo-Summers, "Association of Cocaine Use with Sperm Concentration, Motility and Morphology," *Fertility and Sterility* 53 (1990): 315–322.

163. R. A. Yazigi, R. R. Odem, and K. L. Polakoski, "Demonstration of Specific Binding of Cocaine to Human Spermatozoa," *Journal of the American Medical Association* 266 (1991): 1956–1959.

164. G. Friedler and H. S. Wheeling, "Behavioral Effects in Offspring of Male Mice Injected with Opioids Prior to Mating," *Pharmacology, Biochemistry and Behavior* 11 (1979): 23–28; Gladys Friedler, "Effects of Limited Paternal Exposure to Xenobiotic Agents on the Development of Progeny," *Neurobehavioral Toxicology and Teratology* 7 (1985): 739–743.

165. Zenad El-Gothamy and May El-Samahy, "Ultrastructure Sperm Defects in Addicts," *Fertility and Sterility* 57 (1992): 699–702.

166. These news stories are: N. Angier, "Genetic Mutation Tied to Father in Most Cases," *New York Times* (17 May 1994): C12; S. Blakeslee, "Research on Birth Defects Shifts to Flaws in Sperm," *New York Times* (January 1991): A1; "Cocaine-Using Fathers Linked to Birth Defects," *New York Times* (15 October 1991): C5; "Study Links Cancer in Young to Father's Smoking," *New York Times* (24 January 1991): B8; "Vitamin C Deficiency in a Man's Diet Might Cause Problems for Offspring," *New York Times* (12 February 1992): C12; "Fathers Who Smoke," *Wall Street Journal* (24 January 1991): A1; Tim Friend, "Sperm May Carry Cocaine to Egg," *USA Today* (9 October 1991): 1A; A. Stone, "It's 'Tip of the Iceberg' in Protecting Infants," *USA Today* (25 Au-

gust 25 1989); and Ann Merewood, "Studies Reveal Men's Role in Producing Healthy Babies," *Chicago Tribune* (12 January 1992): 8.

167. Calculated from indexes in the online catalog ProQuest.

168. The personification of sperm is not a new phenomenon, as was seen in chapter 2, but one that has been resurrected in new form in the 1990s. See Davis et al., "Male-Mediated Teratogenesis," 290.

169. A. Merewood, "Sperm under Siege," *Health* (April 1991): 53–76.

170. R. Black and P. Moore, "The Myth of the Macho Sperm," *Parenting* 6 (1992): 29–31.

171. J. R. Schroedel and P. Peretz, "A Gender Analysis of Policy Formation: The Case of Fetal Abuse," presented at the Western Political Science Association Meeting, Pasadena, California, 18–20 March 1993.

172. Brett Wright, "Smokers' Sperm Spell Trouble for Future Generations," *New Scientist* (6 March 1993): 10.

173. See Laura Hewitson, Calvin R. Simerly, and Gerald Schatten, "ICSI, Male Pronuclear Remodeling and Cell Cycle Checkpoints," in *Advances in Male Mediated Developmental Toxicity*, ed. Bernard Robaire and Barbara F. Hales (New York: Kluwer Academic/Plenum, 2003), 200.

174. For these studies, see *Advances in Male Mediated Developmental Toxicity*, ed. Bernard Robaire and Barbara F. Hales (New York: Kluwer Academic/Plenum, 2003).

175. The restoration of sperm production was achieved by a treatment with a testosterone suppressant. Meistriech noted that some men rendered infertile by DBCP regained their fertility more than seven years after toxic exposure. As he surmised, "Perhaps they ate beef with some hormones." Comment made at Male Mediated Developmental Toxicity Conference, Montreal, Canada, 23 June 2001. Also see Marvin L. Meistriech, Gene Wilson, Gunapala Shetty, and Gladis A. Shuttleworth, "Restoration of Spermatogenesis after Exposure to Toxicants: Genetic Implications," in *Advances in Male-Mediated Developmental Toxicity*, ed. Bernard Robaire and Barbara F. Hales (New York: Kluwer Academic/Plenum, 2003), 227–237.

176. In Calgary, R. H. Martin has found that men treated with chemotherapy produced abnormal sperm for up to 18 months after treatment, with some chromosomal abnormalities that might transmit harm far longer. Renee H. Martin, "Chromosome Abnormalities in Human Sperm," in Robaire and Hales, *Advances in Male Mediated Developmental Toxicity*, 181–189.

177. Comment made at the second International Conference on Male-Mediated Developmental Toxicity, June 2001, Montreal, Canada, by Keith Jarvi, University of Toronto-Mt. Sinai Hospital.

178. Colie, "Male Mediated Teratogenesis."

179. Silbergeld interview (22 June 2001).

180. A good example of this is the "crack baby" panic of the 1990s. An article published in the *Journal of the American Medical Association* in March 2001 reviewed the scientific research on the effects of cocaine use during pregnancy and found that there was "no convincing evidence" that prenatal cocaine exposure was associated with "developmental toxic effects different in severity or scope" from other known hazards, such as cigarette smoking. Yet such limited scientific research on cocaine and pregnancy during the 1990s generated a tremendous public response, in terms of research dollars, punitive punishments, and media coverage of the "crack baby epidemic." See Deborah A. Frank, Marilyn Augustyn, Wanda Grant Knight, Tripler Pell, and Barry Zuckerman, "Growth, Development, and Behavior in Early Childhood following Prenatal Cocaine Exposure," *Journal of the American Medical Association* 285 (28 March 2001): 1613.

181. Thalidomide was a drug given to pregnant women to reduce morning sickness during the late 1950s, but it unexpectedly produced severe birth defects, including missing or stunted growth in arms and legs in their children. While approximately 10,000 "thalidomide babies" were born worldwide, only 17 were born in the United States. For more information on this, see www.chm.bris.ac.uk/motm/thalidomide/effects.html. This human tragedy generated intense public attention to prescription drug use by women during pregnancy.

182. The term *teratology* refers traditionally to substances that can cause birth defects, primarily by crossing through the placenta. The term is derived from the Latin root meaning the "making of monsters."

183. Hales interview (23 June 2001).

184. Hales and Robaire interviews (23 June 2001); some substances are mutagenic and may produce harm through chromosomal aberrations. But other toxins that are not mutagenic seem to produce similar harms. Ellen Silbergeld observes that not until advances in developmental biology come together with research in toxicology will those mechanisms become possible to see. Silbergeld interview (22 June 2001).

185. Hales interview (23 June 2001).

186. Hales and Robaire interviews (23 June 2001).

187. Anthony Scialli, "Paternally Mediated Effects and Political Correctness," *Reproductive Toxicology* 7 (1993): 189–190.

188. On this point, see Evelyn Fox Keller, *Secrets of Life, Secrets of Death* (New York: Routledge, 1992), 31.

189. This is a paraphrase of the ethical questions posed by Immanuel Kant. This point was made in a keynote address by Charles Scriver at the second International Conference on Male-Mediated Developmental Toxicity, June 2001, Montreal, Canada.

190. "Women . . . generally bore the onus of a barren marriage," observe Margaret Marsh and Wanda Ronner, in their interesting history of infertility in the United States. See *The Empty Cradle: Infertility in America from Colonial Times to the Present* (Baltimore: Johns Hopkins University Press, 1996), 16.

BIBLIOGRAPHY

AATB, "Ethical Guidelines for Commercial Activities and Advertising," at www.aatb.org.

———, "FDA Final Rule: Registration and Listing." AATB Information Alert XI (18 January 2001) at www.aatb.org.

———, "Statement of Ethical Principles," at www.aatb.org.

Abel, Ernest L., "Gin Lane: Did Hogarth Know about Fetal Alcohol Syndrome?" *Alcohol and Alcoholism* 36 (2001): 131–134.

———, Interview with C. Daniels (24 January 2001).

———, "Paternal Exposure to Alcohol," in *Perinatal Substance Abuse*, ed. T. B. Sonderegger (Baltimore: Johns Hopkins University Press, 1992), 133.

———, *Psychoactive Drugs and Sex* (New York: Plenum, 1985).

Acacio, Brian D., Tamar Gottfried, Robert Israel, and Rebecca Z. Sokol, "Evaluation of a Large Cohort of Men Presenting for a Screening Semen Analysis," *Fertility and Sterility* 73 (March 2000): 595–597.

Alexander, Daryl, Interview with C. Daniels (16 January 2001).

Allan, Bruce B., and Rollin Brant, "Declining Sex Ratios in Canada," *Canadian Medical Association Journal* 156 (1 January 1997): 37.

Anderson, Elizabeth, *Value in Ethics and Economics* (Cambridge, MA: Harvard University Press, 1993).

Angier, N., "Genetic Mutation Tied to Father in Most Cases," *New York Times* (17 May 1994): C12.

Anouna, Albert, Director, BioGenetics, Interview with C. Daniels (27 March 2001).

Ansbacher, Rudi, "Artificial Insemination with Frozen Spermatozoa," *Fertility and Sterility* 29 (April 1978): 375–379.

Appadurai, A., ed., *The Social Life of Things: Commodities in Cultural Perspective* (Philadelphia: University of Pennsylvania Press, 1986).

Araneta, M. R., L. Mascola, A. Eller, L. O'Neil, M. M. Ginsberg, M. Bursaw, J. Marik, S. Friedman, C. A. Sims, M. L. Rekart, et al., "HIV Transmission through Donor Artificial Insemination," *Journal of the American Medical Association* 273 (March 1995): 854–858.

ASRM, "Guidelines for Gamete and Embryo Donation," at www.asrm.org.

Associated Press, "44% of Doctors Report Tests for AIDS on Donated Semen," *New York Times* (11 August 1988): 23, LNAU.

———, "Lawsuit over Infection Settled by Sperm Bank," *Los Angeles Times* (2 November 1990): 9B.

———, "Sperm Counts Reported to Drop," *Boston Globe* (11 September 1992): 19.

Auger, J., F. Eustache, A. G. Andersen, D. S. Irvine, N. Jørgensen, N. E. Skakkebæk, J. Suominen, J. Toppari, M. Vierula, and P. Jouannet, "Sperm Morphological Defects Related to Environment, Lifestyle and Medical History of 1001 Male Partners of Pregnant Women from Four European Cities," *Human Reproduction* 16 (December 2001): 2710–2717.

Auger, J., J. M. Kunstmann, J. Czyglik, and P. Jouannet, "Decline in Semen Quality among Fertile Men in Paris during the Past 20 Years," *New England Journal of Medicine* 332 (2 February 1995): 281–285.

Ayvazian, L. Fred, "Seminal Gelation," *New England Journal of Medicine* 279 (1968): 436.

"Bad Seed: How Sperm Bank Lost Its Deposits," *San Francisco Chronicle* (27 June 1971; 18 July 1975), LNAU.

Baker, Robin, and Mark A. Bellis, "'Kamikaze' Sperm in Mammals?" *Animal Behaviour* 36 (1988): 936–939.

Barkay, Joseph, and Henryk Zuckerman, "Further Developed Device for Human Sperm Freezing by the Twenty-Minute Method," *Fertility and Sterility* 29 (March 1978): 304–308.

Barlow, Susan M., and Frank M. Sullivan, *Reproductive Hazards of Industrial Chemicals: An Evaluation of Animal and Human Data* (New York: Academic Press, 1982).

Barlow, Thomas, "Body and Mind," *Financial Times* (London) (17 February 2001): 2, LNAU.

———, "Is the Number Up for Sperm Counts?" *Financial Times* (London) (17 February 2001): 2.

Barry, Jan, "Troubling Questions about Dioxin," *New York Times* (11 September 1983): 26.

BBC/Discovery Production, "Assault on the Male" (4 September 1994; aired in 1993 in Great Britain).

Beardsley, Grant S., "Artificial Cross Insemination," *Western Journal of Surgery, Obstetrics and Gynecology* 48 (1940): 95.

Behrman, S. J., "Artificial Insemination," in *Progress in Infertility*, 2nd ed., ed. S. J. Behrman and Robert W. Kistner (Boston: Little Brown, 1975), 785.

Behrman, S. J., and D. R. Ackerman, "Freeze Preservation of Human Sperm," *American Journal of Obstetrics and Gynecology* 103 (1969): 660–661.

Bellis, Mark, and Robin Baker, "Do Females Promote Sperm Competition? Data for Humans," *Animal Behaviour* 40 (1990): 997–999.

Ben-Horin, Daniel, "The Sterility Scandal," *Mother Jones* (May 1979): 51–63.

Bergstrom, R., H. O. Adami, M. Mohner, W. Zatonski, H. Storm, A. Ekbom, S. Tretli, L. Teppo, O. Akre, and T. Hakulinen, "Increase in Testicular Cancer Incidence in Six European Countries: A Birth Cohort Phenomenon," *Journal of the National Cancer Institute* 88 (5 June 1996): 727–733.

Berlau, J., "Case of the Falling Sperm Counts," *National Review* (26 June 1995): 45–48.

Betteridge, K. J., "An Historical Look at Embryo Transfer," *Journal of Reproduction and Fertility* 62 (1981): 3.

Black, R., and P. Moore, "The Myth of the Macho Sperm," *Parenting* 6 (1992): 29–31.

Blakeslee, S., "Research on Birth Defects Shifts to Flaws in Sperm," *New York Times* (January 1991): A1.

Blankenhorn, David, *Fatherless America* (New York: Basic Books, 1995).

Bonde, J. P., H. I. Hjollund, T. B. Henriksen, T. K. Jensen, M. Spano, H. Kolstad, A. Giwercman, L. Storgaard, E. Ernst, and J. Olsen, "Epidemiologic Evidence on Biological and Environmental Male Factors in Embryonic Loss," in *Advances in Male Mediated Developmental Toxicity*, ed. Bernard Robaire and Barbara F. Hales (New York: Kluwer Academic/Plenum, 2003), 25–36.

Boseley, Sarah, "Nappies Cause Infertility Claim Stirs Controversy," *Guardian* (London) (26 September 2000): 6.

Bracken, M. B., B. Eskenazi, K. Sachse, J. E. McSharry, K. Hellenbrand, and L. Leo-Summers, "Association of Cocaine Use with Sperm Concentration, Motility and Morphology," *Fertility and Sterility* 53 (1990): 315–322.

Brady, K., Y. Herrera, and H. Zenick, "Influence of Paternal Lead Exposure on Subsequent Learning Ability of Offspring," *Pharmacology, Biochemistry and Behavior* 3 (1975): 561–565.

Brenner, R. B., "Sperm Repository, Marking 10th Year, Still Has Same Goal—Genius," *San Diego Union-Tribune* (22 July 1990), LNAU.

Bronskill, Jim, "Health Woes Plague Gulf War Babies," *Ottawa Citizen* (29 June 1998).

Brooks, Clark, "Fatal Flaws: How the Military Misled Vietnam Veterans and Their Families about the Health Risks of Agent Orange," *San Diego Union-Tribune* (1 November 1998): A1.

Brown, David, "Children's Leukemia Risk Tied to Agent Orange; Panel's Finding of Possible Causation Means Vietnam Vets' Offspring May Be Compensated," *Washington Post* (20 April 2001): A2.

Bunge, R. G., and J. K. Sherman, "Fertilizing Capacity of Frozen Human Spermatozoa," *Nature* 172 (1953): 767–768.

Burger, E. J., R. G. Tardiff, A. R. Scialli, and H. Zenick, eds., *Sperm Measures and Reproductive Success* (New York: Alan R. Liss, 1989).

Burton, A. J., "Are Men Really Necessary?" *Science Digest* 49 (April 1961): 6–7.

C. C. (Author), "Bye Bye, Baby Boys," *Earth Island Journal* 13 (Spring 1998): 12.

California Cryobank, Inc., *Donor Information,* 2000 (www.cryobank.com).

———, *Racial Identification System* (www.cryobank.com/racial.html).

Carlsen, Elisabeth, Aleksander Giwercman, Niels Keiding, and Niels E. Skakkebæk, "Evidence for Decreasing Quality of Semen during the Past Fifty Years," *British Medical Journal* 305 (1992): 609–612.

Castleman, Michael, "Big Drop," *Sierra* 78 (March–April 1993): 38.

———, "Down for the Count," *Mother Jones* (January–February 1996): 20–21.

CBC News Online, "Pentagon Looking at Possible Cause of Gulf War Syndrome" (19 October 1999).

Centers for Disease Control, *2 to 20 years: Boys Body Mass Index-for-Age Percentiles* (2000) at www.cdc.gov/growthcharts.

———, *2 to 20 years: Boys Stature-for-Age and Weight-for-age Percentiles* (2000) at www.cdc.gov/growthcharts.

————, 2000 CDC Growth Charts, National Center for Health Statistics, Centers for Disease Control at www.cdc.gov/nchs (2/10/02).

Centola, G. M., "American Organization of Sperm Banks," in *Donor Insemination*, ed. C. L. R. Barratt and I. D. Cooke (Cambridge: Cambridge University Press, 1993), 143–151.

Cherfas, Jeremy, *The Redundant Male: Is Sex Irrelevant in the Modern World?* (London: Bodley Head, 1984).

Chiasson, M. A., R. L. Stoneburner, and S. C. Joseph, "Human Immunodeficiency Virus Transmission through Artificial Insemination," *Journal of Acquired Immune Deficiency Syndrome* 3 (1990): 69–72.

Cicero, T. J., B. Nock, L. H. O'Connor, B. N. Sewing, M. L. Adams, and E. R. Meyer, "Acute Paternal Alcohol Exposure Impairs Fertility and Foetal Outcome in the Male Rat," *Life Sciences* 55 (1994): 901–910.

"Cocaine-Using Fathers Linked to Birth Defects," *New York Times* (15 October 1991): C5.

Coffey, T. G., "Beer Street: Gin Lane. Some Views of 18th Century Drinking," *Quarterly Journal of Studies on Alcohol* 27 (1966): 669–692.

Cohen, E. N., B. W. Brown, M. L. Wu, C. D. Whitcher, J. B. Brodsky, H. C. Gift, W. Greenfield, T. W. Jones, and E. J. Driscoll, "Occupational Disease in Dentistry and Chronic Exposure to Trace Anesthetic Gases," *Journal of the American Dental Association* 101 (1980): 21–31.

Cohen, Estelle, "'What the Women at All Times Would Laugh At': Redefining Equality and Difference, circa 1660–1760," in *Women, Gender and Science: New Directions*, ed. Sally Gregory Kohlstedt and Helen Longino (*Osiris*, vol. 12, 1997), 127.

Cohn, Carol, "'Clean Bombs' and Clean Language," in *Women, Militarism and War*, ed. Jean Bethke Elshtain and Sheila Tobias (Savage, MD: Rowman and Littlefield, 1990), 35–56.

Colborn, Theo, Dianne Dumanoski, and John Peterson Myers, *Our Stolen Future: Are We Threatening Our Fertility, Intelligence, and Survival? A Scientific Detective Story* (New York: Dutton, 1996).

Colborn, Theo, and Richard Liroff, "Toxics in the Great Lakes," *EPA Journal* 16 (November–December 1990): 5.

Cole, F. J., *Early Theories of Sexual Generation* (London: Oxford University Press, 1930).

Coleman, M. P., J. Esteve, P. Damiecki, A. Arslan, and H. Renard, "Trends in Cancer Incidence and Mortality," *IARC Scientific Publications* 121 (1993): 521–542.

Colie, C. F., "Male Mediated Teratogenesis," *Reproductive Toxicology* 7 (1993): 7.

Committee on Hormonally Active Agents in the Environment, Board on Environmental Studies and Toxicology, Commission on Life Sciences, National Research Council, *Hormonally Active Agents in the Environment* (Washington, DC: National Academy Press, 1999).

Cone, Marla, "Study Supports Finding of Male Fertility Decline," *Los Angeles Times* (2 February 1995): A22.

Connor, Steve, "Fertility Rises Despite Falling Sperm Counts," *Independent* (London) (2 June 2000): 15.

———, "Science: Mystery of the Vanishing Sperm," *Independent* (8 March 1992): 43.

"Counting Sperm," *Pittsburgh Post-Gazette* (28 June 1993): C4.

Cowan, David N., Robert F. DeFraites, Gregory C. Gray, Mary B. Goldenbaum, and Samuel M. Wishik, "The Risk of Birth Defects among Children of Persian Gulf War Veterans," *New England Journal of Medicine* 336 (1997): 1650–1656.

Critser, John K., "Current Status of Semen Banking in the USA," *Human Reproduction* 13 (suppl. 2, 1998): 55–66.

Cullitan, Barbara J., "Sperm Banks Debated," *Science News* 92 (1967): 208–209.

Curie-Cohen, M., L. Luttrell, and S. Shapiro, "Current Practice of Artificial Insemination by Donor in the United States," *New England Journal of Medicine* 300 (1979): 585–590.

Daniels, Cynthia R., *At Women's Expense: State Power and the Politics of Fetal Rights* (Cambridge, MA: Harvard University Press, 1993).

———, "Between Fathers and Fetuses: The Social Construction of Male Reproduction and the Politics of Fetal Harm," *Signs: Journal of Women in Culture and Society* 22 (1997): 579–616.

David, Amnon, and Dalia Avidan, "Artificial Insemination Donor: Clinical and Psychological Aspects," *Fertility and Sterility* 27 (May 1976): 528–532.

Davis, D. L., "Paternal Smoking and Fetal Health," *Lancet* 337 (1991): 123.

Davis, D. L., G. Friedler, D. Mattison, and R. Morris, "Male-Mediated Teratogenesis and Other Reproductive Effects: Biological and Epidemiologic Findings and a Plea for Clinical Research," *Reproductive Toxicology* 6 (1992): 289–292.

Davis, Devra Lee, Michelle B. Gottlieb, and Julie R. Stampnitzky, "Reduced Ratio of Male to Female Births in Several Industrial Countries: A Sentinel Health Indicator?" *Journal of the American Medical Association* 279 (1998): 1018–1023.

Dimid-Ward, H., C. Hertzman, K. Teschke, R. Hershler, S. A. Marion, and A. Ostry, "Reproductive Effects of Paternal Exposure to Cholorophenate Wood Preservatives in the Sawmill Industry," *Scandinavian Journal of World Environmental Health* 22 (1996): 267–273.

Dinwoodie, Robbie, "Warning over Fall in Male Fertility," *Herald* (London) (28 May 1993): 10.

"Disposable Nappies Catch a Spray from Researchers," *The Age* (Melbourne) (27 September 2000), 3.

"Domestic Relations; The Child of Artificial Insemination," *Time* 89 (14 April 1967): 79–80.

"Don't Worry, Be Fertile," *Men's Health* 13 (June 1998): 34.

Douglass, Mary, *Purity and Danger: An Analysis of the Concepts of Pollution and Taboo* (New York: Routledge and Kegan Paul, 1966).

Dunn, Kyla, "'Teeny Weenies,' Alligators in Florida's Lake Apopka Have Smaller Penises," *PBS* (2 June 1998).

Earley, Pete, "Second Federal Study; Agent Orange Risk Doubted," *Washington Post* (17 August 1984): A1.

Editorial, "Andrology as a Specialty," *Journal of the American Medical Association* 17 (1891): 691.

Editorial, "Masculinity at Risk," *Nature* 375 (15 June 1995): 522.

Ekbom, A., and O. Akre, "Increasing Incidence of Testicular Cancer Birth Cohort Effects," *Acta Pathologica, Microbiologica et Immunologica Scandinavica (APMIS)* 106 (January 1998): 225–231.

El-Gothamy, Zenad, and May El-Samahy, "Ultrastructure Sperm Defects in Addicts," *Fertility and Sterility* 57 (1992): 699–702.

Environmental Protection Agency, "Endocrine Disruptor Screening and Testing Advisory Committee, Final Report, Chapter Seven, Compilation of EDSTAC Recommendations" (1998): ES-1. Available at www.epa.gov/scipoly/oscpendo/docs/edstac/chap7v14.pdf.

Environmental Protection Agency Endocrine Disruptor Screening Program, "Report to Congress," August 2000, 16. Available at www.epa.gov/oscpmont/oscpendo/docs/edmvs/edmvsstatusreporttocongressfinal.pdf.

Erickson, J. D., J. Mulinare, P. W. McClain, T. G. Fitch, L. M. James, A. B. McClearn, and M. J. Adams Jr., "Vietnam Veterans Risks for Fathering Babies with Birth Defects," *Journal of the American Medical Association* 252 (August 1984): 903–912.

Ersek, Robert A., "Frozen Sperm Banks," *Journal of the American Medical Association* 220 (1972): 1365.

"Eugenic Babies: Medical Science Finds a Way, Even with Sterile Husbands," *Literary Digest* (21 November 1936): 23–25.

Express Staff, "Plastic Diapers Tied to Infertility," *Daily News* (New York) (26 September 2000): 2.

Ezzell, C., "Eggs Not Silent Partners in Conception," *Science News* 139 (1991): 214.

Facemire, Charles F., Timothy S. Gross, and Louis J. Guillette Jr., "Reproductive Impairment in the Florida Panther: Nature or Nurture?" *Environmental Health Perspectives* (suppl. 4, 1995): 79–86.

Fackelmann, Kathy A., "Zona Blasters: There's More Than One Way to Crack an Egg," *Science News* 138 (15 December 1990): 376–379.

Fader, Sonia, "Sperm Banking: A Reproductive Resource" (California Cryobank, 1993), at www.cryobank.com/history.html.

Farley, John, *Gametes and Spores: Ideas about Sexual Reproduction, 1750–1914* (Baltimore: Johns Hopkins University Press, 1982).

"Fathers Who Smoke," *Wall Street Journal* (24 January 1991): A1.

Federal Register, 43(53)–Friday March 17, 1978. Title 29–Labor, Chapter XVII–Occupational Safety and Health Administration, Department of Labor, Part 1910–Occupational Safety and Health Standards, Occupational Exposure to 1,2–Dibromo-3–Chloropropane (DBCP), [4510–26] 11514–11520.

———, "Guidelines for Preventing Transmission of Human Immunodeficiency Virus Through Transplantation of Human Tissue and Organs," *Federal Register* (Health Care Financing Administration, Department of Health and Human Services, Appendix A to Subpart G of Part 486, effective 2 May 1996).

———, "Suitability Determination for Donors of Human Cellular and Tissue-Based Products," *Federal Register* (Department of Health and Human Services, Food and Drug Administration, 9 January 2001).

Fisch, H., and E. T. Goluboff, "Geographic Variations in Sperm Counts: A Potential Cause of Bias in Studies of Semen Quality," *Fertility and Sterility* 65 (May 1996): 1044–1046.

Fissel, Mary, "Gender and Generation: Representing Reproduction in Early Modern England," in *Sexualities in History: A Reader*, ed. Kim M. Phillips and Barry Reay (New York: Routledge, 2002), 105–128.

Fitzherbert, Claudia, "Commentary: Terror on the Trouser Front," *Daily Telegraph* (12 March 1992): 17.

Food and Drug Administration, "Eligibility Determination for Donors of Human Cells, Tissues, and Cellular and Tissue-Based Products," *Federal Register*, 21 CFR Parts 210, 211, 820, and 1271, May 25, 2004.

————, 21 CFR Parts 210, 211, 820, 1271, Docket #97N-484S, "Suitability Determination for Donors of Human Cellular and Tissue-Based Products."

————, "Meeting–Semen Donor Suitability Issues," February 12, 2001 p. 1–2, accessed from http://www.fda.gov/cber/minuetes/glma021201.htm.

Forsyth, A. J., "Letter," *Independent* (15 March 1992): 23.

Fournier, Ron, "Agent Orange Aid Expanded," *Chicago Sun-Times* (29 May 1996): 31.

Fox, Maggie, "Sperm Counts Falling around the World," *Reuters* (24 November 1997).

Frank, Deborah A., Marilyn Augustyn, Wanda Grant Knight, Tripler Pell, and Barry Zuckerman, "Growth, Development, and Behavior in Early Childhood following Prenatal Cocaine Exposure," *Journal of the American Medical Association* 285 (28 March 2001): 1613–1625.

Frankel, Mark S., "Human-Semen Banking: Implications for Medicine and Society," *Connecticut Medicine* 39 (May 1975): 313–317.

————, "Role of Semen Cryobanking in American Medicine," *British Medical Journal* (7 September 1974): 619–621.

Freed, David, "Male Infertility Is an Overlooked Hazard of Toxic Exposure," *Los Angeles Times*, (6 September 1993): A24.

Freedman, Murray, "Counting Sperm" (Letter), *Times* (London) (24 April 1993).

Friedler, G., and H. S. Wheeling, "Behavioral Effects in Offspring of Male Mice Injected with Opioids prior to Mating," *Pharmacology, Biochemistry and Behavior* 11 (1979): 23–28.

Friedler, Gladys, "Developmental Toxicology: Male-Mediated Effects," in *Occupational and Environmental Reproductive Hazards*, ed. Maureen Paul (Baltimore: Williams and Wilkins, 1993), 52–59.

————, "Effects of Limited Paternal Exposure to Xenobiotic Agents on the Development of Progeny," *Neurobehavioral Toxicology and Teratology* 7 (1985): 739–743.

————, "Paternal Exposures: Impact on Reproductive and Developmental Outcome. An Overview," *Pharmacology Biochemistry and Behavior* 55 (1996): 691–700.

————, Telephone interview with C. Daniels (7 February 2001).

————, Telephone interview with C. Daniels (13 February 2001).

Friend, Tim, "Sperm May Carry Cocaine to Egg," *USA Today* (9 October 1991): 1A.

"Frozen Fatherhood," *Time* (8 September 1961).

Fumento, Michael, "Hormonally Challenged," *American Spectator* 32 (October 1999): 2.

Gardner, M. J., M. P. Snee, A. J. Hall, C. A. Powell, S. Downes, and J. D. Terrell, "Results of Case-Control Study of Leukaemia and Lymphoma among Young People near Sellafield Nuclear Plant in West Cumbria," *British Medical Journal* 300 (1990): 423–429.

Gaul, Gilbert M., "The Blood Brokers—America: The OPEC of the Global Plasma Industry," *Philadelphia Inquirer* (28 September 1989), at www .bloodbank.com/part-5.html (accessed 2/17/02).

"The Gelding of America: Is DDT to Blame?" *Civil Defense Perspectives* 12 (November 1995).

"'Ghost' Fathers: Children Provided for the Childless," *Newsweek* 3 (12 May 1934): 16.

Golden, Janet, "From Commodity to Gift: Gender, Class and the Meaning of Breast Milk in the Twentieth Century," *Historian* 59 (1996): 75–87.

Golden, Janet, and Cynthia R. Daniels, "The Politics of Paternity: Fetal Risks and Reproductive Responsibility," in *Current Issues in Law and Medicine* 3, ed. M. Freeman (London: Oxford University Press, 2000), 363–378.

Goldsmith, J., G. Potashnik, and R. Israeli, "Reproductive Outcomes in Families of DBCP-Exposed Men," *Archives of Environmental Health* 16 (1984): 213–218.

"Grades Aren't All That Are Dropping," *Washington Monthly* 33 (December 2001): 22.

Gray, Chris, "Scientist Hot on Trail of Hormones; Chemical Clues Seen in Animals," *Times-Picayune* (New Orleans) (23 December 1996): A1.

Guillette Jr., Louis J., Timothy S. Gross, Greg R. Masson, John M. Matter, H. Franklin Percival, and Allan R. Woodward, "Developmental Abnormalities of the Gonad and Abnormal Sex Hormone Concentrations in Juvenile Alligators from Contaminated and Control Lakes in Florida," *Environmental Health Perspectives* 102 (August 1994): 680–688.

Guttmacher, Alan Frank, "A Physician's Credo for Artificial Insemination," *Western Journal of Surgery, Obstetrics and Gynecology* 50 (1942): 358–359.

————, "Practical Experience with Artificial Insemination," *Journal of Contraception* 3 (1938): 76.

Guzick, David S., James W. Overstreet, Pam Factor-Litvak, Charlene K. Brazil, Steven T. Nakajima, Christos Coutifaris, Sandra Ann Carson, Pauline Cisneros, Michael P. Steinkampf, Joseph A. Hill, Dong Xu, and Donna L. Vogel, for the National Cooperative Reproductive Medicine Network, "Sperm Morphology, Motility, and Concentration in Fertile and Infertile Men," *New England Journal of Medicine* 345 (2001): 1388–1393.

Hales, Barbara, interview with C. Daniels (23 June 2001).

Halwell, Brian, "Plummeting Sperm Counts Cause Concern," *Futurist* (November 1999): 14–15.

Hamilton, Doug, "Interview with Fredrick vom Saal," *Frontline* (PBS, 2 June 1998).

Haraway, Donna, "Investment Strategies for the Evolving Portfolio of Primate Females," in *Body/Politics*, ed. Mary Jacobus, Evelyn Fox Keller, and Sally Shuttleworth (New York: Routledge, 1990), 155–156.

Harris, John F., and Bill McAllister, "President Adds VA Benefits after AO Study; Prostate Cancer; Nervous Disorder Covered," *Washington Post* (29 May 1996): A01.

Hewitson, Laura, Calvin R. Simerly, and Gerald Schatten, "ICSI, Male Pronuclear Remodeling and Cell Cycle Checkpoints," in *Advances in Male Mediated Developmental Toxicity*, ed. Bernard Robaire and Barbara F. Hales (New York: Kluwer Academic/Plenum, 2003).

Highfield, Roger, "Folic Acid 'Is the Key to Fertility in Males,'" *Daily Telegraph* (London) (10 February 2001), 12.

————, "Goodbye Macho Man?" *Daily Telegraph* (London) (30 November 1992): 16.

Hoppe, Arthur, "Dealing with Heir Loss," *San Francisco Chronicle* (16 September 1992): A17.

Houston Chronicle News Service, "Environment Pollutants Linked to a Large Drop in Sperm Count," *Houston Chronicle* (11 September 1992): 24.

Hubbard, Ruth, "Have Only Men Evolved?" in *Discovering Reality: Feminist Perspectives on Epistemology, Metaphysics, Methodology and the Philosophy of Science*, ed. Sandra Harding and Merrill B. Hintikka (Dordrecht: Reidel, 1983).

"Human Sperm Count Peaks in Winter, Studies Say," *Toronto Star* (22 May 1993): A3.

Hunter, Bob, "Plastics Ain't So Fantastic, Lovers," *Eye Weekly* (Toronto) (15 February 1996); accessed at www.eye.net/eye/issues/, 3/19/02.

Hyde, Lewis, *The Gift: Imagination and the Erotic Life of Property* (New York: Vintage, 1983).

Inskip, H., "Stillbirth and Paternal Preconceptional Radiation Exposure," *Lancet* 354 (1999): 1400–1401.

Institute of Medicine, National Academy of Sciences, *Veterans and Agent Orange: Health Effects of Herbicides Used in Vietnam* (Washington, DC: National Academy Press, 1994).

———, *Veterans and Agent Orange: Update 1996* (Washington, DC: National Academy Press, 1997).

International Society of Andrology, web site http://andrology.org/.

Irvine, Stewart, "Is the Human Testis Still an Organ at Risk?" *British Medical Journal* 312 (22 June 1996): 1557–1558.

Isreal, S. Leon, in "Discussion," following reprint of Behrman and Ackerman's lecture in "Freeze Preservation" (1969): 662.

James, P. D., *The Children of Men* (London: Faber, 1992).

James, W. H., "The Human Sex Ratio, Part 1: A Review of the Literature," *Human Biology* 59 (1987): 721–752.

———, "Male Reproductive Hazards and Occupation," *Lancet* 347 (1996): 773.

———, "The Sex Ratio of Offspring Sired by Men Exposed to Wood Preservatives Contaminated by Dioxin," *Scandinavian Journal of World Environmental Health* 23 (1997): 69.

———, "What Stabilizes the Sex Ratio?" *Annals of Human Genetics* 59 (1995): 243–249.

Jenkins, Phil, "Mystery Master Probes a Bleak and Barren Future," *Ottawa Citizen* (24 October 1992): B7.

Jensen, Tina Kold, Jorma Toppari, Niels Keilding, and Niels Erik Skakkebaek, "Do Environmental Estrogens Contribute to the Decline in Male Reproductive Health?" *Clinical Chemistry* 41 (1995): 1897.

Jørgensen, Niels, Anne-Grethe Andersen, Florence Eustache, D. Stewart Irvine, Jyrki Suominen, Jørgen Holm Petersen, Anders Nyboe Andersen, Jacques Auger, Elizabeth H. H. Cawood, Antero Horte, Tina Kold Jensen, Pierre Jouannet, Niels Keiding, Matti Vierula, Jorma Toppari, and Niels E. Skakkebæk, "Regional Differences in Semen Quality in Europe," *Human Reproduction* 16 (2001): 1012–1019.

Kaiser, Jocelyn, "Endocrine Disrupters: Scientists Angle for Answers," *Science* 274 (13 December 1996): 1837–1838.

Kanamine, Linda, "Congress Considering Children-of-War Measure," *USA Today* (12 September 1996): 4A.

Katcher, Brian S., "The Post-Repeal Eclipse in Knowledge about the Harmful Effects of Alcohol," *Addiction* 88 (1993): 729–744.

Kavlock, Robert J., George P. Daston, Chris DeRosa, Penny Fenner-Crisp, L. Earl Gray, Steve Kaattari, George Lucier, Michael Luster, Michael J. Mac, Carol Maczka, Ron Miller, Jack Moore, Rosalind Rolland, Geoffrey Scott, Daniel M. Sheehan, Thomas Sinks, and Hugh A. Tilson, "Research Needs for the Risk Assessment of Health and Environmental Effects of Endocrine Disruptors: A Report of the U.S. EPA-Sponsored Workshop," *Environmental Health Perspectives* 104 (suppl. 4, 1996): 715–740.

Keettel W. C., R. G. Bunge, J. T. Bradbury, and W. O. Nelson., "Report of Pregnancies in Infertile Couples," *Journal of the American Medical Association* 160 (January 1956): 102–105.

Keller, Evelyn Fox, *Secrets of Life, Secrets of Death* (New York: Routledge, 1992).

Kevles, Daniel J., "Brave New Biology: The Dreams of Eugenics" http://invisible .gq.nu/wake/texts/BRAVENEWBIOLOGY.html (accessed 5/21/03).

———, *In the Name of Eugenics: Genetics and the Uses of Human Heredity* (Cambridge, MA: Harvard University Press, 1985).

Kharrazi, M., G. Patashnik, and J. R. Goldsmith, "Reproductive Effects of Dibromochloropropane," *Israel Journal of Medical Science* 6 (1980): 403–406.

Kimmel, Michael S., ed., *The Gendered Society Reader*, 2nd ed. (London: Oxford University Press, 2004).

Kipen, Howard M., and Nancy Fiedler, "Invited Commentary: Sensitivities to Chemicals—Context and Implications," *American Journal of Epidemiology* 150 (1999): 13–16.

Kolata, Gina, "Measuring Men Up," *New York Times* (May 5, 1996): 4.

Kong, Dolores, "Study Says Fetal Estrogen Exposure May Explain Male Ills," *Boston Globe* (28 May 1993): 3.

Krier Beth Ann, "King of the Anonymous Fathers," *Los Angeles Times* (21 April 1989): 10.

Krimsky, Sheldon, *Hormonal Chaos: The Scientific and Social Origins of the Environmental Endocrine Hypothesis* (Baltimore: Johns Hopkins University Press, 1999).

Lambton, Christopher, "Mamas Maketh Man," *Guardian* (11 February 1993): 12.

Lancranjan, H., I. Popescu, O. Gavanescu, I. Klepsch, and M. Serbanescu, "Reproductive Ability of Workmen Occupationally Exposed to Lead," *Archives of Environmental Health* 30 (1975): 396–401.

Landis, David, "Sperm Count Slide," *USA Today* (September 11, 1992): 1D.

Lane, Earl, "Study: Agent Orange Linked to Spina Bifida," *Houston Chronicle* (15 March 1996): 10.

Laqueur, Thomas, *Making Sex* (Cambridge, MA: Harvard University Press, 1990).

Larkin, Marilynn, "Male Reproductive Health: A Hotbed of Research," *Lancet* 352 (15 August 1998): 552.

Laurance, Jeremy, "Hormone Linked to Falling Fertility," *Times* (London) (28 May 1993).

Lean, Geoffrey, and Richard Sadler, "Chemicals in Water 'Lower Sperm Counts,'" *Independent* (17 March 2002): 10; accessed LNAU, 3/27/02.

Lees, Hannah, "Born to Order," *Collier's* (April 1946): 20.

Le Fanu, James, "Behind the Great Plastic Duck Panic," *New Statesman* (22 November 1999): 11.

———, "The Cure for Which There Is No Disease," *Daily Telegraph* (London) (3 October 2000): 22; accessed LNAU, 3/28/02.

Leslie, W., G. Quinlivan, and Herlinda Sullivan, "The Immunologic Effects of Husband's Semen on Donor Spermatozoa during Mixed Insemination," *Fertility and Sterility* 28 (April 1977): 448–450.

Linklater, Magnus, "Why We Should Welcome Strangers Bearing Gifts," *Scotland on Sunday* (July 23, 2000); accessed LNAU, 3/28/02.

Macilwain, Colin, "U.S. Panel Split on Endocrine Disruptors," *Nature* 395 (1998): 828.

Mann, Thaddeus, "Advances in Male Reproductive Physiology," *Fertility and Sterility* 23 (October 1972): 699.

Marchione, Marilynne, "Potent News," *Milwaukee Journal Sentinel* (27 March 2000): 15.

Marmor, D., V. Izard, D. Schahmaneche, G. Genoit, and A. Jardin, "Is Today's Man Really Less Fertile?" *Presse Med* 27 (October 1998): 1484–1490.

Marsh, Margaret, and Wanda Ronner, *The Empty Cradle: Infertility in America from Colonial Times to the Present* (Baltimore: Johns Hopkins University Press, 1996).

Marsiglio, William, *Procreative Man* (New York: New York University Press, 1998).

Martin, Emily, "The Egg and the Sperm: How Science Has Constructed a Romance Based on Stereotypical Male-Female Roles," *Signs: Journal of Women in Culture and Society* 16 (1991): 485–501.

Martinez, Fernando, Anne Wright, Lynn Taussig, and Group Health Medical Associates, "The Effect of Paternal Smoking on the Birthweight of Newborns Whose Mothers Did Not Smoke," *American Journal of Public Health* 84 (1994): 1489–1491.

Mason, George, "Female Infidelity: May the Best Sperm Win," *New Scientist* (January 1991): 29.

Maugh, Thomas H., II, "Protein's Discovery May Aid Birth Control," *Chicago Sun-Times* (19 March 1992): 3.

May, Elaine Tyler, *Barren in the Promised Land* (New York: Basic Books, 1995).

Mazzocchi, Anthony, Interview with C. Daniels (19 January 2001).

McDiarmid, M. A., J. P. Keogh, F. J. Hooper, K. McPhaul, K. Squibb, R. Kane, R. DiPino, M. Kabat, B. Kaup, L. Anderson, D. Hoover, L. Brown, M. Hamilton, D. Jacobson-Kram, B. Burrows, and M. Walsh, "Health Effects of Depleted Uranium on Exposed Gulf War Veterans," *Environmental Research* 82 (February 2000): 168–180.

McGrory, Mary, "Justice for Vietnam Veterans," *Washington Post* (9 May 1989): A2.

McLaren, Angus, *A History of Contraception from Antiquity to the Present Day* (Oxford: Basil Blackwell, 1990).

———, *Reproductive Rituals, The Perception of Fertility in England from the Sixteenth to the Nineteenth Century* (London: Methuen, 1984).

Meirow, D., and J. G. Schenker, "The Current Status of Sperm Donation in Assisted Reproduction Technology: Ethical and Legal Considerations," *Journal of Assisted Reproduction and Genetics* 14 (March 1997): 133–138.

Meistriech, Marvin L., Gene Wilson, Gunapala Shetty, and Gladis A. Shuttleworth, "Restoration of Spermatogenesis after Exposure to Toxicants: Genetic Implications," in *Advances in Male-Mediated Developmental Toxicity*, ed. Bernard Robaire and Barbara F. Hales (New York: Kluwer Academic/Plenum, 2003), 227–237.

Merewood, Anne, "Sperm under Siege," *Health* (April 1991): 53–76.

———, "Studies Reveal Men's Role in Producing Healthy Babies," *Chicago Tribune* (12 January 1992): 8.

Mihill, Chris, "Raised Levels of Oestrogen Linked to Male Sex Disorders," *Guardian* (28 May 1993): 7.

Mirer, Frank, Interview with C. Daniels (2 February 2001).

Mocarelli, Paolo, Paolo Brambilla, Pier Mario Gerthoux, Donald G. Patterson Jr., and Larry L. Needham, "Change in Sex Ratio with Exposure to Dioxin," *Lancet* 348 (10 August 1996): 409.

————, "Paternal Concentrations of Dioxin and Sex Ratio of Offspring," *Lancet* 355 (27 May 2000): 1858–1863.

Moehringer, J. R., "Legacy of Worry," *Los Angeles Times* (22 October 1995): A3.

Moline, Jacqueline M., Anne L. Golden, Natan Bar-Chama, Ernest Smith, Molly E. Rauch, Robert E. Chapin, Sally D. Perreault, Steven M. Schrader, William A. Suk, and Phillip Landrigan, "Exposure to Hazardous Substances and Male Reproductive Health: A Research Framework," *Environmental Health Perspectives* 108 (September 2000): 803–813.

Moller, Henrik, "Change in Male:Female Ratio among Newborn Infants in Denmark," *Lancet* 348 (21 September 1996): 828–829.

Moscucci, Ornella, *The Science of Woman: Gynaecology and Gender in England, 1800–1929* (Cambridge: Cambridge University Press, 1990).

Moure, Rafael, Telephone interview with C. Daniels (25 January 2001).

Munkelwitz, Robert, and Bruce Gilbert, "Are Boxer Shorts Really Better? A Critical Analysis of the Role of Underwear Type in Male Subfertility," *Journal of Urology* 160 (October 1998): 1329–1333.

Nagourney, Eric, "American Sperm, as Hardy as Ever," *New York Times* (28 March 2000): F8.

Nehmer v. U. S. Veterans' Administration, 712 F. Supp. 1404 (N.D. Cal.1989).

Nicolson, Adam, "Sunday Matters," *Daily Telegraph* (12 December 1993): 16.

Nicosia, Gerald, *Home to War* (New York: Crown, 2001).

Office of Technology Assessment, Congress of the United States, *Artificial Insemination Practice in the United States. Summary of a 1987 Survey. Background Paper* (Washington, DC: Office of Technology Assessment, Congressional Board of the 100th Congress, U.S. Congress, 1988).

O'Leary, L. M., A. M. Hicks, J. M. Peters, and S. London, "Parental Occupational Exposures and Risk of Childhood Cancer: A Review," *American Journal of Industrial Medicine* 20 (1991): 17–35.

Oliva, Alejandro, Alfred Spira, and Luc Multigner, "Contribution of Environmental Factors to the Risk of Male Infertility," *Human Reproduction* 16 (August 2001): 1768–1776.

Olshan, A. F., and E. M. Faustman, "Male-Mediated Developmental Toxicity," *Reproductive Toxicology* 7 (1993): 191–202.

Olshan, A. F., and D. R. Mattison, *Male-Mediated Developmental Toxicity* (New York: Plenum, 1994).

Olshan, Andrew, and Edwin van Wijngaarden, "Paternal Occupation and Childhood Cancer," in *Advances in Male Mediated Developmental Toxicity*, ed. Bernard Robaire and Barbara F. Hales (New York: Kluwer Academic/Plenum, 2003), 147–162.

Oren, Laura, "Protection, Patriarchy, and Capitalism: The Politics and Theory of Gender-Specific Regulation in the Workplace," *UCLA Women's Law Journal* 6 (Spring 1996): 321–373.

Oudshoorn, Nelly, *Beyond the Natural Body: An Archeology of Sex Hormones* (New York: Routledge, 1994).

———, *The Male Pill: A Biography of a Technology in the Making* (Durham, NC: Duke University Press, 2003).

Pallot, Peter, "Tight Pants and Too Much Drinking Hit Sperm Count," *Daily Telegraph* (9 March 1992): 3.

Parker, G. A., "Sperm Competition and Its Evolutinary Consequences in the Insects," *Biological Review* 45 (1970): 525–567.

Parker, L., M. S. Pearce, H. O. Dickinson, M. Aitkin, and A. W. Craft, "Stillbirths among Offspring of Male Radiation Workers at Sellafield Nuclear Reprocessing Plant," *Lancet* 354 (23 October 1999): 1407–1414.

Partsch, C.-J., M. Aukamp, and W. G. Sippell, "Scrotal Temperature Is Increased in Disposable Plastic Lined Nappies," *Archives of Disease in Childhood* 83 (October 2000): 364–368.

Paul, Diane B., *Controlling Human Heredity, 1865 to the Present* (New York: Humanities Press, 1995).

Paulsen, C. A., N. C. Berman, and C. Wang, "Data from Men in Greater Seattle Area Reveals No Downward Trend in Semen Quality: Further Evidence That Deterioration of Semen Quality Is Not Geographically Uniform," *Fertility and Sterility* 65 (1996): 1015–1020.

Payton, Jack R., "It's the Weird, the Wild, and the Wacky from around the World," *St. Petersburg Times* (21 July 1993): 2A.

Penman, Alan D., Russell S. Tarver, and Mary M. Currier, "No Evidence of Increase in Birth Defects and Health Problems among Children Born to Persian Gulf War Veterans in Mississippi," *Military Medicine* 161 (January 1996): 1–6.

Perrick, Penny, "Future Shock," *Sunday Times* (London) (20 September 1992).

Peterson, Karen, "Decreasing Sperm Counts Blamed on Environment," *USA Today* (28 May 1993): 1A.

Pinchbeck, Daniel, "Downward Motility," *Esquire* (January 1996): 79–84.

Pinto-Correia, Clara, *The Ovary of Eve: Egg and Sperm and Preformation* (Chicago: University of Chicago Press, 1997).

"Potent News," *Milwaukee Journal Sentinel* (24 March 2000): 2G.

Potashnik, G., J. Goldsmith, and V. Insler, "Dibromochloropropane-Induced Reduction of the Sex-Ratio in Man," *Andrologia* 39 (1984): 85–89.

"Proxy Fathers," *Time* (26 September 1938): 28.

Radin, Margaret Jane, *Contested Commodities* (Cambridge, MA: Harvard University Press, 1996).

Raines, Lisa J., and Stephen P. Push, "Protecting Pregnant Workers," *Harvard Business Review* (May–June, 1986): 26–30.

Raloff, Janet, "Common Pollutants Undermine Masculinity," *Science News Online* 155 (3 April 1999): 1–4; accessed at www.sciencenews.org, 3/20/02.

———, "The Gender Benders," *Science News Online* (22 January 1994), accessed LNAU 3/20/02.

———, "That Feminine Touch," *Science News Online* (22 January 1994), accessed LNAU, 3/20/02.

Ralt, D., M. Goldenberg, P. Fetterolf, D. Thompson, J. Dor, S. Mashiach, D. L. Garbers, and M. Eisenbach, "Sperm Attraction to a Follicular Factor(s) Correlates with a Human Egg Fertilizability," *Proceedings of the National Academy of Sciences* 88 (1991): 2840–2844.

Ratcliff, J. D., "Are These the Most Loved Children?" *Women's Home Companion* 82 (March 1955): 46–47, 51, 54, 56.

Reuters, "Male Infertility May Be Linked to Pesticides," *Toronto Star* (27 July 2001): D02; accessed LNAU, 3/27/03.

Richter, Paul, "Clinton Expands U.S. Benefits for Veterans Exposed to Agent Orange," *Los Angeles Times* (29 May 1996): 18.

Rizza, John R., Director, New England Cryobank, Interview with C. Daniels (24 October 2001).

Robaire, Bernard, Interview with C. Daniels (23 June 2001).

Robaire, Bernard, and Barbara F. Hales, eds., *Advances in Male Mediated Developmental Toxicity—International Conference on Male Mediated Developmental Toxicity 2001*, (New York: Kluwer Academic/Plenum, 2003).

Robinson, James C., *Toil and Toxics: Workplace Struggles and Political Strategies for Occupational Health* (Berkeley: University of California Press, 1991).

Robotham, Julie, "Speedy Sperm, and Plenty of It," *Sydney Morning Herald* (Feb. 20, 2002): 3; accessed LNAU, 3/27/02.

Rogan, W. J., G. C. Gladen, Y.-L. Guo, and C. C. Hsu, "Sex Ratio after Exposure to Dioxin-Like Chemicals in Taiwan," *Lancet* 353 (1999): 206.

Rosemberg, Eugenia, "American Society of Andrology: Its Beginnings," *Journal of Andrology* 7 (1986): 72–75.

Rosenberg, P. H., and H. Van Hinen, "Occupational Hazards to Reproduction and Health in Anaesthetists and Paediatricians," *Acta Anaesthesiology Scandinavia* 22 (1978): 202–207.

Rosenfeld, Albert, "The Futuristic Riddle of Reproduction," *Coronet* 54 (1959): 122.

Rubin, Rita, "Shapely Swimmers Win Fertility Race," *Herald Sun* (Durham, NC) (10 November 2001): i; accessed LNAU, 3/27/02.

Ruestow, Edward, "Images and Ideas: Leeuwenhoek's Perception of the Spermatozoa," *Journal of the History of Biology* 16 (Summer 1983): 185–224.

———, *The Microscope in the Dutch Republic: The Shaping of Discovery* (Cambridge: Cambridge University Press, 1996).

Rupa, D. S., P. P. Reddy, and O. S. Reddi, "Reproductive Performance in Population Exposed to Pesticides in Cotton Fields in India," *Environmental Research* 55 (1991): 123–128.

Safe, Stephen H., "Endocrine Disruptors and Human Health: Is There a Problem? An Update," *Environmental Health Perspectives* 108 (June 2000): i; accessed online at http://ehpnet1.niehs.nih.gov, 11 April 2000.

———, "Environmental and Dietary Estrogens and Human Health: Is There a Problem?" *Environmental Health Perspectives* 103 (April 1995): 346–351.

Sander, Warren G., and James D. Eisen, "Cryogenically Preserved Human Semen: Clinical Applications," *Nebraska Medical Journal* (December 1977): 422.

Sapolsky, Robert M., "Testosterone Rules," in *The Gendered Society Reader*, 2nd ed., ed. Michael Kimmel (London: Oxford University Press, 2004).

Savitz, David A., "Paternal Exposure to Known Mutagens and Health of the Offspring: Ionizing Radiation and Tobacco Smoke," in *Advances in Male Mediated Developmental Toxicity*, ed. Bernard Robaire and Barbara F. Hales (New York: Kluwer Academic/Plenum, 2003), 49–58.

Savitz, David A., and J. Chen, "Parental Occupation and Childhood Cancer: Review of Epidemiological Studies," *Environmental Health Perspectives* 88 (1990): 325–337.

Savitz, D., and D. P. Sandler, "Prenatal Exposure to Parents' Smoking and Childhood Cancer," *American Journal of Epidemiology* 133 (1991): 123–132.

Savitz, D., P. J. Schwingle, and M. A. Keels, "Influence of Paternal Age, Smoking and Alcohol Consumption on Congenital Anomalies," *Teratology* 44 (1991): 429–440.

Savitz, David A, Nancy L. Sonnenfeld, and Andrew F. Olshan, "Review of Epidemiologic Studies of Paternal Occupational Exposure and Spontaneous Abortion," *American Journal of Industrial Medicine* 25 (1994): 361–383.

Schettler, Ted, Gina Solomon, Maria Valenti, and Annette Huddle. *Generations at Risk: Reproductive Health and the Environment* (Cambridge, MA: MIT Press, 1999).

Schiebinger, Londa. *The Mind Has No Sex?* (Cambridge, MA: Harvard University Press, 1986).

Schmidt, K. F., "The Dark Legacy of Fatherhood," *U.S. News and World Report* (14 December 1992): 92.

Schmit, Julie, "Countries Consider Joint Study of Agent Orange," *USA Today* (16 March 2000): 15A.

Schnorr, Theresa, Telephone interview with C. Daniels (18 January 2001).

"Scholars Find Drop in Sperm Counts," *Houston Chronicle* (16 November 1992): 3.

Schottenfeld, D., and M. E. Warshauer, "Testis," in *Cancer Epidemiology and Prevention*, ed. D. Schottenfeld and J. F. Fraumeni Jr. (Philadelphia: Saunders, 1982), 947–957.

Schrader, Steven M., "Towards a Safer Occupational Environment: The U.S. Approach, the Example of Glycol Ethers," *Middle East Fertility Society Journal* 3 (1998): 70.

Schrader, Steven M., R. E. Chapin, E. D. Clegg, R. O Davis, J. L. Fourcroy, D. F. Katz, S. A. Rothmann, G. Toth, T. W. Turner, and M. Zinaman, "Laboratory Methods for Assessing Human Semen in Epidemiological Studies: A Consensus Report," *Reproductive Toxicology* 6 (1992): 275–279.

Schroedel, J. R., and P. Peretz, "A Gender Analysis of Policy Formation: The Case of Fetal Abuse," presented at the Western Political Science Association Meeting, Pasadena, California, 18–20 March 1993.

Schull, W. J., M. Otake, and J. V. Neel, "Genetic Effects of the Atomic Bombs: A Reappraisal," *Science* 213 (1987): 1220–1227.

Scialli, Anthony, "Paternally Mediated Effects and Political Correctness," *Reproductive Toxicology* 7 (1993): 189–190.

Seashore, R. T., "Artificial Impregnation," *Minnesota Medicine* 21 (1938): 641–644.

Serrano, Richard, "Birth Defects in Gulf Vets' Babies Stir Fear, Debate," *Los Angeles Times* (14 November 1994): A1.

Sever, Lowell E., Tye E. Arbuckle, and Anne Sweeney, "Reproductive and Developmental Effects of Occupational Pesticide Exposure: The Epidemiologic Evidence," *Occupational Medicine: State of the Art Reviews* 12 (April–June 1997): 305–325.

Seymour, Frances I., "Eugenics in Practice: Cross Artificial Insemination," *Marriage Hygiene* 3 (1936): 46.

Seymour, Frances I., and Alfred Koerner, "Medicolegal Aspects of Artificial Insemination," *Journal of the American Medical Association* 107 (1936): 1531–1534.

Shapiro, Bennett M., "The Existential Decision of a Sperm," *Cell* 49 (1987): 293–294.

Sharpe, R. M., and N. E. Skakkebaek, "Are Oestrogens Involved in Falling Sperm Counts and Disorders of the Male Reproductive Tract?" *Lancet* 341 (29 May 1993): 1392–1395.

Shenon, Philip, "Air Force Links Agent Orange to Diabetes," *New York Times* (29 March 2000): A23.

Sherins, R. J., "Are Semen Quality and Male Fertility Changing?" *New England Journal of Medicine* 332 (2 February 1995): 327–328.

Silbergeld, Ellen, interview with C. Daniels (22 June 2001).

Silbergeld, Ellen K., Betzabet Quintanilla-Vega, and Robin E. Gandley, "Mechanisms of Male Mediated Developmental Toxicity Induced by Lead," in *Advances in Male Mediated Developmental Toxicity*, ed. Bernard Robaire and Barbara F. Hales (New York: Kluwer Academic/Plenum, 2003), 37–48.

Small, Meredith, "Sperm Wars," *Discover* (July 1991): 48–53.

Smith, Keith D., and Emil Steinberger, "Survival of Spermatozoa in a Human Sperm Bank: Effects of Long-Term Storage," *Journal of the American Medical Association* 223 (12 February 1973): 774.

Sonderegger, T. B., ed., *Perinatal Substance Abuse* (Baltimore: Johns Hopkins University Press, 1992).

"Sperm Banks: Fatherhood on Ice," *Chicago Tribune* (18 November 1972).

"Sperm Counts Declining," *Buffalo News* (1 December 1992): 3.

"Sperm Shape, Swimming Ability Prove to Be Better Indicator of Fertility," *USA Today* (8 November 2001): 1, accessed LNAU, 3/27/02.

Starr, Douglas, *Blood: An Epic History of Medicine and Commerce* (New York: Alfred A. Knopf, 1998).

"Stat Bite: U.S. Incidence of Testicular Cancer" [News], *Journal of the National Cancer Institute* 91 (1999): 1803.

State of New York, Public Health Law, Section 4365, Part 52, "Tissue Banks and Nontransplant Anatomic Banks," Subpart 52-8.

Stellman, Jeanne, Interview with C. Daniels (22 March 2001).

———, Interview with C. Daniels (12 June 2001).

———, Telephone interview with C. Daniels (21 March 2001).

Stellman, S., and J. Stellman, "Health Problems among 535 Vietnam Veterans Potentially Exposed to Herbicides," *American Journal of Epidemiology* 112 (1980): 444.

Stepita, C. Travers, "Physiologic Artificial Insemination," *American Journal of Surgery* 21 (1933): 450–451.

Stewart, G. J., J. P. Tyler, A. L. Cuningham, J. A. Barr, G. L. Driscoll, J. Gold, and B. J. Lamont, "Transmission of Human T-Cell Lymphotropic Virus Type III (STLV-III) by Artificial Insemination by Donor," *Lancet* 2 (14 September 1985): 581–585.

Stokes, Walter R., "Artificial Insemination," *Medical Annals of the District of Columbia* 7 (1938): 218–219.

Stone, A., "It's 'Tip of the Iceberg' in Protecting Infants," *USA Today* (25 August 1989).

Stowe, V. M., and R. Goyer, "Reproductive Ability and Progeny of Fi Lead-Toxic Rats," *Fertility and Sterility* 22 (1971): 755–760.

Strathern, Marilyn, "Displacing Knowledge: Technology and the Consequences for Kinship," in *Conceiving the New World Order*, ed. Faye D. Ginsburg and Rayna Rapp (Berkeley: University of California Press, 1995), 346–364.

"Study Links Cancer in Young to Father's Smoking," *New York Times* (24 January 1991): B8.

Sullivan, Kathleen, "Lawyers Badger VA to Help Vets Hurt by Dioxin," *San Francisco Chronicle* (11 March 2001): A17.

Sutton, H. Eldon, and Robert P. Wagner, *Genetics: A Human Concern* (New York: Macmillan, 1985).

Swan, Shanna, Eric P. Elkin, and Laura Fenster, "Have Sperm Densities Declined? A Reanalysis of Global Trend Data," *Environmental Health Perspectives* 105 (1997): 128–132.

———, "Letter," *New York Times* (29 March 2000).

Swan, Shanna H., Eric P. Elkin, and Laura Fenster, "The Question of Declining Sperm Density Revisited: An Analysis of 101 Studies Published 1934–1996," Environmental Health Perspectives 108 (October 2000): 961–966.

Taylor, Pennie, Scotland on Sunday (31 October 1993).

Terry, Jane, "Conflict of Interest: Protection of Women from Reproductive Hazards in the Workplace," Industrial and Labor Relations Forum 15 (1981): 48.

"Test Tube Babies: The Controversy over Artificial Insemination," Good Housekeeping 166 (February 1968): 163–165.

"Testicular Dysgenesis Syndrome: Newly Coined TDS Encompasses Symptoms of Deteriorating Male Reproductive Function," Health and Medicine Week (6 August 2001): 49.

"The Sperm Count of Our Species Is in Serious Decline," ToxCat 2–2 (Spring 1996), www.communities-against-toxics.org.uk/.

Thompson, Sylvia, "The Vanishing Sperm," Irish Times (19 October 1992): 10.

Tisdall, Simon, "Gulf Babies Maimed at Birth," Guardian (23 December 1993): A1.

Titmuss, Richard M., The Gift Relationship: From Human Blood to Social Policy (London: Pantheon, 1971).

Toppari, Jorma, John C. Larsen, Peter Christiansen, Aleksander Giwercman, Philippe Grandjean, Louis J. Guillette Jr., Bernard Jégou, Tina K. Jensen, Pierre Jouannet, Niels Keiding, Henrik Leffers, John A. McLachlan, Otto Meyer, Jørn Müller, Ewa Rajpert-De Meyts, Thomas Scheike, Richard Sharpe, John Sumpter, and Niels E. Skakkebæk, "Male Reproductive Health and Environmental Xenoestrogens," Environmental Health Perspectives 104 (suppl. 4, 1996): 768.

"Toward a 'Sperm Bank,'" Newsweek (18 April 1966): 101.

Troen, Philip, "Andrology: Origins and Scope," in Encyclopedia of Reproduction, vol. 1 (New York: Academic Press, 1999), 214.

Trotter, Stewart, "Letter," Independent (London) (15 March 1992): 23.

Trotter, Thomas, An Essay, Medical, Philosophical, and Chemical, on Drunkenness, and Its Effects on the Human Body (Philadelphia: Anthony Finley, 1813).

Turano, Anthony M., "Paternity by Proxy," American Mercury 43 (1938): 418–424.

UAW v. Johnson Controls, 111 S.Ct. 1196 (1991).

"Urge Human Sperm Banks," Science News Letter 80 (9 September 1961): 163.

U.S. Census Bureau, Population Estimates Program, Population Division, 2002, www.census.gov/popest/estimates.php.

——, 1990 U. S. Population Census, available at http://eire.census.gov/popest/archives/national/nation3/intfile3-1.txt.

U.S. General Accounting Office, "Agent Orange: Actions Needed to Improve Communications of Air Force Ranch Hand Study Data and Results," in Report to the Ranking Minority Member Committee on Veterans Affairs, House of Representatives (December 1999): GAO/NSIAD-00-31.

——, "Gulf War Illnesses: Improved Monitoring of Clinical Progress and Reexamination of Research Emphasis Are Needed," Report to the Chairmen and Ranking Minority Members of the Senate Committee on Armed Services and the House Committee on National Security, GAO/NSIAD-97-163, June 1997, www.gao.gov/archive/1997/ns97163.pdf.

——, "Gulf War Illnesses: Understanding of Health Effects from Depleted Uranium Evolving but Safety Training Needed," in Report to Congressional Requesters, GAO/NSIAD-00-70, March 2000, www.gao.gov/new.items/ns00070.pdf.

"U.S. Men Face Extinction," Earth Island Journal (Winter 1999–2000): 3.

"Vitamin C Deficiency in a Man's Diet Might Cause Problems for Offspring," New York Times (12 February 1992): C12.

Wang-Cheng, Becky, "Dispelling a Myth about Boxer Shorts and Fertility," Milwaukee Journal Sentinel (2 October 2000): 1G.

Warner, Rebecca H., and Henry L. Rosett, "The Effects of Drinking on Offspring: An Historical Survey of the American and British Literature," Journal of Studies on Alcohol 36 (1975): 1395.

Watson, Rory, "Chemicals Concern over Falling Sperm Counts," Herald (Glasgow) (May 5, 2000): 11.

Weisman, Abner I., "The Selection of Donors for Use in Artificial Insemination," Western Journal of Surgery, Obstetrics, and Gynecology 50 (1942): 144.

"Western Man's Fertility Counts Are Falling Fast: 12 Ways to Beat Sperm Crisis," Sunday Mail (SA) (18 February 2001): 118. Accessed LNAU 3/28/03.

Whorton, M. Donald, "Male Occupational Reproductive Hazards," in Occupational Medicine, 3rd ed., ed. Carl Zenz, O. Bruce Dickerson, and Edward P. Howarth (St. Louis, MO: Mosby-Year Book, 1994): 871.

Williams, Wendy, "Firing the Woman to Protect the Fetus: The Reconciliation of Fetal Protection with Employment Opportunity Goals under Title VII," Georgetown Law Journal 69 (1981): 641–704.

Witherington, Roy, John B. Black, and Armand M. Karow Jr., "Semen Cryopreservation: An Update," Journal of Urology 118 (1977): 510.

Wray-McCann, Hugh, "Fatherhood in Deep Freeze," *Science Digest* 60 (14 July 1966): 12–14.

Wright, Brett, "Smokers' Sperm Spell Trouble for Future Generations," *New Scientist* (6 March 1993): 10.

Wright, Lawrence, "Silent Sperm," *New Yorker* (15 January 1996): 42–55.

Xytex Corporation, *Donor Screening Guide*.

Yazigi, R. A., R. R. Odem, and K. L. Polakoski, "Demonstration of Specific Binding of Cocaine to Human Spermatozoa," *Journal of the American Medical Association* 266 (1991): 1956–1959.

Yoshimoto, Y., "Cancer Risk among Children of Atomic Bomb Survivors: A Review of RERF Epidemiologic Studies," *Journal of the American Medical Association* 264 (1990): 596–600.

Younglai, E. V., J. A. Collins, and W. G. Foster, "Canadian Semen Quality: An Analysis of Sperm Density among Eleven Academic Fertility Centers," *Fertility and Sterility* 70 (July 1998): 76–80.

Zelizer, Viviana, *Pricing the Priceless Child: The Changing Social Value of Children* (New York: Basic Books, 1985).

Zhang, Jun, and Jennifer Ratcliffe, "Paternal Smoking and Birthweight in Shanghai," *American Journal of Public Health* 83 (1993): 207–210.

Zhang, Jun, David A. Savitz, Pamela J. Schwingle, and Wen-Wei Cai, "A Case-Control Study of Paternal Smoking and Birth Defects," *International Journal of Epidemiology* 21 (1992): 273–278.

INDEX

Abel, Ernest, 114–16
abortions, 15, 79, 101, 200–201n111
    spontaneous, 121, 124, 125, 126, 133
Abzug, Bella, 55
accreditation, 99, 198nn93,98
acupuncture, 98
Adopt-a-Sperm program (Univ. of
    Utah), 94
adultery, 80, 84, 98
advertising, 89, 99, 106
Aeschylus, 15
African Americans, 39, 73, 93, 97,
    196n74. *See also* black
    populations
Agent Orange, 129–37, 209–10nn104,117,
    211nn119,123,128,131
aggression, 27–28, 175n69
aggressive egg theory, 116–18, 204–
    5nn41,42
agricultural workers, male, 44, 50, 125
AID (artificial insemination donor),
    75–80, 82–84, 90, 98,
    197–98n91
AIDS, 89, 98, 100. *See also* HIV
AIH (artificial insemination homologous),
    75–76, 189n6, 193n55
airport workers, male, 37, 177nn15,16

alcohol abuse, 7
    and drop in sperm counts, 48, 51, 61
    and feminization of men, 58
    and male-mediated fetal harm, 125,
        126, 141–44, 152, 154
        all or nothing theory, 112, 114, 201–
            2n8
    and maternal transmission, 110–11
    and sperm donors, 199–200nn98, 104
Alexander, Daryl, 127–28
alienation of reproductive assets, 85–86,
    92, 105
alligators, 46, 51, 57, 65
all or nothing theory, 112–16, 203–
    4nn18,21,23,25
alternative forms of parenting, 95, 107–8
altruism, 105
American Association of Obstetricians
    and Gynecologists, 82
American Association of Tissue Banks
    (AATB), 90, 99, 196n80,
    198nn93,95, 199–
    200nn98,101,104,108
American Cyanamid (Willow Island,
    Va.), 121–24, 206n66
American Fertility Society, 83, 196n80,
    198n93

Gulf War babies, 111, 137–40
heavy metals exposure, 112, 150,
202n11
ICSI technique, 146
mercury exposure, 206n67
and maternal impressions theory, 19
and norms of masculinity, 70
and regulation of pollution, 62
and sperm donors, 199–200n104
and thalidomide, 48, 111, 148, 150,
216n181
and tobacco use, 142–43
birth sex ratios, 15, 31, 42–45, 66,
180nn46,47, 181nn51,58
birth weight, 142, 145, 155
Bishop, Jack, 148
black populations, 44, 195–96n72. *See
also* African Americans
Blankenhorn, David, 102–3, 107
blood donors, 86
BMI (body mass index), 96
body piercing, 98, 100, 198n95
body types, 93
Boston University, 109
boxer shorts, 48–49
boxing metaphors, 53
Boy Scouts, 95
brain tumors, 124, 125
breast cancer, 55, 62–63, 68
breast milk, 86–87
Brewer, Herbert, 201n114
British Medical Journal, 52, 60
British soldiers, 212–13n144
Buck v. Bell, 78
Bunge, R. G., 81, 83
bus drivers, 58–59
Bush, George H. W., 133, 136
Bush administration (George H. W.),
127–28
"Bye Bye, Baby Boys," 42, 180n46

cadmium, 138, 207n75
caffeine, 126, 183n82
California Cryobank (Los Angeles), 94,
195n66, 197n84, 199n101
Canadian soldiers, 212–13n144

cancers, 50, 115, 123, 125, 126
and Agent Orange, 129, 131–34,
211n123
breast, 55, 62–63, 68
of Gulf War babies, 137
liver, 137
prostate, 133–34
respiratory, 133
scrotal skin, 112, 202n10
testicular, 31, 37, 41–42, 56, 58, 66, 68,
133, 159, 180n42, 187n141
cancer treatments, 89, 115, 144–45,
215nn175,176
carcinogens, 119–20, 147
caregiving, 27, 29, 158
cathode-ray tube radiation, 58
Catholics, 94, 197–98n91
Caucasians, 39, 73, 93, 97, 104, 178n24,
195–96nn71,72
causality, 67, 148, 150
Cell, 203n18
cell theory, 23, 26
Centers for Disease Control (CDC), 96,
100, 130–31, 197nn82,86,88,
200n109, 212n140
chemical castration, 32, 58, 61
chemical exposures, 50–51, 125, 184n85
and birth sex ratios, 43
and drop in sperm counts, 38
and feminization of men, 57–58
and maternal transmission, 55–56
regulatory response to, 62–64
and sperm donors, 199–200n104
wildlife studies of, 45–47
See also names of chemicals
See also names of estrogenic
chemicals
chemical industry, 63, 68, 131
chemical plant explosion (Seveso, Italy),
43, 180n47, 206n67
chemotaxis sperm theory, 116
chemotherapeutic drugs, 89, 115, 144–45,
215n176
Cherfas, Jeremy, 28
Chesney, Murphy, 130
child support, 80

ethical issues (*continued*)
  and sperm banking industry, 99,
    193n52, 198–99nn93,96
ethnic differences
  and birth sex ratios, 45, 181n58
  and drop in sperm counts, 39, 178n24
  and sperm donors, 74, 77, 93, 104, 195–
    96nn71,72
ethylene dibromide, 207n75
ethylene oxide, 207n75, 209n94
eugenics
  and artificial insemination, 8, 76–81,
    84, 190nn14,24, 191nn29,30,35
  and paradoxes of reproductive
    masculinity, 102, 201n114
  and sperm banking industry, 89, 96
eutelegenesis, 106, 201n114
Evans, Lane, 129, 133
exercise, 61
exposure of newborn, 15, 172n13
extrovert-introvert scales of behavior, 94

factory imagery, 54, 59, 68
Fairfax Cryobank (Va.), 93, 94, 195n66,
  196nn77,79
Farley, John, 21–22, 25, 174n52
farmers, 44, 50, 125
FDA (Food and Drug Administration),
  100–101, 196n80
feminism, 48, 54–55, 62, 184n103,
  185n104
feminization of men, 32, 42, 56–60, 158,
  186n124
  and nationhood, 59–60, 186–
    87nn134,135
Fertility and Sterility, 83
Fertility Center (Calif.), 198n94
fertility clinics, 36, 40
fertility drugs, 44
fertility researchers, 203–4n25
fetal hazards, paternal. *See* male-
  mediated fetal harm
fetuses, 18–19, 24
  and maternal transmission, 55–56, 69
  and state protection, 70
Fiedler, Nancy, 140

Fisch, Harry, 39
fish, 45–46, 57, 64
Fissel, Mary, 172n18
"Fitter Families" contests, 77
Florida panther, 47–48, 52, 54
folic acid, 49–50
FQPA (Food Quality Protection Act), 63
Frankel, Mark S., 192n37
Friedler, Gladys, 109–11, 114, 116, 143, 146,
  150, 155
Friedman, Jan, 145
frozen sperm. *See* cryopreservation
Fumento, Michael, 67
fungicides, 50
The Futurist, 59

Galen, 14, 16
gay donors, 74, 95, 98–101, 167, 196n80,
  200n109
gender difference. *See* reproductive
  differences
gender discrimination, 123, 147–48,
  216n180
gendered norms, 68–69, 87
gender inequalities, 5, 9, 101, 150–51, 154,
  175n62, 200–201n111
gender politics, 121–23
gender privilege, 70, 74, 157, 167
gender roles. *See* division of labor,
  reproductive
gender wars, 54–55, 70
genetic defects. *See* birth defects
genetic/hormonal difference model, 13,
  26–30, 175n69
genital deformations, 36–37, 41–42, 57–
  58, 180n42, 187n141
geniuses, 82, 89, 191n30
Georgetown University School of
  Medicine, 79
gift giving, 85, 105, 192–93n48
gin epidemic in England, 112, 201–2n8
Glasgow Royal Infirmary (Scotland), 60
global doom, 60–62, 68–69,
  187nn139,141,144
global warming, 68
glycol ethers, 112, 127, 207n75

God, 17–18
Goluboff, E. T., 39
Graham, Robert Clark, 89
Great Depression, 79
GRE scores, 94
growth charts (CDC), 197nn82,86
Guillette, Louis, 46, 65
Gulf War syndrome, 140
Gulf War veterans, 111, 133, 136, 137–41,
    212–13nn138,140,144
Guttmacher, Alan, 78–79
gynecology, 25, 27, 33–34, 83–84

HAAs (hormonally active agents), 65–67
Hales, Barbara, 115–16, 145–46, 148–50,
    202n14
halogenated hydrocarbon, 119
handwriting samples, 94
Hard, Addison Davis, 75–76
Hartsoeker, Nicolaas, 173n40
Harvard University, 94
hashish, 143
hat sizes, 93, 96
"healthy warrior" effect, 138–39
heavy metals, 112, 123, 138–39, 202n11,
    207n75
height of donors, 92, 95–97, 104,
    197nn82,89
Herald (Glasgow, Scotland), 60
herbicides, 44, 50, 124. *See also* Agent
    Orange
Heredity Choice, 94, 197n90
heritable characteristics. *See also*
    eugenics
  and artificial insemination, 79–80
  and paradoxes of reproductive
    masculinity, 107
  and sperm banking industry, 73, 89
    donor physical traits, 92–94
    donor social traits, 94–98, 196–
    97nn75,78,81
Herman J. Muller Repository for
    Germinal Choice, 89, 194n56
hermaphroditism, 46, 56–57
heroin, 143
Hindus, 94

Hippocrates, 15–16, 34, 172n10, 173n35
Hiroshima (Japan) atomic bombing,
    123–24
Hispanics, 39, 93, 97, 104, 178n24, 195–
    96nn71,72
HIV, 90–91, 95, 99–101, 189n3, 193n54,
    196n80, 198n95, 200n109. *See also*
    AIDS
hobbies, 96, 97
Hodgkin's disease, 133, 211n123
homosexuality, 74, 95, 98–101, 167,
    196n80, 200n109
Hoppe, Arthur, 53
hormonal difference. *See* genetic/
    hormonal difference model
hormonal exposures. *See* estrogenic
    chemicals
hormonally active agents (HAAs), 65–
    66
*Hormonally Active Agents in the
    Environment* (HAAE), 65–67
human body, commodification of, 85–88
Human Reproduction, 145
Hunter, John, 75
hunting metaphors, 54
Hyde, Lewis, 192–93n48
hydrocarbons, 124, 125
hydrocephalus, 142
hypospadias, 41–42, 66

ICSI (intra cytoplasmic sperm
    injection), 146
IDANT Corporation (New York City),
    194n57, 197n90, 199n101
ideals of masculinity, 3–4, 9, 53, 71, 157–
    59
  and male-mediated fetal harm, 154
  and sperm donors, 74, 95–98, 104–5,
    196–97nn81,82,84,86,88-90
illicit drugs, 111, 143–44, 154, 216n180
Immigration Act (1924), 77
immigration restrictions, 77, 190n24
Imperial School of Medicine (London,
    Eng.), 179n35
"impotence," 39, 58, 178n25
inbreeding, 52

polychlorinated biphenyl (PCB) exposure, 45, 50, 62, 181n58
polyvinyl chloride (PVC) exposure, 55
positive eugenics, 77, 81–82, 89, 191nn29,30,35
posttraumatic stress disorder, 138
Potts, Percival, 112
Prader Willi syndrome, 147
preformation theory, 13, 17–23, 173nn33,35,40, 174n48
pregnancy
    and conception theories, 23, 24
    and environmental toxins, 183n82
    and maternal transmission, 56
    "time to pregnancy," 40, 179n35
    use of drugs during, 48
prison inmates, 36, 74, 98, 100–101, 167
private female sphere, 22
procreation. See conception theories
Procreative Technologies (St. Louis, Mo.), 196n77
prostate cancer, 133–34
prostates, 47
prostitution, 98
psychosocial screening, 99
public male sphere, 22
PVC (polyvinyl chloride) exposure, 55

questionnaires, reproductive, 196–97n81

raccoons, 48
racial differences, 167
    and birth sex ratios, 44
    and eugenics, 80, 190n24
    and sperm donors, 73–74, 77, 80, 93–94, 97, 104, 195–96nn71,72,74
    and tobacco use, 142
racial hygiene policies, 190n14
racial politics. See eugenics
radiation, 82, 123–24, 199–200n104, 207n73
radiation therapies, 144–46, 215n175
Ranch Hand study, 130, 134–35
rat studies, 49–51, 62, 109–10, 113
Reagan administration, 127–28

Register of Toxic Effects of Chemical Substances, 209n94
regulation, 166–68
    of male-mediated fetal harm, 126–27
    of male reproductive health risks, 62–68
    of sperm banking industry, 90, 98–101, 198–99nn93-96,98,101
        federal/state, 99–101, 199–200nn104,108,109
reinstatement, social processes of, 69, 83
religious beliefs, 17–18, 60
religious differences, 74, 79, 93, 94, 104, 196n75, 197–98n91
Repository for Germinal Choice, 89, 194n56
reproductive differences, 5–6, 8, 9, 12–13, 25–29, 150–51, 159–62, 175nn62,69
respiratory illnesses, 124, 133, 211n123
Reuters, 53–54
Rh incompatibility, 80–81
risk factors, 48, 51
    of male-mediated fetal harm, 126, 152
    and norms of masculinity, 68–70
    regulatory response to, 64, 67
    and reproductive differences, 150–51
    and sperm banking industry, 99–101, 107
"rival father," 83–84
Robaire, Bernard, 115–16, 145–46, 148–50, 202n14
Rockefeller, Jay, 135
Ronner, Wanda, 217n190
RU 486, 200–201n111
Ryan, Michael, 129

Safe, Stephen, 42, 51–52, 64–65
Safe Drinking Water Act, 63
salicylate, 183n82
Sander, Warren G., 192n37
San Francisco Chronicle, 53
sarin, 139–40
SAT scores, 94, 96
Savitz, David, 125, 142
Schnorr, Theresa, 128
Schwarzenegger, Arnold, 159

testicles
  and conception theories, 14–15, 24
  undescended, 36–37, 41, 47
testicular atrophy, 119
testicular cancer, 31, 37, 41–42, 56, 58, 66,
    68, 133, 159, 180n42, 187n141
testicular temperature, 49, 58–59
testosterone, 28, 51, 55–56, 157, 175n69,
    215n175
Texas A&M, 65, 178n24
thalidomide, 48, 111, 148, 150, 216n181
Third World, 59
thyroid hormones, 64
Time, 79
"time to pregnancy," 40, 179n35
tissue banks, 99–100, 193n54, 199n98
tobacco use
  and drop in sperm counts, 51, 61
  and male-mediated fetal harm, 125,
    126, 142–44, 152, 154
tolerance to drugs, 109–10
toluene, 124, 138, 207n75
Tour de France, 159
toxic exposures. *See* alcohol abuse;
    drug abuse; environmental
    toxins; workplace toxins
trichloroethylene (TCE) exposure, 50
Trotter, Thomas, 141
Tufts University School of Medicine,
    184n85
turtle egg shells, 45
twelve-step plans, 61

"unfit," 77–78
University of Florida, 46
University of Pittsburgh, 144
University of Southern California, 59
University of Southern California–Los
    Angeles, 94
  Medical Center, 40
University of Texas, 45
University of Utah Medical Center, 94
unmanliness, 36, 162. *See also*
    masculinity; reproductive
uranium, 137, 139

urology, 33
U.S. Air Force, 129–30, 132, 134–35,
    210n117, 211n119
USA Today, 56, 61
U.S. Census Bureau, 97, 195–96n72
U.S. Chamber of Commerce, 128
U.S. Department of Defense, 140
U.S. Department of Health and Human
    Services, 63
U.S. Department of Interior, 64
U.S. Department of Veterans Affairs,
    129–34, 139–40, 212n140
U.S. Environmental Protection Agency,
    63–64, 188n152
U.S. Food and Drug Administration,
    100–101, 196n80
U.S. General Accounting Office (GAO),
    134, 138, 210n117
U.S. Marines, 133
U.S. National Institutes of Health, 115
U.S. Supreme Court, 123
uterine insemination, 189n6
uterus, 14, 20, 56

vasectomies, 89, 120–21
Veterans Administration (VA), 129–34,
    139–40, 212n140
video recordings, 93
Vietnamese, 129, 136
Vietnam veterans, 111, 123, 129–37, 141, 153
Vietnam Veterans of America, 136
vinyl chloride, 124
Virchow, 26, 175n62
virility, 6, 7, 8, 33–34, 164–65
  and nationhood, 59–60, 186–
    87nn134,135
  and norms of masculinity, 69–71
  and paradoxes of reproductive
    masculinity, 102–3, 106
  and sperm donors, 74, 95
vitamin C, 143–44
voice recordings, 93
Vom Saal, Fredrick, 47
vulnerability, 6–7, 68–70, 102, 108, 151,
    153, 162–64